Raymond Williams

WITHDRAWN FROM
THE LIBRARY
UNIVERSITY OF
WINCHESTER

...ring, controversial and brimming with intellectual rigour and integrity, ...ymond Williams's work is increasingly regarded as one of the milestones in ...entieth-century criticism. Williams successfully challenged the reigning ...demic orthodoxy in such seminal works as *Culture and Society*, *Drama from ...en to Brecht*, *The Country and the City* and *Marxism and Literature*.

...*aymond Williams: Literature, Marxism and Cultural Materialism* offers the ...ngle most comprehensive historical and theoretical account of Williams's work ...date. John Higgins examines what Williams termed his prolonged argument ...h 'official English culture', focusing in particular on the complex and ...bivalent relation of his thinking to its two main sources: Marxist cultural ...ory and Cambridge English studies. Higgins provides a detailed account of ...different contexts and occasions of Williams's arguments and interventions, ...g the dynamic development of his work from its beginnings in the 1940s' ...s on Marxism and culture, through the cultural politics of the New Left ...e later critique of structuralism, to its culmination in the theory and ...e of cultural materialism. This book vigorously challenges many of the ...d ideas and images of the value and substance of Williams's work, ...ng new light on his crucial relation to figures such as T.S. Eliot, ...pher Caudwell and Mikhail Bakhtin, and offers a powerful argument for ...ntinued relevance of Williams's thought to contemporary debates.

... **Higgins** is Senior Lecturer in the Department of English at the ...rsity of Cape Town, and a Convenor of the Theory of Literature ...ramme. He is the founding editor of the South African journal, *Pretexts: ...es in Writing and Culture*, and the author of numerous articles on film, ...ture and cultural politics.

To

Critics of the Twentieth Century

General editor: Christopher Norris

University of Wales, Cardiff

Raymond Williams

Literature, Marxism and cultural materialism

John Higgins

London and New York

KING ALFRED'S COLLEGE
WINCHESTER

801.95
/WIL

KA02596059

First published 1999
by Routledge
11 New Fetter Lane, London EC4P 4EE

Simultaneously published in the USA and Canada
by Routledge
29 West 35th Street, New York, NY 10001

© 1999 John Higgins

Typeset in Baskerville by Routledge
Printed and bound in Great Britain by MPG Books Ltd, Bodmin

All rights reserved. No part of this book may be reprinted or
reproduced or utilised in any form or by any electronic,
mechanical, or other means, now known or hereafter
invented, including photocopying and recording, or in any
information storage or retrieval system, without permission in
writing from the publishers.

British Library Cataloguing in Publication Data
A catalogue record for this book is available from the British Library

Library of Congress Cataloguing in Publication Data
Higgins, John. Raymond Williams: literature, Marxism, and cultural
materialism. Includes bibliographical references and index.
1. Williams, Raymond – Knowledge and learning.
2. Literature – History and criticism – Theory, etc.
3. Criticism – England – History – 20th century.
4. Marxist criticism – England. 5. Culture –
Historiography. 6. Historical materialism. I. Title. II. Series: Critics
of the twentieth century (London, England).
PR6073.I4329768   1999
98–31008
828'.91409–dc21
CIP

ISBN 0–415–02344–0 (hbk)
ISBN 0–415–02345–9 (pbk)

In memory of Margaret Higgins 1921–1981

Contents

Acknowledgements

'he is trying to write down a book he wrote years ago in his head'

'South America'

Tom Raworth's line, from his fine poem 'South America', always seemed to capture something of my predicament with this project. It would never have made it on to the page without the encouragement of friends and family too numerous to mention, but they all know who they are, and what their kind support has meant to me over the years, whether in Great Britain, Switzerland or South Africa.

More formally, though the substance of the debt goes beyond formality, I take the opportunity to thank those who provided some of the concrete occasions for writing or speaking on Williams's work. Many thanks are due to both Bruce Robbins and Jonathan Arac for their early encouragement to write on Williams for *boundary 2*, and similarly to Michael Sprinker (*the minnesota review*); thanks also to Susan van Zyl (*Journal of Literary Studies*) and Christopher Prendergast (*Social Text Collective*) for later opportunities.

I am also grateful to Peter de Bolla (formerly University of Geneva), Peter Kohler (University of the Western Cape), Reingard Nethersole (University of the Witwatersrand), Maud Ellmann (King's College, Cambridge), Stewart Crehan (University of the Transkei), and Fredric Jameson (Duke University) for invitations to speak on Williams at their respective institutions. All of these occasions contributed in some way to the formulations presented here.

More specifically, thanks are due to Tina Barsby, Louise Green and David Schalkwyk, who each read parts of the manuscript and gave their always welcome and insightful advice. Christopher Prendergast read an early draft of the book as a whole, and his critical comments were acute and stimulating. A number of informal conversations with Terry Eagleton, Edward Said and Gareth Stedman Jones were also very useful to me, as was the general encouragement of both Tony Tanner[*] and Gayatri Spivak. My most pervasive debt is to Frances Long-Innes, for more than a decade of ever-stimulating and critical dialogue.

I benefited enormously in the final stages of writing and revision from my sustaining dialogue with Jessica Dubow; and the very careful readings of the book made by John Coetzee, Anthony Morphet and John Kench: to respond adequately to their probing critical concerns – as to those of Routledge's readers (Christopher Norris, who also first suggested the idea for the book, Graham Martin, and Terry Eagleton) – would have made it necessary to write a different and better study than this. I should also record that the late Raymond Williams was kind enough to offer help and encouragement at an early stage in the planning of this work.

My thanks also to the staff at the University Library in Cambridge, the British Museum Reading Room, and the library of the University of Cape Town, who were unfailingly patient and helpful with my search for materials and information; and to the King's College Research Centre for kindly allowing me office space during a visit to Cambridge.

---

* Sadly, Tony Tanner died in his rooms at King's on December 5, 1998. My intellectual debts to him go far beyond what can be acknowledged with respect to this particular project.

Introduction

Raymond Williams died, more than a decade ago now, in January 1988. The immediate response was overwhelming: progressive intellectuals throughout the world mourned the passing of one of the foremost socialist thinkers, intellectuals and cultural activists of the postwar period. In the obituary columns of leading newspapers, at conferences and on television, and in the pages of academic journals, we saw the public mourning of a figure who was, in Patrick Parrinder's words, 'father-figure to thousands', who was, for Juliet Mitchell and many more like her, 'an intellectual and moral touchstone'.[1] Who was this remarkable figure and why should his work continue to hold our interest and attention? We can begin to answer these questions by looking briefly at the background and career of Britain's most distinguished socialist thinker on culture of the past forty years.

Raymond Henry Williams was born in the small Welsh village of Pandy in 1921, the son of a railway signalman. He won a scholarship to Cambridge in 1939 where he was active in the student branch of the Communist Party and the Cambridge University Socialist Club.[2] He was called up in 1941 and fought as a tank commander in a number of the most bloody battles of the Second World War, returning to Cambridge in 1946 to complete his degree in English with a powerful dissertation on Ibsen in which some of his own sense of vocational crisis came through. For the next fourteen years, Williams worked as a tutor in adult education.[3] This move, and the consequent departure from the usual university syllabus of English studies, provided some of the ground for the writing of two seminal works which challenged the existing paradigm of literary studies, and did much to help the emergence of the new disciplines of cultural studies. *Culture and Society 1780–1950* (1958) and *The Long Revolution* (1961) established his reputation as the leading thinker of the New Left; in the words of the historian Edward Thompson, 'our best man'.[4]

In 1961, Williams received a letter from the English Faculty of the University of Cambridge informing him that he had been appointed Lecturer in English; a few days later, other letters arrived, encouraging him to apply for the post![5] Discouraged by the shift of emphasis in adult education away from working-class education and towards middle-class provision, Williams accepted the post and was to spend the rest of his working life at Cambridge, first as a lecturer and then, from 1974, as Professor of Drama. It was from here, the centre of Britain's elite educational system, that Williams was to produce a body of work which challenged many of that elite culture's central assumptions, not only as they appeared in English studies, but also as they informed the dominant modes of thinking about politics and society, and as they swayed assessments of the very possibility of progressive social and political action. As he clarified during the exhaustive interviews with the *New Left Review*, published as *Politics and Letters* in 1979, his work was above all the work of an oppositional intellectual: 'If you look at the implied relationships of nearly all the books I have written, I have been arguing with what I take to be official English culture' (Williams 1979: 316).

This study takes that argument with 'official culture' as its guiding thread, and follows it across the twenty-four or so volumes of his academic writing. On the way, it challenges some of the received ideas concerning his work. Chapter 1 examines Williams's earliest writings, and particularly the essays written for the journals he helped to found in the late 1940s, *Politics and Letters* and *The Critic*, as well as his first major study, *Reading and Criticism* (1950). Drawing attention to the pervasive influence of Eliot (rather than Leavis, as is commonly assumed), it argues that the tensions between literary and Marxist analysis which Williams found so crippling in this early period in fact provided the motor of his development as a whole. Chapter 2 argues for the formative (rather than marginal) role usually assigned to Williams's early thinking on drama, and examines neglected works such as *Drama from Ibsen to Eliot* (1952), the first version of *Drama in Performance* (1954), and the book co-written with Michael Orrom, *Preface to Film* (1954). The third chapter focuses on the largely neglected context of cultural, educational and political debate from which *Culture and Society* and *The Long Revolution* emerged, while Chapter 4 concentrates on the significant detail of Williams's oppositional relation to 'Cambridge English' in his books *Modern Tragedy* (1966), *The English Novel from Dickens to Lawrence* (1970), and *The Country and the City* (1973), and the way these studies also carried on his critical dialogue with Marxism. Chapter 6 investigates the ways in which cultural materialism is offered as the theoretical alternative to existing formations of English studies, while Chapter 7 examines the final, interrupted, stage of Williams's argument with 'official culture' through his renewed attention to the ideological and disciplinary forces at work in the related formations of modernism and English studies, both in their historical trajectory and in terms of their contemporary theoretical assessment and practice.

The guiding principle of this study is that Williams's engagement with English studies cannot be understood in terms purely internal to the discipline of English. As well as writing against the official culture of liberal and conservative literary studies, he also wrote in opposition to what he read as the orthodoxies of Marxist thinking on literature, culture and politics. Arguing first against Marxist literary criticism as he knew it from the 1930s, he maintained an ever-sceptical and ever-critical stance towards the later trends of Althusserian and post-structuralist theory, while at the same time continuing his always defining commitment to socialist politics. While the terms of this larger argument are necessarily present throughout, Chapter 5 focuses on them more narrowly, and traces their development in Williams's thinking from the late 1950s through to the development of the concept of cultural materialism in *Marxism and Literature* in 1977.

Similarly, no one can read Williams's work without becoming aware just how far its concerns reach beyond the bounds of the academy and extend the usual confines of a professional academic identity. The single most striking characteristic of his work is its commitment to the connection of literary argument and debate with the broader issues of politics and society. This account seeks to foreground some of the ways in which it always interacted with the cultural and political debates of his day. He was never just an academic, but always, to borrow Edward Said's terms, a public and fully secular intellectual.[6] The study closes with an examination of the difficult dynamics of settling Williams's intellectual legacy in the decade since his death.[7]

I make no claim to cover every aspect of the extraordinary range of Williams's writing and thinking. Conspicuously absent are any assessment of his own fictional and dramatic writing, which was so deeply and interestingly connected to his academic work; any substantial account of his specifically political ideas and activities, or even a full engagement with his important work on television and mass communication; Chapter 3 focuses on *Culture and Society* at the expense of *The Long Revolution*.[8] The focus is narrow, but, I hope, productive. While this study is not intended as a final word or judgement on Williams's work as a whole, it is intended as a counter to some of the 'final words' that have been offered, to my mind prematurely. For there seems to be an implicit (and at times explicit) judgement in some recent accounts that 'we can now only read Williams's work historically', as if its relevance has dissipated.[9] My own feeling is that reading Williams historically – as is attempted here – can be a salutary challenge to any tendency on our own parts to either theoretical or political complacency. This study therefore presents an account and analysis of the interaction in his thinking between the principled opposition to and questioning of both Marxist cultural theory and Cambridge literary criticism across some forty years of academic writing and debate.

1 The tight place

Marxism or literature? 1947–50

Raymond Williams's first critical writings – from, for example, the essays and reviews in *Politics and Letters* (1947–8) to *Preface to Film* (1954) – have been powerfully characterised as 'left-Leavisite'. Perhaps in consequence, they have been too little read. As Williams himself noted in *The Long Revolution*, sometimes the very availability of a description and the ascription of a name can work to block fully historical analysis (Williams 1961a: 89–90). The aim of the first two chapters of this study is to prise open some of the internal complexities and contradictions that the label 'left-Leavisite' works to contain, and to provide a more historically nuanced account and assessment of the early criticism than is generally available.[1] In so doing, I shall challenge the dominant view that this early period is best viewed as a merely probationary, and easily superseded, moment in Williams's formation. I argue that, duly considered, the early work presents us with the constitutive dynamic of his intellectual identity. This first chapter examines the uneasy development of his thought from the autumn of 1939, when he began his undergraduate studies in English at Cambridge University, through the first years of his work as staff tutor for the Oxford University Tutorial Committee, to the publication of his first book, *Reading and Criticism*, in 1950.

Terry Eagleton, probably Williams's single most extensive critic, proposed the term 'left-Leavisite' in his provocative and polemical assessment of Williams's work, first published as an essay in *New Left Review* and then as the opening chapter of his *Criticism and Ideology*, both in 1976.[2] Of course, others had remarked on the importance to Williams of his formation in the discipline of English, but no one had done so with as much vigour as the self-consciously iconoclastic Eagleton.[3] In *Criticism and Ideology*, 'left-Leavisism' figures as the first of the three main stages in an incomplete move towards a genuinely Marxist criticism.

In an important but little-known interview with the Cambridge journal *Red Shift* in 1977, Williams said that although he 'would accept much of [Eagleton's] account', he was disturbed by some aspects of it. Questioned about the contradictions of his own position and intellectual history, he responded wryly: 'What I want to ask is who Eagleton is?'. He went on to argue vigorously that the 'basic fault of the kind of formalist Marxism which Eagleton is now in is that it assumes that by an act of intellectual abstraction you can place yourself above the lived contradictions both of the society and of any individual you choose to analyse, and that you are not yourself in question'. Against this, he asserted that 'the belief that one is above that deeply contradictory situation is a fantasy.... There is no position except in fantasy where one can merely examine what others are inscribing' (Williams 1977b: 12, 15).

A year later, in a discussion with *New Left Review* which was in part prompted by Eagleton's essay, Williams had sharpened his response, and now rejected 'the general label left-Leavisism' because it implied far too unified and far too comfortable a position. Except in fantasy, 'left-Leavisism' could only be an 'inherently unstable' position (Williams 1979: 195). As we shall see, what was troubling was the way in which Eagleton's confidently theoretical description glossed over instabilities and contradictions which had been felt very deeply and very painfully, and which the writing itself had struggled but failed to resolve.

The tight place

'The tight place, where you stick fast; there is no going forwards or backwards.' Ibsen's words – from *When We Dead Awaken* - held a particular resonance for Raymond Williams as he completed his undergraduate studies in Cambridge in 1946.[4] He quoted them in his final year dissertation on Ibsen (an essay which later formed the basis for the first chapter of *Drama from Ibsen to Eliot*); and some thirty years later, he recalled how that sense of being unable to move, of being trapped, which he had found in Ibsen, seemed to sum up his own intellectual and political predicament, his own troubled sense of self and vocation. 'That was exactly my sensation. The theme of my analysis of Ibsen is that although everybody is defeated in his work, the defeat never cancels the validity of the impulse that moved him; yet that the defeat has occurred is also crucial' (Williams 1979: 62–3).

What were the terms of this defeat? Why did the young Williams suffer from such a sense of failure when, by all ordinary standards, he already appeared to be an achiever, indeed a success? He had, after all, survived the war and come through some of its bloodiest fighting in the Normandy and Ardennes offensives. He had married in 1942, and he and his wife Joy had their first child in 1944. He graduated from Cambridge with a first-class degree in English and was offered a place to do research, but chose instead to become a tutor in the burgeoning adult education movement. Between 1946 and 1953 he completed three books, wrote most of a fourth, collaborated as editor of and contributor to two new (though short-lived) journals, and at the same time worked through the preliminary drafts and versions of his first novel. On the surface, Raymond Williams in the late 1940s and early 1950s was already a successful academic and intellectual. Why then this troubled sense of blockage and of failure?

To understand this, we need to grasp something of the depth of Williams's commitment, one which we can read in the terms he appropriated from Ibsen as commitment to a vocation, and as a commitment always under threat of failure. If we see his vocation as, in the first instance, that of a socialist literary critic, then we can read that commitment as riven by a conflict between its two main components. Literary criticism provided him with both something of an intellectual base and the superstructure of a professional identity; but its generally apolitical or even conservative stance was deeply unattractive to him, as were its usually apolitical and ahistorical modes of analysis. In a sense, the discourse of literary criticism was the 'tight place' in which Williams felt so trapped. At this point, as we shall see, he was unable either to go back to the Marxist literary criticism which he decisively abandoned – on professional grounds – in the course of his undergraduate studies; but neither was he able to move forwards beyond the terms of existing literary studies.

At the same time, we need to understand that it was just this sense of being stuck which proved to be the necessary ground for Williams's major work. The deep feelings of failure and defeat which dogged him in this early period provided the necessary dynamic for a reworking not only of the possible relationships between Marxism and literary studies, but for a significant revision and recasting of both. This first chapter examines the constitutive tensions of that 'tight place', of the young Williams caught unhappily between a literary criticism he could not accept politically and a Marxism he could not reproduce professionally. It was the extreme discomfort of this 'position' in this period that proved to be the very motor and motive of his intellectual development.

Beginnings

In the autumn of 1939, Raymond Williams arrived at Trinity College Cambridge to begin his studies for a BA degree in English literature. It was the beginning of a combative relationship with 'Cambridge English' which was to structure and define the main contours of his intellectual identity. It was to shape the nature of his particular contribution to both Marxism and literary studies that together form the focus of this account: that attention to the politics of culture, and to the primacy of culture in politics, which he finally came to name a 'cultural materialism'.

Unlike most students at Trinity, and indeed in the university as a whole, Williams did not belong to the privileged elite who had received their secondary education in one of Britain's so-called public schools. For these, three years study at 'Oxbridge' was simply a stepping stone to an already established place in the natural hierarchy of British society.[5] Instead, Williams 'came up' to Cambridge as what was to become a familiar icon of 1950s culture, as a 'scholarship boy', one of a number of students from working-class families who won a place in one of the prestige universities through the highly competitive entrance examinations.[6]

Born in the Welsh village of Pandy, and educated first at the local primary school and then at King Henry VIII Grammar School for Boys four miles away in Abergavenny, Williams arrived at Cambridge unwilling to be intimidated, and, initially at least, with a sturdy self-confidence and political identity which were the products of a deeply supportive family environment.[7] Trinity had no Fellow responsible for teaching English, so in the first year he was tutored by Lionel Elvin and had his weekly discussions on Shakespeare and the literature of the Renaissance at Trinity Hall. As a member of the Communist Party – which he joined in December – he devoted a great deal of his time to the Cambridge Socialist Club, writing for the Club Bulletin, participating in debates at the Cambridge Union and, at the urging of the Communist Party, acting as editor for the *Cambridge University Journal*. As a member of the ironically named Aesthetes, Williams also showed a keen interest in film. Far from being the alienated figure suggested by critics such as Jan Gorak, the young Williams found a ready place in the active socialist life of the university: as he was later to put it, 'I had to dine in Hall and the class stamp of Trinity at that time was not difficult to spot. But it did not have to be negotiated as the only context at Cambridge. The Socialist Club was a home from home' (Williams 1979: 40).[8]

Certainly the details of an average week's activities in the Club show the fullness of its timetable. We might take the week-long period beginning 6 March 1940 as presenting an average week's activities in the Club:

Wednesday: 12.30 Hands Off Russia – Lobbying and Poster Parade
Friday: Hand's Off Russia – Meeting in The Dorothy
Saturday: 2.30 Film Club – Pabst's Westfront; 8.00 pm Social
Sunday: 2.00 Film Show; 4.30 Tea; 8.00 Film
Monday: 8.00 pm Business Meeting
Tuesday: Union Debate – Intervention against the USSR
Wednesday: 8.00 pm – 1.30 am Dance

In addition, there were three faculty group meetings for students in history, physics and English. Williams gave a short paper, 'Culture and the People', on Friday 1 November 1940 which CUSBC reports was 'followed by keen discussion providing enough questions to keep the group going for the rest of the year.'[9]

And yet a notable feature of the later *Culture and Society* was its hostile chapter on the Marxist literary criticism which was the staple diet of young socialists like the undergraduate Williams. The 'home from home' was to be repudiated. Chapter 5 of Part 3 – 'Marxism and Culture' – is the only place in *Culture and Society* where the famously balanced and objective tone of the book breaks down, most obviously in its notorious judgement on Caudwell, whose writing is described with contempt as 'not even specific enough to be wrong' (Williams 1958a: 277). The 1930s had seen the publication of a number of works which became standard reading for socialist students of literature: in 1937 alone, Alick West's *Crisis and Criticism*, Ralph Fox's *The*

Novel and the People, Christopher Caudwell's *Illusion and Reality*, and the Day-Lewis collection, *The Mind in Chains*, all appeared. These were all the targets of Williams's sharpest criticism. What it is important to recognise, and what is in any case evident from the angry tone of the account, is that it was just these works which formed the initial basis for his literary analyses as he worked for Part One of the English Tripos. The savageness of his later criticism should alert us to the existence of what he was later to acknowledge as a painful – and determinant – break with these available forms of Marxist literary analysis under the pressures of the availability of the techniques and skills of Cambridge English. That this break was to be the very condition for the formation of Williams's own distinctive version of literary and cultural studies is relatively easy to see in hindsight. It did not and could not appear to be anything so promising at the time.

Impasse

The first cracks began to appear in the second year of his studies at Cambridge, when he moved from Elvin's sympathetic supervision to a more challenging encounter with E.M.W. Tillyard at Jesus College.[10] Tillyard – one of the first lecturers to be appointed to teach the new Cambridge degree in the 1920s, and the pioneer of studies in the historical 'background' of English literature that Williams was later to attack with regularity –   raised a number of questions which the young Williams was unable to answer.

The second year of the English Tripos focused on the history of the novel and Romantic poetry. In his tutorials with Tillyard, Williams sought to apply the stock responses of the 1930s Marxist criticism he had been reading. In this 'proleptic criticism', the literature of the present and of the past is read and evaluated in terms of future needs. In his introduction to *The Mind in Chains* (1937), the poet Cecil Day-Lewis repeated with approval Edward Upward's contention that 'the most enduring books are those in which the writer has seen so deeply into contemporary reality that he has exposed "the shape of things to come" latent there' (Day-Lewis 1937a: 16). Upward himself argued that for the Marxist 'a good book is one that is true to life.... For the Marxist critic, therefore, a good book is one that is true not merely to temporary existing situations but also to the future conditions which are developing within that situation' (Day-Lewis 1937: 46). In the same vein, Ralph Fox, in his *The Novel and the People*, also stresses the need for a new Marxist realism:

> The new realism it is our task to create must take up the task where bourgeois realism laid it down. It must show man not merely critical, or man at hopeless war with a society he cannot fit into as an individual, but man in action to change his conditions, to master life, man in harmony with the course of history and able to become the lord of his own destiny.
>
> (Fox 1937: 100)

In this view, novels of the past should be judged in terms of how novels should be written in the present; Romantic poetry represented an unfinished project of human liberation.[11] Tillyard's reply to this was apparently blunt and forceful: 'He told me this was not a tenable procedure; it was a fantasy' (Williams 1979: 52). Williams found the encounter very stressful:

> I was engaged in having to satisfy somebody who was professionally teaching a subject that my ideas were tenable and reasonable, and I could not. I was continually found out in ignorance, found out in confusion.... You must remember that a hell of a lot of my self-image was devoted to the notion that I could handle academic work. It now became clear to me that I could not.
>
> (Williams 1979: 51)

What was at stake were the very terms of his developing sense of a self and a vocation, and it is significant that he later remembered his call-up and entry into the army in July of 1941 as something of a relief, as a temporary way out of the tight place he had found himself in.

But only temporary. Williams spent the next four years in the army, but was given the early release available to university students who had interrupted their studies to take part in the war. He returned to Cambridge in the autumn of 1945 and went on to complete the third year of the Tripos with a special paper on George Eliot and a 15,000 word essay on Ibsen. In both of these areas of work, he remained troubled by the arguments raised by Tillyard, arguments he still felt unable to resolve. He felt he had reached an impasse, one in which a major part of his own sense of self-identity and self-esteem was at stake: his professional identity as a literary scholar. In this crisis, we can recognise what was to become a central and defining characteristic of his work: its unusual biographical impetus, its powerful sense of an integrity and focus located in the personal voicing of the academic.

The feeling of impasse is crucial to an understanding of the forces which drove Williams in his attempt to forge a new way of doing literary studies. By his return to Cambridge in 1945, he had rejected the available forms of Marxist literary criticism. At the university, the energies of the Socialist Club had waned, though Williams found society and stimulus with two new friends, Henry Collins and Wolf Mankowitz, both enthusiastic Leavisites. Together, the three were keen to promote left-wing literary and cultural criticism which, while it accepted the Leavisite criticism of Marxist literary analysis, refused their rejection of politics.

Politics and Letters

In an early review, Williams repeats the standard Leavisite line, and writes of the failure of Marxist literary criticism to 'emerge from theory into respectable practice' (1947b: 52). The practice in question was literary criticism, and the first attempt to force such an emergence came with the founding of the journal *Politics and Letters* in 1947. Williams put the journal together with the help of his two Cambridge friends, Wolf Mankowitz and Henry Collins. Its contributors, over its short lifespan, included Jean-Paul Sartre, George Orwell, Christopher Hill and F.R. Leavis. A 'complementary' journal – one more purely concerned with the 'literary', *The Critic* – also began at the same time, but was amalgamated with *Politics and Letters* after the second issue. *Politics and Letters* itself ran for four issues before it collapsed in 1948.

As Williams was later to put it, the journal signalled an attempt to 'unite a radical left politics with Leavisite literary criticism. We were to be to the left of the Labour Party, but at a distance from the CP. Our affiliation to *Scrutiny* was guarded, but it was none the less quite a strong one' (Williams 1979: 65). This is the position now generally known as 'left-Leavisism', though the term is rejected by Williams for implying too unitary and too static a position.

Politics and Letters defined itself in opposition to three currents of thought. First of all, it was directed against the failed Marxist literary theory of the 1930s; second, it rejected the (a)political stance of Leavis's *Scrutiny*, by now the key journal in literary studies; and third, it was set against what was seen as the self-conscious metropolitanism and self-indulgent aestheticism of Cyril Connolly's *Horizon* (1940–9). It was here that, in April 1947, Connolly saw fit to declare that 'the honeymoon between literature and action...is over...the left-wing literary movement has petered out'.[12] In positive terms, *Politics and Letters* was intended as the spearhead of political activism in the adult education movement and sought to ensure that the Labour government did not ignore the importance of cultural politics in the struggle for working class emancipation and the achievement of a participatory democracy.[13]

The very title of its first editorial – 'For Continuity in Change' – embodied the difficult reliance on and yet combative relation to Leavisism in its repetition and adjustment to the title of Leavis's most polemical collection of essays, *For Continuity* (first published by the Minority Press in Cambridge in 1933). The editorial chose the literary scandal of 1946 known as the Zoschenko debate as the grounds of the journal's first public intervention. The central argument was that the usual 'dichotomy between politics and letters' – exemplified in Leavis's writing of the period, and in the pro- and anti-Marxist stances of *Modern Quarterly* and *Horizon*, respectively – needs to be challenged. A proper understanding of the issues involved in the Soviet literary debate shows why this challenge is necessary. For Williams and his co-editors, both Marxists and anti-Marxists miss what Leavis had grasped: the 'real nature' of literature. The *Horizon* moralists miss the 'detailed experience of living' which literature embodies, and are therefore unable to prevent their 'values' from being too abstract, or worse, too self-indulgent. The ideologues of the *Modern Quarterly* are blind to the very existence of a professional literary criticism whose tools and methods should be brought to bear in any cultural debate. Against these positions, the editors suggest the following:

What is valid, and in our opinion supremely important, is that the structure of society, its institutions and directions, should be constantly assessed by standards resting on certain immediate qualities of living, qualities which social history scarcely records, but which, 'for continuity', our cultural tradition embodies.

(Williams *et al.* 1947a: 3–4)

'Embodies' is the key term. It articulates the journal's debt to the 'Cambridge English' of the *Scrutiny* school, where literature is not merely a record of past experience; it is the still living embodiment of that experience. According to the metaphysics of this school, the literary critic enjoys a highly privileged relation to history; somehow, through the experience of reading literary texts, the critic can re-experience the structure and specificity of any historical moment. Hence the idea – first put forward by I.A. Richards, and later taken up by F.R. Leavis – that the 'standard of living' of a society could best be judged – indeed, could only be judged – by the literary critic.[14] The editors of *Politics and Letters* allowed this same centrality to the critic, but went on to point out that the critic needs to be concerned with more than the understanding of literature alone.

There were then two primary tasks for the journal: the creation of 'an intelligent reading public', and the creation of a group which could and would intervene politically. The problem was, of course, that there was no necessary connection between the two groups, any more than there was a necessary connection between the two journals originally imagined as 'complementary'. Despite the desire to go beyond *Scrutiny*'s apolitical stance, *Politics and Letters* remained, in the end, trapped by its inadequate conceptualisation of politics. As the second editorial, 'Culture and Crisis', put it, in the rather desperate terms which signalled the journal's imminent collapse:

The critic stands subject to two autonomies: that of planning for material survival and prosperity (it is an estimate we must make objectively and with the methods of science); and that of allowing for and fostering *responsibility* in society, an effort in which we are supported by that evidence there is of human maturity, by tradition evidenced by literature and social history, by experience. We have at present to make separate estimates of these problems remembering that as literary critics we have training to aid us in the latter, while in politics we are undoubtedly naive.

(Williams *et al.* 1947b: 7)

Subject to two autonomies, trained in one and yet naive in the other, it is hardly surprising that *Politics and Letters* could only reproduce in the end the tight place of Williams's frustrations.

Williams contributed some thirteen essays and reviews to the two journals and these reflect his interests and preoccupations of the time.[15] His single most important essay was 'Soviet Literary Controversy in Retrospect', published in the first issue of *Politics and Letters* (Summer 1947). Many of the principles outlined in the 'For Continuity in Change' editorial are here put into practice (the editorial itself states that it 'brings our outlined preoccupation to bear on current disagreement in this country, as well as in the Soviet Union' (Williams *et al.* 1947a: 4). The essay is worth some detailed attention as it marks his definitive and public break with Communist Party orthodoxy as well as representing the first of his attempts to move beyond that orthodoxy through the practice of literary analysis.

Soviet literary controversy

1946 had seen an intensification of repression in the Soviet Union as Stalin responded to the pressures of a disastrous harvest and the beginnings of Cold War attitudes in Britain and the USA.[16] As a part of a renewed drive to discipline and cow the intelligentsia, Andrei A. Zhdanov, a key figure in the elaboration of Socialist Realism in the 1930s and now Secretary of the Central Committee of the Communist Party, launched an attack on two avant-garde Leningrad journals, *Zvezda* and *Leningrad*. He was particularly scathing about the work of the modernist poet Anna Akhmatova, and a short story – 'Adventures of an Ape' – by the satirical writer Mikhail Zoschenko.[17] At a meeting of the Leningrad Party Committee, Zhdanov declared: 'Why should we provide a literary platform for all these decadent literary tendencies so completely alien to us?' His criticisms were picked up by Cyril Connolly in the October issue of *Horizon* and read as a warning of what socialism could mean in Britain.[18] The Soviet position was defended in turn by John Lewis in the editorial to the Winter 1946 issue of the Communist Party journal, the *Modern Quarterly*, as an exemplary instance of democratic self-criticism: 'what we witness is not the spectacle of cowed and intimidated writers reluctantly toeing the Party line, but writers, readers and critics everywhere in the Union overhauling their work.... Nothing can be done in the Soviet Union that is dictated from above' (Lewis 1946–7a).

Williams saw the debate itself as symptomatic of the emerging Cold War. How else to explain the attention paid to it in a press usually hostile to literary discussion? Nonetheless, it was useful in revealing the 'prevailing muddle about the relation of politics and letters' (Williams 1947c: 21), and particularly so in regard to two topical questions – 'the place of literature in the modern, centralised state, and...the obligation of such a state towards literature'.[19] For Connolly, the stakes were 'the principle and practice of state interference in cultural affairs'; while for John Lewis, Zhdanov's intervention was a prime example 'not of interference, but of healthy self-criticism, [one] which might be expected to arise in a country where human values are assured by a rational social organisation' (Williams 1947c: 22).

According to Williams, Lewis's editorial is 'typical of the popular Marxist writing on culture' in that it simply fails to understand anything about the 'the nature of literature itself' (1947c: 22–3). Drawing on Leavis's literary empiricism to argue his case, he insists that 'the practice of literary criticism, and of creative literature, is bound to be different from the administrative self-criticism to which he has attempted to relate it' (1947c: 23). It is bound to be so because above all literature is concerned with 'realised immediate experience' and not the dry abstractions which form social theory. 'The function of literature in keeping society healthy', he concludes, in full Leavisite tones, 'is that it injects realised immediate experience, personal and traditional, into the abstractions which inevitably form the body of social thinking' (1947c: 23). All in all, Lewis can do nothing to prove his central assertion that the Soviet literary controversy is a good example of how self-criticism works in a socialist society. On the contrary, 'Criticism from below is the essence of the democratic safeguard in Soviet society. The way this business has gone does nothing, in itself, to disprove allegations that Soviet government is based on decision from the top, followed by organized and manipulated public approval' (1947c: 23). Small wonder that Williams had allowed his membership of the Communist Party to lapse in 1941. He later did not recall or choose to recall and was not asked the precise circumstances of this. Certainly his assertion of the necessity for 'criticism from below' ran directly counter to the prevailing Communist Party practice of 'democratic centralism', in which, according to Raphael Samuel in a fine historical and autobiographical account, the 'Party allowed no conceptual space...for dissent'.[20]

As far as *Horizon* is concerned, Williams cannot agree with Connolly's complacent suggestion that judgement of art should always be left to the 'Reading Public'. How could Connolly not be aware that such a cohesive 'Reading Public' no longer existed? After all, this had been the burden of Q.D. Leavis's *Fiction and the Reading Public* as well as Leavis and Thompson's *Culture and Environment*, the very centre of *Scrutiny*'s whole intervention. 'It is no use saying', he argued:

> that state interference with art, or the suppression of non-conforming writers which may be involved in state patronage, is worse than the effects of commercialism or of advertising manipulation. Both are bad; neither is admissible...to ignore the destructive elements in our own society, and to concentrate on them in another (a society moreover which can hardly be criticised without large political repercussions) – surely that is not a defence of culture but rather political opportunism in the real sense of that abused term?
>
> (Williams 1947c: 25)

The attack on Connolly continued in the following issue of *Politics and Letters*, where he was challenged to write about the American Congress Committee on UnAmerican Activities with as much passion as he had about Russia (Williams 1947d: 105–6). For Williams, as he was later to record, Connolly represented 'a self-indulgent decadence' which he attacked 'with ferocity' (Williams 1979: 72).

Williams then turns to examine Zhdanov's criticisms. 'The disturbing thing', he writes, 'is the exclusiveness, the narrowness, of the role which literature is called upon to play' (1947c: 27). Against this, it is urged that:

> We must, then, retain the right to judge a civilization by its culture. For culture is the embodiment of the quality of living of a society; it is the 'standard of living' with which the critic is concerned. Assessment of it is the social function of the critic and the creative writer...Our precept is clear: we must, negatively, by the application of the strictest critical standards, ensure that inwardness is neither abused (becoming 'profitable introspection') nor set up for sale in the commercial market; and positively, we must attempt, however often we fail, to ensure that in our own inevitable development towards a planned, rational, society, the distinctive values of living embodied in our literary tradition are preserved, re-created, expanded, so that ultimately with material may grow human richness.
>
> (1947c: 30–1)

The 'standard of living argument' had become a commonplace of literary studies, adequate testimony to the strength of I.A. Richards's founding rhetoric of the 1920s. Williams sees little chance of the raising of this standard in the Soviet Union, where he fears that 'Soviet Man' will become a comparably caricatural figure to the West's 'Average Man', or the 'Successful Man' of the advertising world. Both East and West show signs of failing to understand the nature and importance of culture and the literary tradition insisted on by the Cambridge school.

In the end, the *Politics and Letters* project proved (to borrow Williams's own later terms) to be emergent rather than – as Jan Gorak suggests – residual. For Gorak, 'Williams and his fellow editors ventured into the postwar world with the prejudices of prewar intellectuals. A new cultural politics could hardly be constructed from materials such as these' (Gorak 1988: 47). But *Politics and Letters* is better understood as challenging rather than confirming the prewar attitudes to be found in *Scrutiny*, *Horizon* and the *Modern Quarterly*. Though the two journals only survived for two years, and though they owed something to the Leavisite orthodoxy, they did none the less signal an important challenge to it.[21]

Reading and Criticism revalued

When *Reading and Criticism*, Williams's first published book, is mentioned it is usually in dismissive terms. *Reading and Criticism* is treated as the expression of his most complete accommodation to orthodox literary studies, and, as such, something better left alone. Terry Eagleton writes of 'the techniques of textual analysis which Williams inherits from *Scrutiny* and reproduces without question in *Reading and Criticism*' (Eagleton 1976b: 38). Jan Gorak sees the book as an act of significant intellectual dishonesty on Williams's part, accusing him of employing in it 'a style of literary criticism he had intellectually repudiated' (Gorak 1988: 47). Fred Inglis asserts that it 'came directly out of his teaching, and that teaching was in the direct line of Leavis's famous journal *Scrutiny*' (Inglis 1995: 126). All agree on the identification of *Reading and Criticism* with the practical criticism of the *Scrutiny* school. Even Williams's most respectful interrogators, the *New Left Review* team, seem to support this identification when they conclude that *Reading and Criticism* not only reproduces 'the classic Leavisite argument', but reproduces it 'at its most circular' (Williams 1979: 238). Nonetheless, they feel obliged to allow an opportunity for self-defence, and ask whether he was aware of 'any substantive divergences...[any] unexpressed differences' (1979: 237) between the positions advocated in *Reading and Criticism* and the work of the *Scrutiny* tradition.

We need to examine both Williams's reply in the late 1970s – that he took a distance from *Scrutiny* through his criticism of the method of evaluating an author by extract only – and the evidence offered by a closer examination of *Reading and Criticism* itself. *Reading and Criticism* deserves more careful attention than it has hitherto been given: it needs to be read as a formative work in his intellectual and theoretical development, rather than left largely unread and avoided as an embarrassment to the usual image of him. Once this is done, we see that it helps to throw some light on the development of one of his most central and most problematic ideas, that of the 'structure of feeling'.

Reading and Criticism was written in 1948 and can certainly be taken as a partial record of Williams's teaching as a tutor in adult education. It was published in 1950 in the *Man in Society* series, edited by three leading figures in the adult education movement: Thomas L. Hodgkin, S.G. Raybould, the Director of the Leeds branch and Vice-President of the Association, and Lady Simon of Wythenshawe. The books in the series were 'intended for the use of students in adult classes such as those promoted by the WEA' – just the classes which he taught for fully the first third of his academic career. The main aim of the series was introductory: they were how-to books, designed to help students acquire the dominant skills and practices appropriate to particular subjects and disciplines.

In this sense, it is hardly surprising that *Reading and Criticism* can offer plenty of evidence for Williams's accommodation to existing literary studies since the basic purpose of the book was to be an introduction to them. However, we should also be aware of an important recommendation of the series editors, one crucial to the ethos of WEA policy. This is that even introductory texts should not 'exclude topics which are matters of current controversy'. Simple reproduction or critical distancing? We certainly need to examine *Reading and Criticism* with both options in mind, as the expression of his debt to the dominant *Scrutiny* positions, but also with an awareness of the ambivalence inherent in any indebtedness.

How did Williams – at the age of twenty-eight – see his own relation to the literary studies of the late 1940s? And how do we assess that self-image? Perhaps the strongest element in this is the assertion, however qualified, of independence.

In the Preface to the book, he makes three basic moves. First, he acknowledges his debts to a whole catalogue of critical influences. Eliot, Middleton Murry, I.A. Richards, Empson and L.C. Knights are all given honourable mention; F.R. Leavis is singled out as being 'largely responsible for the intelligent development of critical analysis as an educational discipline'. 'To his work, and to that of *Scrutiny*, I am indebted' Williams admits. But in the next breath, in what was to become a characteristically distancing gesture, he asserts that he has 'never consciously or formally belonged to any "school of criticism" '. This assertion is then itself qualified by the admission of a common point of departure: 'As an independent student I have found the work of these critics valuable because it insisted on "the text as the starting-point of criticism" ' (Williams 1950: ix–x). This movement – from indebtedness, to independence, to the acceptance of the text as the 'starting-point of criticism' – suggests that at this point in his career, Williams was perhaps more able to articulate a desire for intellectual autonomy rather than to achieve it.[22] Nonetheless this desire is itself crucial for any understanding of his development. It is the source of all his later achievements. We need then to be aware of the strong desire to make *Reading and Criticism* somehow independent of the tradition it was its primary task to teach.

From a first reading, it is clear that the nine chapters of *Reading and Criticism* largely reproduce and embody the conventional terms and assumptions of literary criticism. I.A. Richards's *Principles of Literary Criticism* (1924) and *Science and Poetry* (1926), Leavis's seminal pamphlet 'Mass Civilization and Minority Culture' (1930), and Q.D. Leavis's authoritative *Fiction and the Reading Public* (1932) all leave their traces, and are acknowledged in the bibliographies, as are such secondary school textbooks as Leavis and Thompson's *Culture and Environment* (1933) and Thompson's own *Reading and Discrimination* (1934). In a repetition of the founding gesture of Cambridge English, the Introduction defines criticism as a practice of reading and not just the accumulation of the rote-facts of a literary history. In Chapter 1, criticism is defined as a 'mature reading' to set against the reading habits spawned by the mass culture of advertising, journalism and popular fiction, that 'mechanization' of reading which stems from 'the influence of newspapers and deliberately written-down publications' (Williams 1950: 9). Chapter 2, 'The Way We Read Now', examines, in a way familiar from Leavis and Thompson's *Culture and Environment*, an advertisement for tea, a newspaper report and some examples of 'popular' fiction in order to argue that the 'last thing which writing of this kind encourages is a conscious and disciplined attention to the words which comprise the statement' (1950: 14). Chapter 3 locates the position of the critic as the 'mediator between the artist and the serious reading-public', a position all the more necessary in the fallen world of mass culture where 'the facts of our reading being what they are', he has to be 'increasingly concerned…with the extension of literacy in the fullest sense' (1950: 21). Chapters 4–6 show analysis at work in a number of comparative passages of verse and prose, while Chapter 7 seeks to show what an analysis of a whole work might look like (Conrad's *Heart of Darkness*).[23] The two final chapters offer brief discussions of drama, where Williams anticipates the central theme of *Drama from Ibsen to Eliot*, the tendency 'to believe that the naturalist method is the permanent and universal dramatic method' (1950: 91); while 'Literature and Society' argues for a distinction between the reductive view of literature as evidence and 'the fact of the text', suggesting that it should be read as 'a highly aware and articulate record of individual experience' (1950: 101). All in all, Williams's 'mature reading' is concerned with the three *mots d'ordre* of *Scrutiny* criticism, with 'evaluation, with comparison, and with standards'.

Yet though *Reading and Criticism* repeats so many of the orthodox pieties of *Scrutiny* criticism, and reads at times like nothing so much as an updated version of *Culture and Environment* (1933) or *Reading and Discrimination*, the repetitions are not complete and there are numerous points at which Williams seeks to give substance to his claims for intellectual autonomy.[24] In the most general terms, we can cite his concern, expressed in self-consciously socialist terms which recall the polemics of *Politics and Letters*, to stress the social nature of critical judgement against the *Horizon* and *Scrutiny* emphasis on criticism as essentially a matter of personal taste or individual judgement:

> Criticism...is essentially a social activity. It begins in individual response and judgement.... But its standards of value, if it is to acquire meaning, must be ultimately matters of agreement between many people: values which are instinct in the culture of a society. The doctrine of the self-sufficiency of personal taste is hostile to criticism for the same reason that the doctrine of individual self-sufficiency is hostile to society.
>
> (Williams 1950: 29)

There is also a major difference of attitude towards the very idea of a reading public. The Leavisite version worked to establish a hierarchy of high and low culture, between minority literature and mass culture, one in which the task of the critic was to fight for higher standards. In Leavis's seminal pamphlet, the argument runs as follows:

> In any period it is upon a very small minority that the discerning appreciation of art and literature depends: it is only a few who are capable of un-prompted, first-hand judgement. They are still a small minority, though a larger one, who are capable of endorsing such first-hand judgement by genuine personal response.... The minority capable not only of appreciating Dante, Shakespeare, Donne, Baudelaire, Hardy (to take major instances) but of recognising their latest successors constitute the consciousness of the race (or of a branch of it) at a given time...
>
> (Leavis 1933: 13–15)

Williams takes issue with this representation of those who appear to be innately capable of 'unprompted, first-hand judgement' in his own emphasis on literary criticism as a training in 'mature reading'. Against the implicit emphasis (and mystification) surrounding the abilities of the literary critic in the *Scrutiny* mode, with its emphasis on the creative and reparative powers of the critic himself, he offers a down-to-earth reminder of the fact that skills in literary criticism may be acquired – indeed, have to be acquired – just like any others, through hard work and practice. 'To be able to read serious literature requires training. A "born reader" is just as much a fantasy as a "born writer": there are no such persons' (Williams 1950: 8). It is hardly then surprising that he differs from the *Scrutiny* assessment regarding the possible size of the 'minority culture' of critically trained readers. He doubts whether 'the present intelligent reading public…is anything like as large as it might be', and urges

> There is no need to surrender to popular sentimentalities in this matter, but the aristocratic converse is no more acceptable. There exist what would seem to be remediable reasons for the smallness of the serious reading public…one should remember that an increase in the serious reading public by the number of students who annually attend formal courses – some 100,000 – would revolutionise the material situation of literature…
>
> (1950: 4,6)

Against the gifted few of Leavis's account, there are the capable many of Williams's adult education experience.

In response to the *New Left Review*'s prompting, Williams himself drew attention to another point of difference with Leavis, one 'which may not appear obvious now, but was important then' (Williams 1979: 237). This was his challenge to the standard *Scrutiny* practice of assessing the quality of a novel or a novelist through the careful analysis of an extract from the work. This overt attack was mounted in Chapter 4 of the book, 'What is Analysis?'.

He begins by quoting Leavis's definition of analysis, from *Education and the University*, as 'the process by which we seek to attain a complete reading of the poem' (Williams 1950: 31). For Williams, there is a problem whenever this kind of analysis is applied to a longer work, and particularly to the novel. What is at stake is the status of the extract through which such analysis then necessarily works, and the principles of selectivity which govern the choice of such passages. He easily demonstrates, through an examination of two sets of paired extracts from George Eliot and D.H. Lawrence, that either can be made to appear the better writer depending on the selection of the passages. 'When we make a judgement by analysis we commit ourselves to a judgement *on that piece of writing alone*', he insists. 'We do not say that the analysis of a short extract is sufficient analysis of the work of an author' (Williams 1950: 43). At the same time, the aim of the critic must always be to arrive at 'a total judgement of a work and of an author' (1950: 45). 'A writer's work is integral' (1950: 74) he urges; and for this reason, the question of selection is crucial. Williams foregrounds the practice of selection itself, and argues for it as a fundamental feature of interpretation or 'response':

The structure or pattern of a work is more than the text; it is the text *and* the response. It goes without saying that such response must be everywhere actual, and its elements justifiable from the text which is the only fact of the work.

(1950: 73)

Though the elementary rules of textual evidence must always be adhered to, Williams recognises something like the agency of the critic and of criticism itself in the fact of the work performed on the text. The 'structure or pattern' is at once a property of the text, and of the critic's response: 'A critic assessing a writer's work as a whole will find that his primary task is the perception of this fundamental pattern, and then the finding of adequate passages which convey this pattern...' (1950: 74). In the next chapter, we shall see how the 'structure or pattern', which the critic finds in the text, is the forerunner of the idea of the 'structure of feeling' which, argues Williams, the author articulates from the culture and experience of his or her time.

In the Conclusion to *Reading and Criticism*, Williams seeks to sum up his understanding of the importance of literature not just for the literary critic, but also for the social critic. It is a statement which is torn and tortured by the tensions in his attempt to find a position which can supersede – that is, both retain and go beyond – the insights available from either a dogmatic Marxism or an orthodox Leavisism:

What is it that literature represents which has reference to our social needs? It is valuable primarily as a record of detailed individual experience which has been coherently stated and valued. This may be the commentary of a fully intelligent mind – informed, detached, emotionally aware – on the society and culture of its day. Or it may be the articulate statement of a perception of certain individual relationships which set the pattern of a culture. Or it may be the coherent evaluation of close personal relationships, or the exposition of intense and considered personal experience.... Literature is communication in written *language*. To the language of a people, which is perhaps the fundamental texture of its life, literature is supremely important as the agent of discovery and analysis.

(1950: 107)

While Williams accepts the conventional focus on literature as valuable 'as a record of detailed individual experience', he is keen to twist that expression of individual experience to a social end. This record need not then be concerned only with 'close personal relationships' or 'intense and considered personal experience'. It may instead be a commentary on contemporary 'society and culture', the framing, in Ruth Benedict's phrase, of the 'pattern of a culture' (Benedict 1934). In other words, *Reading and Criticism*, just at the moment when it looks back to *Politics and Letters*, also looks forward to and anticipates, and not by verbal echo alone, something of the project of *Culture and Society*.

What we can see at work in the formulations of *Reading and Criticism* are Williams's attempts to think for himself, beyond the available formulae of literary criticism. For this reason alone, *Reading and Criticism* needs to be read with more attention than it is usually given, and not passed over as quickly as possible, as something best forgotten in the Williams canon. With his emphasis on criticism as 'mature reading', and his concern with 'the extension of literacy in the fullest sense', he is struggling to articulate what will become the focus of his later work. For what comes into play in the critic's assessment of the 'structure of pattern' in a writer's work is no less than the whole of a person's experience. Already, mature reading is not only a literary critical method; it is an ethical and implicitly political practice, a dialectical positioning of both self and text. 'Mature reading' is the name he gives at this early moment to the practice of a critical literacy which defines much of the distinctiveness of his work as a whole, that unusual combination of the academic and the autobiographical which is the trademark of later works such as *Modern Tragedy* and *The Country and the City*.

However, at this stage the formulations are often hesitant, often awkward. Still in the tight place of contradiction, Williams's resort to the impersonal pronoun is most unlike him at the moment he is most like himself:

> one wishes to read adequately, and to set one's reading in order with rela-
> tion to one's personal experience and to the experience of the culture to
> which one belongs. The basic standards one seeks are those traditional
> valuations which have been re-created in one's own direct experience.
>
> (1950: 26)

To describe and then to see these early works as merely probationary is to blind oneself to their tortuous internal dynamic, and to their significance for any assessment of Williams's developing project. For in these early writings we can see something of the contradictory dynamic of his thought. This is a deeply formative period for Williams, one in which we can see the first attempts to bring literary studies and socialist cultural criticism together by partially rejecting both. For Williams, 'left-Leavisism' was not simply an assured position he held for a while and then quite naturally grew out of: it was the tight place in which he felt trapped and unable to move. These attempts to get out of that trap can help us to better understand the nature, limits and success of his entire *oeuvre*.

2 Drama and the structure of feeling 1947–54

Williams's reputation as a public intellectual was formed in the late 1950s as the author of *Culture and Society* (1958), and consolidated by the publication of *The Long Revolution* in 1961. This fact has tended to obscure the earlier and formative years of his academic and intellectual development. It is the early writings on drama which have suffered most from this neglect, and many commentators have found it difficult to get his work on drama as a whole into proper focus. This chapter examines the writing on drama published between 1947 and 1954, but leaves aside the later – and better known – recastings of it in order to emphasise and understand the contribution this early work made to the formation of his distinctive theoretical vocabulary. I argue that this writing on drama was the crucible in which he forged some of his central theoretical ideas, including that most contested and most characteristic item in his conceptual repertoire, the idea of the 'structure of feeling'. Properly under-stood, this notion represents Williams's first direct conceptual challenge to Marxist literary orthodoxy.

A significant portion of Williams's work was devoted to the history and analysis of dramatic forms. Cambridge University acknowledged and celebrated his scholarly stature by appointing him Professor of Drama in 1974. No less than three of his first four books were concerned with drama and naturalism, and he retained a consistent interest in the history and dynamics of dramatic production, whether on stage, in film or on television. In 1964 and 1968, the early studies *Drama from Ibsen to Eliot* and *Drama in Performance* were revised, extended and republished; and these were joined by a new work, *Modern Tragedy*, in 1966. He wrote a regular column on television for *The Listener* between 1968 and 1972, and in 1974 published his influential study, *Television: Technology and Cultural Form*. Chapter 6 of *Culture* (1981) deploys a 'breathtaking chronological sweep' of the history of drama in order to substantiate his claims for what 'comparative formal analysis' of a cultural form can yield. All the essay collections – *Problems in Materialism and Culture* (1980a), *Writing in Society* (1984a) and posthumous collections such as *What I Came to Say* (1989c) and *The Politics of Modernism* (1989a) – contain essays on film and drama, and show his continued interest in the history of dramatic forms.[1] Drama was certainly one of Williams's persistent preoccupations; and yet, many commentators insist on viewing this considerable body of work as somehow peripheral to his main interests.

In this, many students of his thought appear to follow the lead given by Terry Eagleton in his powerful assessment (Eagleton 1976b). Here Eagleton noted that 'a volume of dramatic criticism has regularly punctuated his production of "social" texts', but wrote that although he found 'the place of dramatic criticism within his work...an interesting, even intriguing one', in the end could only suggest that 'the relations between the two bodies of work are not easy to decipher' (Eagleton 1976b: 37). J.P. Ward, in the first monograph on Williams, describes drama as the one area of his writing that is 'insulated, as though an interest that is sealed off and self-contained' (Ward 1981: 28). Similarly, for Jan Gorak, his 'dramatic interests remain difficult to place in the light of his work as a whole' (Gorak 1988: 15). Even the scrupulously attentive *New Left Review* team could only suggest, in the course of their exhaustive interrogations, that his work on drama represents a 'central paradox' for any of his readers (Williams 1979: 201). In the general view, the writings on drama are eccentric to the main body of his work, and his interest in it is peripheral. This chapter takes a contrary view, and argues that Williams's work on drama – and particularly the early writings – are central to the foundation and formation of his whole intellectual project.[2]

In this general neglect, the early writings on drama have been even less attended to. Few have sought to establish any significant distinctions between the early body of writing and what came to replace it, or any significant connections between it and the rest of Williams's work.[3] In part, this may be due to its relative inaccessibility, and the fact that two of the three early books have been superseded by later versions: commentators focus on the revised editions. *Drama from Ibsen to Eliot*, written between September 1947 and completed by April 1948, was published in November 1952. *Drama in Performance* and *Preface to Film* (with Cambridge friend Michael Orrom) were both written in 1953 and published in 1954. In 1968, *Drama in Performance* was republished in an enlarged edition; and *Drama from Ibsen to Eliot* was similarly revised and enlarged to become *Drama from Ibsen to Brecht*. Only *Preface to Film* has been out of print since its first publication.

As in some academic version of the mystic writing pad, this early work is hidden beneath layers of subsequent rewriting and revision. *Drama from Ibsen to Eliot* disappears beneath *Drama from Ibsen to Brecht*. The first version of *Drama in Performance* is lost beneath the second. This chapter recovers some of what has been lost or hidden in revision and rewriting in order to better understand the difficult dynamic of Williams's developing thought. One consequence of this is to further challenge the orthodox view of his 'left-Leavisism' as it becomes clear that the single most powerful influence on his thinking about drama was T.S. Eliot. That this was an influence he was later to do his best to forget perhaps only makes the point more strongly: the most positive references to Eliot are silently removed from the later versions of *Drama from Ibsen to Eliot* and *Drama in Performance*.[4]

Against Naturalism

The early writings on drama express the sense of commitment common to socialist intellectuals of the 1940s and 1950s. They seek, in the first instance, to intervene in the contemporary cultural situation, and to subordinate academic analysis to cultural effectivity. The young Williams intended his writings on drama to have a practical effect on the dramaturgy of his time. In the process of revision, some of the urgency of this address has been lost, and these studies have come to be treated as textbooks and reference points in the history of naturalism.[5]

He was not alone in perceiving something of a crisis in the contemporary theatre. British drama in the late 1940s and early 1950s was widely seen to be in the doldrums. That deadly calm was not to be broken until the acclaimed first performance of John Osborne's *Look Back in Anger* in May 1956. *Observer* critic Kenneth Tynan, writing in 1954, gives something of the flavour of the pre-Osborne theatrical scene in his essay 'West-End Apathy':

> The bare fact is that, apart from revivals and imports, there is nothing in the London theatre that one dares discuss with an intelligent man for more than five minutes. Since the great Ibsen challenge of the nineties, the English intellectuals have been drifting away from drama.
>
> (Tynan 1964: 31)

Four years later, Tynan offered a succinct and perceptive analysis of the power and appeal of John Osborne's work. In his 1958 essay 'The Angry Young Movement', he describes *Look Back in Anger* as a major breakthrough in British drama in terms very appropriate to understanding some of the thrust of Williams's own project:

> The new intelligentsia created by free education and state scholarships was making its first sizeable dents in the facade of public-school culture....For the first time the theatre was speaking to us in our own language, on our own terms....For too long British culture had languished in a freezing-unit of understatement and 'good taste'. In these chill latitudes Jimmy Porter flamed like a blowtorch....The ivory tower has collapsed for good. The lofty, lapidary, 'mandarin' style of writing has been replaced by a prose that has its feet on the ground. And the word 'civilized', which had come to mean 'detached, polite, above the tumult', is being restored to its old etymological meaning: to be civilized nowadays is to care about society and to feel oneself a responsible part of it.[6]
>
> (Tynan 1964: 56, 57, 62)

For Williams, as for Tynan and others, the prewar dramas had no purchase on the new world of the 1950s. For a time, the appearance of verse-dramas such as Eliot's *The Cocktail Party* seemed to promise a new vitality, but this was not to last. In his writings on drama, Williams sought to help revitalise the dramatic scene.[7] The first blows were struck in a number of essays and reviews written for *The Critic* and *Politics and Letters*.

Actors

Williams's first essays on drama were published in 1947, in the two journals he helped to edit, *The Critic* and *Politics and Letters*.[8] The most substantial of these was the essay 'A Dialogue on Actors', which appeared in the first issue of *The Critic*. Here the debt to Eliot is evident throughout. The essay is consciously modelled on Eliot's own 'A Dialogue on Dramatic Poetry' (1928), and adopts virtually all of Eliot's main ideas on drama.[9] Eliot was keen to stress three main points: first, the importance of convention in drama; second, the new possibilities and energies offered by the new poetic drama; and third, the insistence that good drama had to be good literature as well. All of these come through in his influential essay, 'Four Elizabethan Dramatists'.

Eliot argues that Lamb's selections of the Elizabethan dramatists set the terms for contemporary attitudes towards drama in which the reader is committed 'to the opinion that a play can be good literature but a bad play and that it may be a good play and bad literature' (Eliot 1924: 110); while William Archer's *The Old Drama and the New* fails largely because of Archer's inability to see that the 'faults' of Elizabethan drama may be due to simply the existence of different and non-naturalistic conventions, or more accurately, the unsettledness of Elizabethan conventions. He chooses the figure of a great dancer of the Russian school as a model for what the actor should be like: 'a true acting play is surely a play which does not depend upon the actor for anything but acting, in the sense in which a ballet depends upon the dancer for dancing' (Eliot 1924: 114).

In William's dialogue, all of these points are picked up. There are four 'speakers' in the dialogue – L, M, N and O – but these enjoy little characterisation and tend to speak only variants of Williams's own ideas. The main problem of the modern theatre is identified by N as a problem of acting and actors: 'It is the most fashionable current heresy to regard drama and acting as one and the same thing.... Because people identify drama with acting, because they judge the plays and performances by acting standards, real dramatic values are neglected' (Williams 1947a: 17). He asserts while the current vogue for actor-directors is responsible for the 'lie' 'that a play can be a good play without at the same time being good literature' (1947a: 21). Crucial to the whole discussion is the problem of naturalism. N argues that: 'You cannot condemn contemporary actors without an inclusive condemnation of naturalism' (1947a: 22), and insists that: 'A competent analysis of naturalism, with the record of its growth, would be the most important piece of scholarship our dramatic literature could receive' (1947a: 22). M sums up the case as a whole:

Our specific point here is that naturalism involves, inevitably, the actor's attitude we have condemned. Constructively, we can only say this: that revival in quality of drama (quantity can wait) depends on the use of dramatic conventions, within which dramatists and actors can collaborate; which will enable the dramatist, and the actors who complete his work on the stage, to penetrate below the superficial verisimilitude which has been the curse of naturalism, and to produce work which is likely to remain powerful and valid regardless of superficial social changes, work which is central in the whole human situation and which does not depend on chance audience-identification.

(1947a: 23–4)

This was the basis of the case which was to be argued at greater length and with greater detail in his study *Drama from Ibsen to Eliot*.

From Eliot to Ibsen

Drama from Ibsen to Eliot is the first of three works which will seek to provide that 'analysis of naturalism, with the record of its growth' that Williams had deemed necessary in his 1947 essay. It extends Eliot's insights into a fully historical and academic account, one which can be used to support the contemporary argument for the reform of the drama.

The Introduction to *Drama from Ibsen to Eliot* states that the aim of the book is to give 'not so much a history of the drama of these hundred years [1850–1950] as a critical account and revaluation of it' (Williams 1952: 11). As the term 'revaluation' suggests, the project is conceived in terms of the application of practical criticism to the drama. 'My criticism is', writes Williams 'or is intended to be, literary criticism. It is literary criticism, also, which in its major part is of the kind based on demonstrated judgements from texts, rather than on historical survey or generalized impressions' (1952: 12). The study is a 'working experiment in the application of practical criticism methods to modern dramatic literature', and follows the lead given by Eliot on Elizabethan drama and L.C. Knights and G. Wilson Knight on Shakespeare.[10] It is 'practical criticism' in a very direct sense: 'not as a part of that process of tidying-up which we sometimes call literary history, but as an expression of values in the drama, from which we may assess our position, and decide upon future directions' (1952: 38).

The first stage in this project is to place drama firmly as a worthy object of critical scrutiny, to establish the literary status of drama. Following Eliot, Williams argues that this status is one that has been obscured by the 'popular habit' of distinguishing drama sharply off from literature 'while the terms "drama" and "acting" are often virtually exchangeable'. 'It is assumed' he writes, in the scornful accents of an Eliot, 'very widely, that the value of a play has not necessarily anything to do with its literary value; it is held, and firmly asserted, that a play can quite commonly be good, without at the same time being good literature' (1952: 13). For Williams, the 'average playgoer assumes that the attitudes and practices of the contemporary theatre are things necessary and permanent in drama itself' (1952: 13). He attributes this prejudice to the dominance of theatrical naturalism, which he sees as 'a particular stage in the development of the drama' and which, he insists, 'as a form is only a phase in the drama's long and varied history'. Against this, he submits his own definition of literature, and of drama as literature:

> Literature, in its most general definition, is a means of communication of imaginative experience through certain written organisations of words. And drama, since it has existed in written plays, is clearly to be included under this general definition. A play, as a means of communication of imaginative experience, is as clearly the controlled product of an author – the control being exerted in the finalised organisation of words – as any other literary form. But, in the drama, when the actual and specific means of communication are considered, what is essentially a singular literary statement becomes, in performance, apparently plural.
>
> (Williams 1952: 14)

We see here Williams's commitment (articulated in *Reading and Criticism*) to the idea of literature as 'the controlled product of the author', extended to drama. The main problem for drama – and here he returns to the themes he had sketched out in his 'Dialogue on Actors' – is the expectation that drama is primarily a vehicle for actors, rather than a means of using actors in a certain way. 'All we are obliged to remember, for ordinary purposes, is that character and action, in any good play, are ordered parts of a controlled expression, and that the author's control over their presentation ought to be final...the literary nature of drama needs re-emphasis' (1952: 18). The model of expression and artistic control which Williams draws on begins as Eliot's; but, as we shall see, he was to make it his own through the insistence on the possibility of drama – and particularly film – as a form of total expression, the interpretation of the social totality at one particular historical moment.

In the first instance, though, we can read the various histories, or moments of history, which are discussed in the naturalist trilogy as exemplifications of the ideas and insights of Eliot's work on drama. *Drama from Ibsen to Eliot* sees Ibsen as the exemplification of the urge towards controlled dramatic expression argued for by Eliot. Ibsen's purpose 'was the re-establishment of a total dramatic form' (1952: 96) in the wake of Romantic drama; his failure was largely due to the retention of a naturalist 'representational language' (1952: 96). *Peer Gynt* is the play which most successfully realised Ibsen's formal intentions. In much the same way, Strindberg also hoped to overcome the limitations of naturalist drama. Williams finds evidence of this in the distinction which Strindberg attempts between naturalism and realism where 'true naturalism' is that which 'seeks out those points in life where the great conflicts occur' (1952: 103), though in practice Strindberg is limited by the existing naturalist conventions. This limitation, writes Williams 'as in *The Father* and *Lady Julie*, is in the incongruity between the bared, elemental experience of crisis and the covering apparatus of seen and spoken normality' (1952: 110). Chekhov's use of symbolism signals another attempt to escape the confines of naturalist drama; and it too fails due to the lack of enough vital language: 'this [the seagull] is a poor substitute for the concrete and precise realisation of the central experience of the play which is achieved in more formal drama by conventionally exact speech', he argues. 'Rejection of convention, in the interest of character-drawing and lifelike speech, is the root of the difficulty' (1952: 130).

On the positive side, Synge, Yeats and Hauptmann all move towards the kind of speech necessary to great drama. In the best of Synge's work:

> language is no longer confined to 'flavouring', but uses metaphor and verbal symbolism for strict dramatic ends...[*Deirdre*] approaches those permanent levels of great drama which seem to be accessible only when a major dramatist subordinates all else to the exploration of a major experi-ence, through a language which the experience alone determines.
>
> (1952: 168)

William Butler Yeats 'first showed poetic drama to be possible again in our century' (1952: 221): he 'restored to words "their ancient sovereignty" in the drama' (1952: 222); while Hauptmann's *The Weavers* is that rare thing, a successful realist play, and this is 'because its realism operates at every level of creation – action, persons, and speech, instead of being reserved mainly for the convenient elements' (1952: 178–9). But for all his appreciation of these earlier writers, Williams reserves his greatest praise for Eliot's work. It is in his writing that such speech is best represented.

Eliot's plays are 'experiments in a new dramatic form' (1952: 223), one which is particularly important for its 'experiments in language' (1952: 225), and its move towards 'the discovery of a dramatic method which should have the status of poetry' (1952: 227). In *Murder in the Cathedral*, Williams writes with approval, 'language reasserts control in performance' (1952: 229). His only criticisms are directed at moments where that control is weak and falters. These are usually the moments where the acting is too apparent, and draws attention to itself. He singles out Irene Worth's performance as Celia in Eliot's *The Cocktail Party* as an example. At a climactic moment, the 'gestures of her hands were not controlled by the movement of the words, but by the movement of the general emotion. Now this is normal naturalist acting, but in this case, when the words were so adequate and so final, the essentially separate "acting" not only did not support the words, but actually distracted attention from them' (1952: 246). Though Eliot's experiments are not completely successful, they none the less represent 'a very considerable achievement, whatever the immediate future of the drama may be; and in its nature it is beyond the mode of praise' (1952: 246).

As it happened, despite such enthusiasm, the 'immediate future of drama' did not prove to follow Eliot's lead.[11] Nonetheless, for the young Williams, Eliot's ideas on drama, and their partial realisation in his plays, seemed to represent the most promising way forward. This judgement is later abandoned and forgotten, and is carefully excised in the revision of *Drama from Ibsen to Eliot* and its working over into *Drama from Ibsen to Brecht*.

Differences

Jan Gorak has been one of the few critics to register Williams's debt to Eliot; but he underestimates the characteristic attempts, even at the early stage, to assert independence. According to Gorak, Williams 'remained locked within Eliot's guiding assumptions and values' even though he 'signalled his partial independence from Eliot by electing to study nineteenth-century drama' (Gorak 1988: 21). But as we shall see, Williams's attempts to take a distance from Eliot go beyond the mere selection of a canon, and reveal the processes of a thought in formation.

First, let us examine the central idea of the place of speech in drama. Of course, the emphasis which Williams gives to speech in drama connects across Eliot to what were by the 1940s the standard terms of the *Scrutiny* critique of modernity. In *Drama from Ibsen to Eliot* Williams also writes, in the familiar terms of Leavisite literary criticism, that 'contemporary spoken English is rarely capable of exact expression of anything in any degree complex', and this is due in large part to 'that pressure of forces which we call industrialism' (Williams 1952: 26) . We need only compare contemporary with Elizabethan drama to see that 'the medium of naturalism – the representation of everyday speech – is immeasurably less satisfying in the twentieth century than in the sixteenth' (1952: 26). This decline in the richness of dramatic speech is 'related, in fact, not only to the impoverishment of language but to changes in feeling' (1952: 22–3). As the *New Left Review* team are quick to observe, 'The set of propositions here is quite unlike anything else in your work. It seems to be a pure distillation of Leavis' (Williams 1979: 194). But with that single word 'feeling', Williams seeks to give his own twist to the orthodox line, and as he does so, he starts the slow elaboration of his own distinctive concepts. For, as we shall see, 'feeling' will become the key element in the idea of 'structure of feeling'.

Another moment at which he seeks to take a distance from the existing orthodoxy is with regard to the more authoritarian implications at work in the usual representation of Elizabethan drama and its society. Yes, Elizabethan drama enjoyed a moment where the common language contained all the 'elements of literary precision and complexity' (1952: 26) necessary to poetic drama. Because of the existence of a 'community of expression', the limitations of naturalism were invisible: there was an indiscernible blending of the 'lowest naturalism' with the 'highest conventionalism' (1952: 26). For Eliot and others, all this was evidence for 'the idea that a fully serious drama is impossible in a society where there is no common system of belief' (1952: 26).[12] Williams rejects this implication and asserts that 'the condition of a fully serious drama is less the existence of a common faith than the existence of a common language' (1952: 26). The existence of a common language does not imply the existence of a unitary moral – or political – outlook. It is not necessarily authoritarian. 'Morality in literature is not necessarily the assumption of certain ethical conclusions as background against which the immediate experience of the drama is paraded and tested' he argues,

> The moral activity of the artist can also be an individual perception of pattern, or structure, in experience; a process which involves the most intense and conscious response to new elements of substantial living, so that by this very consciousness new patterns of evaluation are created or former patterns reaffirmed.
>
> (1952: 27)

Against the authoritarian emphasis of a 'community of belief', he calls for a 'community of sensibility', one which would function in the open and democratic fashion he was to make central to *Culture and Society* and *The Long Revolution*:

> The artist's sensibility – his capacity for experience, his ways of think-ing, feeling, and conjunction – will always be finer and more devel-oped than that of the mean of his audience. But if his sensibility is at least of the same kind, communication is possible. Where his sensibility is of the same kind, his language and the language of his audience will be closely and organically related; the common language will be the expression of the common sensibility. There is no such common sensi-bility today.
>
> (1952: 26)

In this 'community of sensibility' somehow the right ideas will win the arguments in the end. Though there is no such common sensibility today, the implication is that it will come through in the end, communication will triumph. This is one of the weakest points of Williams's thought, as critics like Thompson were to pick up in relation to *The Long Revolution*. Nonetheless, it marks an attempt at moving away from the conservative and authoritarian implications of Eliot's general cultural views.[13]

Williams also chooses to disagree explicitly with Eliot over one very signifi-cant idea. Characteristically, this comes at a moment where the flow of argument demands that he acknowledge his full debt to Eliot. He finds in so doing that he wishes to establish a distance from Eliot. 'Story, character, idea, seem to have two related uses to the artist' he writes:

In one sense, they serve as a formula for the expression of his experience, in the way defined by T.S. Eliot: 'The only way of expressing emotion in the form of art is by finding an "objective correlative", in other words, a set of objects, a situation, a chain of events which shall be the formula of that particular emotion; such that when the external facts, which must terminate in sensory experience, are given, the emotion is immediately evoked.

(1952: 17)

The quotation is one of Eliot's most famous formulations, taken from his 1919 essay on *Hamlet* (Eliot 1966: 145). The formulation – and the essay as a whole – powerfully expresses Eliot's own ambivalence with regard to the notion of expression.[14] On the one hand, there is what was picked up by many *Scrutiny* critics, and by Williams himself on the whole: the idea of the ideal of artistic expression which lies in the extraordinary ability of the artist to use language as an instrument for the expression of his experience. Yet at the same time there is some implicit fascination with the idea that the very power and appeal of artistic expression may lie in what the artist has been unable to master, which may be the effect, in part, of the breakdown of the artist's control over the instrumentality of language. What interests Williams is Eliot's emphasis on the use of language as instrument, its ability, when controlled by the artist, to fully express experience and emotion. He criticises this instrumental view in the following terms:

In another sense, they may serve as a precipitant to the artist, in that through their comprehension the artist is able to find a provisional pattern of experience. By the force of his own grasp on their actuality, the artist is able to release his own, and their, reality. The only difference in the senses here outlined concerns the placing of these stages in the artistic process. Mr. Eliot's statement of the matter implies an ordered process, in which the particular emotion is first understood, and an objective correlative subsequently found for it. The second statement suggests that finding the objective correlative may often be for the artist the final act of evaluation of the particular experience, which will not have been completely understood until its mode of expression has been found.

(1952:17)

For a moment, but only for this moment in this period of his work, Williams questions the view that understanding precedes expression, and that language is simply the instrument of expression, and argues for the view in which language – figured here as the 'finding of an objective correlative' – is necessarily prior to the formation of understanding. This is a moment of real contradiction. For, as will be clear from the upcoming discussion of 'film as total expression', so many of the arguments in this early work on literature and drama tend towards just the instrumental view which he criticises here.[15] This is a moment of contradiction, in which Williams contradicts his own most powerful influence, and a great deal of the theoretical structure he has taken as his own. It is a focus on the question of language and expression that will not come into its own until the chapter on language in *Marxism and Literature*.

All in all, *Drama from Ibsen to Eliot* is a book deeply influenced by Eliot's ideas. Contemporary drama had come to lose the power proper to drama because it had forgotten that this power was above all generated by a vigorous but controlled use of language. The naturalist insistence on preserving the 'illusion of reality' is the single factor most responsible for the disabling restriction of dramatic speech to everyday prose. Though many have tried to get round this through the use of symbols, or an elevated language at moments of crisis, the problem of speech remains as 'the central one in modern drama' (1952: 26). In the end, the modes of naturalism are the problem and the techniques of Eliot offer the answer: 'The reform of modern English drama has two main phases: first, the development of naturalism; and, second, the establishment of verse plays in the theatre' (1952: 269–70).

In *Drama in Performance* and *Preface to Film*, Williams extends and develops the main argument against naturalism. Where *Drama from Ibsen to Eliot* emphasised the lack of any fully historical grasp of dramatic conventions in the available literary criticism, *Drama in Performance* sets out to provide at least a few moments from such a history, while *Preface to Film* goes on to argue that cinema might represent the possibility of a successful new convention of dramatic performance. In this new convention, the limitations of naturalism would finally be overcome. The new mode of total expression would return absolute control over expression to the author, and so fulfil the ideal of artistic instrumentality so dear to Eliot – and, with the exception of that one moment in *Drama from Ibsen to Eliot*, to Williams as well.

Performance and convention

Reading and Criticism had noted the tendency 'to believe that the naturalist method is the permanent and universal dramatic method' (Williams 1950: 91). At the centre of *Drama in Performance* is the argument that naturalism is a convention with a history, but a history that has been forgotten. The book traces the shape and structure of this forgetting. It shows how the dominant naturalist attitude has led to an anachronistic reading of some of the major texts in the Western dramatic canon. In line with the strictures of *Drama from Ibsen to Eliot*, it seeks to bridge the gap between *theatrical* criticism, the criticism of a play's performance, and *literary* criticism, the analysis of a play as a written text, though one written for performance. Williams, following Eliot, finds the usual separation of these two elements 'deeply disabling', and he therefore proposes to examine 'as a formal point of theory, the relation between text and performance' (Williams 1991: 18). This, in turn, can throw light on the nature of the contemporary failure of naturalism, and even suggest remedy for it, once we realise how the success of these early works depends largely on the working of conventions eclipsed by the moment of naturalism.

This is the challenge Williams issues by suggesting that the usual response to a play such as Shakespeare's *Antony and Cleopatra* is anachronistic. 'The construction of the play has often been condemned,' he notes:

> on the grounds of its frequent shifts and apparent disintegration. But this is to look for integration in the wrong place: in the realistic representation of time and place which have little to do with this kind of drama. The measure of time in the play is the dramatic verse; the reality of place is the reality of played action on the stage.
>
> (Williams 1991: 67)

The *Antigone* of Sophocles and the drama of the Medieval period present examples of the successful integration of writing and performance: 'Sophocles, working through the known conventions, has written the words so that they are necessarily enacted in this way, and with this issue. The words are the whole situation, for they contain and compel the intense physical realization' (1991: 31–2); *Everyman* is 'not only a masterpiece of literature, but a masterpiece of *dramatic* literature.... For a compelling feeling, at once individual and general, has been realized in a fully dramatic pattern, where speech, action and design are one' (1991: 58). These earlier – and often misunderstood – dramas were able to embody in performance a more coherent realization of the dramatic author's intentions than is possible in the conventions of contemporary drama.

Crucial to this success was the availability of coherent conventions of performance, conventions which, in turn, were made possible by the existence of a certain 'structure of feeling' shared by dramatist and audience. The problem for the present is that no new conventions have been formed which fully express the contemporary structure of feeling. Dramatists and their audiences are trapped in the tight place of a transitional moment. Williams argues – at least in the 1954 edition of *Drama in Performance* – that a comparative moment of transition can be found between 1896 and 1898, between the disastrous reception given to the first production of Chekhov's *The Seagull* by Karpov at the Alexandrinsky Theatre, and the extraordinary success of Stanislavsky's production only two years later. For the present, all that can be said is that:

> many writers no longer conceive their themes in a naturalist way. The emphasis has changed, in the mind, from the representation of apparent behaviour to a very different process: the process of attempting to discover a pattern, a structure of feeling, which is adequate to communicate, not merely the acknowledged and apparent, but the whole and unified life of man. One can see, in certain contemporary novels, and in certain plays, that the theme is obviously of this kind.
>
> (Williams 1954: 116)

Not merely 'the acknowledged and apparent, but the whole and unified life of man'. The phrase is worth pausing over, as it indicates the work to be done by Williams's emerging idea of the structure of feeling. To put it in a different theoretical idiom, the new drama will have at its core the desire to represent a social totality which is otherwise invisible, otherwise inaccessible to empirical human scrutiny. This social totality can none the less be adequately communicated by the structure of feeling which the dramatist expresses in his or her work. The structure of feeling can somehow represent the inexpressible social totality. That is the very promise of representation; that is, the necessary aporia of what it means for expression to stand in for something.

But, to return to the focus of Williams's own attention, what counts is that the naturalist attitude still prevails, despite the efforts of dramatists of the past thirty years or so to break with it. Eliot has been the closest to realising such a break; but even he has been unable to overcome the disabling contradiction between the naturalist representation of speech and the need for a non-naturalist dramatic action. Naturalism has no adequate convention for the proper linking of speech and action in drama. In the conclusion to the 1954 edition, he can only offer the argument that:

> certain changes in the minds of writers and others have made naturalism outmoded; and that a conscious acceptance of a different dramatic intention can be realised, in practical terms, by the full use and development of skills that already exist in the theatre.
>
> (Williams 1954: 122)

But he has to accept that these 'have not been integrated into a satisfactory general form' (1954: 122). Drama, then, and even Eliot's drama, seemed at a dead end. What was needed was some new convention of performance which could break the stranglehold of a naturalism which had even repressed the existence of previous conventions in the history of drama. It was film which seemed to provide exactly the right ground for the emergence of a new convention and a newly realised structure of feeling. Film promised to return the dramatic performance to a condition of singular utterance, one in which the intentions of the dramatic author could be fully realized without the distortions imposed through actual production and direction.

Film as total expression

Preface to Film is the only one of the three books on naturalism which has never been republished, and this may account for its relative neglect in critical accounts of the Williams canon. Yet the main essay in the book, 'Film and the Dramatic Tradition', is the most powerful version of Williams's critique of naturalism, and gives the most insight into the development of the concept of structure of feeling.

As an undergraduate, Williams had developed an interest in film as a regular spectator at the Socialist Film Club's weekend shows, and this interest ran against the grain of Leavisism. Leavis had given a notable characterisation of film in his early pamphlet, 'Mass Civilisation and Minority Culture'. Here, because of its greater power and immediacy, the cinema was seen as more of a threat to the vitality of culture than even the emergent tabloid press pioneered by Lord Northcliffe. 'Films have a so much more potent influence' wrote Leavis:

> They provide now the main form of recreation in the civilised world; and they involve surrender, under conditions of hypnotic receptivity, to the cheapest emotional appeals, appeals the more insidious because they are associated with a compellingly vivid illusion of actual life. It would be difficult to dispute that the result must be serious damage to the 'standard of living'…it will not be disputed that broadcasting, like the films, is in practice, mainly a means of passive diversion, and that it tends to make active recreation, especially active use of the mind, more difficult.
>
> (Leavis 1933: 20–1)

In brief, if the purpose of the new literary studies was to save the world from mass culture, as it was for Leavis, then film should *never* receive a place in the curriculum. Implicit in Leavis's argument is, of course, the idea of English studies as a form of 'active recreation', a training in the 'active use of the mind'. Leavis's argument relied upon a claim that literary texts were intrinsically capable of generating intellectual activity, and refused to see that this activity of the mind might itself be simply a product of critical attention and analysis when devoted to texts of any kind, whether of high or low culture. No such prejudice informs Williams's approach to cinema. In 'Film as a Tutorial Subject', he had argued against the Leavisite line, and for the addition of film to WEA tutorials, insisting that film 'provides opportunities for criticism' just as much as literature, and promised to extend his arguments in the forthcoming *Preface to Film*.[16]

The first imperative of *Preface to Film* is to connect cinema to the history of the traditional dramatic canon, and this is the aim of the first chapter by Williams, 'Film and the Dramatic Tradition'. Michael Orrom contributes a chapter, 'Film and its Dramatic Techniques', and the book as a whole concludes with a postscript by Williams.

'Film and the Dramatic Tradition' argues that criticism to date has been marred by its refusal to understand cinema in relation to the history of drama. Properly understood, the advent of cinema may represent a shift in the possibilities of dramatic expression equivalent to Aeschylus's introduction of the second actor, thus subordinating the words of the chorus to the now newly dramatic dialogue. Only when seen in this large historical perspective can the essential novelty and importance of film be grasped. Most important is: 'the fact that the performance which it embodies is recorded and final. It is, that is to say, a total performance, which cannot be distinguished from the work that is being performed' (Williams and Orrom 1954: 1). Film, in other words, seemed to offer what was most lacking in contemporary drama: a convention of performance which would guarantee the full and singular communication of the dramatic author's intentions, without the distortions characteristic of dramatic production in Britain since the advent of the theatre director.[17]

Once again, Eliot's verse-drama provides the necessary limit-case of existing naturalist conventions, particularly with regard to a naturalist style of speech *and* movement. Williams sees this style as a major drawback, 'the familiar one of naturalism: that the concern is to represent "real life", rather than to communicate a dramatic emotion' (1954: 48). Eliot's verse-drama, which tried to break away from this style, could only enjoy partial success and this was a symptom of the general crisis of naturalist convention. 'What is necessary' he argues 'is that dramatists, in collaboration with actors, think again in terms of writing for speech and movement, as an integrated dramatic form' (1954: 49). What is necessary is a convention which would re-establish the possibility of 'total expression' which had existed for Sophocles, and for some Medieval drama:

> a play written from this idea of total expression contains, in its essential conception, the total performance which is necessary to communicate it in the theatre. That is to say, not only the speech, but also the movement and design, have been devised by the dramatist, in terms of his understanding of the appropriate conventions of actions and designers, so that the written play contains everything that is to be performed; the performance itself is the communication of this.
>
> (1954: 50)

At the centre of this theory of total expression lies the idea of a fully realised authorial intention drawn from Eliot. It was above all the iterability of film which appealed to the young Williams: the pure artistic expression of the author/director could never be betrayed by the intermediary figure of the actor/director. The new medium of cinema offered significant opportunities for the realisation of this total expression. 'The moving-picture camera itself is', he concludes, 'a most effective agent for the kind of controlled total effect which I have been urging' (1954: 51).[18] All in all, cinema presents a 'practical alternative' to the problems inherent in 'the methods of naturalism' (1954: vii–viii).

Tony Pinkney has recently offered a summary of Williams's position in his early writings on drama. His assessment differs from mine, and I think he is only able to justify his central points by bending the evidence a little.[19] He emphasises repeatedly the importance of German Expressionism, and concludes that certainly

Williams had his reservations, about the occasional externality of expres-
sionistic devices of spectacle and its relative devaluation of dramatic speech,
but these are only qualifications within a deep overall endorsement.

(Pinkney 1989b: 22)

As a key piece of evidence, he cites the apparent enthusiasm and endorsement
for German Expressionist cinema present in Williams's statement that this is
'the kind of film which has most nearly realized the ideal of a wholly conceived
drama' (Williams and Orrom 1954: 52), that is, the ideal of total expression.
But while he registers that there were 'significant qualifications' to this claim, he
does not detail them, for the very simple reason that the claim for the interest of
German Expressionist film is so limited by Williams's reservations that his
position could never count as a 'deep overall endorsement'. The simple fact is
that films like *Dr Caligari* were silent films, and most of Williams's interests – as
we have seen – in going beyond naturalism were concerned with the problem of
the dramatic and controlled use of speech in drama. As Williams goes on to say:

it has always seemed to me significant that the most successful examples
were in silent film. For, if one looks at expressionist drama as a whole, one
sees a very exciting new convention of movement and design, which has
been achieved, however, at the cost of a radical neglect of speech...it is
clear that the use of sound, particularly for dramatic speech, would have
presented the expressionists with very difficult problems, which might have
ruined such conventional integrations as they had achieved.

(Williams and Orrom 1954: 52)

In terms of the general argument which Williams was maintaining, and which
focuses on the difficulty and importance of dramatic speech, Expressionism
cannot be given the centrality that Pinkney lends it. The main point is that
Expressionist cinema proved to be a dead end, despite its early promise.
Similarly, Pinkney's claim that *Drama from Ibsen to Eliot* (though in a 'displaced
way') 'engages the great Expressionist debates of the 1930s' (Pinkney 1989b:
21) is exaggerated, and can only be sustained by selective quotation. Though
Williams does indeed state that it is 'very common, in England, to be
patronising about the expressionist experiment', he does not lend it his 'deep
endorsement'. Once again, the claims for Expressionism are severely limited:
when 'expressionist drama is set against the poetic drama, or against the very
best of the naturalists...it is true that it must be judged inferior' – and the
reason for this lies with the same fault as he had observed *vis*-à-*vis* Expressionist
cinema – 'it served to confirm the impoverishment of dramatic *language*'
(Williams and Orrom 1954: 184). Each time the point is the same: Expressionism is only partially successful, it suffers too much from impoverished dramatic
language. In the end it is Eliot's verse-dramas which point the way forward; a
claim that Pinkney can only ever diminish and read anachronistically, from the
point of view of Williams's later change of heart.[20]

Structure of feeling

Most commentaries treat 'structure of feeling' as if it were a concept which emerged in Williams's work in the late rather than the early 1950s, and, as such, it has been the object of considerable discussion and criticism. But something is lost when the history of the emergence of the term is not fully traced. *Preface to Film* is the first work in which the term is deployed, and which seeks to establish the distinctive reach and explanatory power which made it a *point de repère* of the later work. Duly examined, it becomes clear that the idea of 'structure of feeling' is used as a deliberate challenge and alternative to the existing explanatory framework of Marxist literary and cultural analysis.[21]

By the time of the interviews with the New Left Review team, published as *Politics and Letters* in 1979, structure of feeling had become known as one of Williams's most characteristic concepts, a keyword of Williams's own vocabulary, and just as shifting and unstable in its conceptual identity as any item in *Keywords* itself. David Simpson – though he neglects its emergence in *Preface to Film* – has given an excellent survey of its mutation in Williams's thinking from its use in *Culture and Society* (1958), where 'it occurs somewhat casually ...[and] seems to define something like ideology in its classic and negative sense', across 'his first sustained account' of it in *The Long Revolution* (1961), through to its reappraisal in *Marxism and Literature* (1977), where 'for all its appearance in a modernized and theoretical format, the spirit and most of the letter...has not much changed' since 1961 (Simpson 1995b: 42).[22]

The discussion of 'structure of feeling' in *Politics and Letters* brings out some major theoretical problems with the term, though here again, the *New Left Review* team concentrate on the deployment of the concept in *The Long Revolution*, ignoring the fact of its first appearance in *Preface to Film* until Williams draws their attention to it. The interviewers point to difficulties with the point of reference for the term: structure of feeling seems to refer to a generation, and yet at times to have a longer lifespan than any single generation, it seems far too unitary in its expression of social consciousness with its casual reference across classes (Williams 1979: 156–62). Nonetheless, for the *New Left Review* team, the concept of 'structure of feeling' remains 'one of the most notable theoretical innovations of *The Long Revolution*' (1979: 156).

In his replies to their various criticisms, Williams accepts many of their arguments, and yet manages to defend his basic positions in a complex and nuanced defence of his arguments and their original context of discussion and debate. He suggests that the proper starting point for any discussion of the idea of the structure of feeling is with its first appearance and definition in 1954. 'The first time I used it was actually in *Preface to Film*' he notes, and insists that the key to the notion, both to all it can do and to all the difficulties it still leaves, is that it was developed as an analytic procedure for actual written works, with a very strong stress on forms and conventions.

(Williams 1979: 159)

'To this day', he notes, 'I find that I keep coming back to this notion from the actual experience of literary analysis rather than from any theoretical satisfaction with the concept itself' (1979: 159). In other words, under the pressure of the *New Left Review*'s probing questions, he admits that there are problems with the use of the term as a concept, but then defends its use pragmatically as 'an analytic procedure for actual written works' (1979: 159). Quite aside from the question of whether the two uses can be so easily separated, it is important to ask whether the original use of the term was pragmatic or conceptual in the senses at work here. We shall see that he gives a selective account of its original use in *Preface to Film*, one which does its best to conceal the term's original ambitious valency; for despite the emphasis on the casually pragmatic usefulness of the term for literary analysis, it did begin life very much as a direct challenge to the existing explanatory orthodoxy of Marxist literary criticism. There is a forgetting at work in Williams's own account of the term's origin just as important as its neglect in most of the existing secondary material.

This forgetting comes through in a quite literal elision in Williams's discussion. In support of this emphasis on the textual and pragmatic nature of the idea (that it is an 'analytic procedure for actual written works') he quotes the following section from *Preface to Film*:

> In the study of a period, we may be able to reconstruct, with more or less accuracy, the material life, the social organization, and, to a large extent, the dominant ideas. It is not necessary to discuss here which, if any, of these aspects is, in the whole complex, determining; an important institution like the drama will, in all probability, take its colour in varying degrees from them all....To relate a work of art to any part of that observed totality may, in varying degrees, be useful, but it is a common experience, in analysis, to realize that when one has measured the work against the separable parts, there yet remains some element for which there is no external counterpart. This element, I believe, is what I have named the *structure of feeling* of a period and it is only realizable through experience of the work of art itself, as a whole.

> (Williams 1979: 158–9)

The emphasis here falls on the idea of the structure of feeling as the result of a work of textual analysis, 'only realizable through experience of the work of art itself'. What is de-emphasised – through selective quotation – is the larger theoretical point Williams was seeking to make in his original formulation. Structure of feeling was intended as a direct challenge to the Marxist explanation of cultural reproduction. As we shall see, the first sentence of the quoted extract reads differently if we see it in the context of the whole paragraph from which it is extracted, and in relation to the flow of argument as a whole. But let us first of all relocate this selective quotation in the context of argument at work in *Preface to Film*.

Structure of feeling as convention

In theoretical terms, what interests Williams most in *Preface to Film* is the necessity for understanding dramatic conventions not merely as questions of technique and staging but as themselves forms of social consciousness. There are in fact two senses at work in the idea of convention, 'convention covers both *tacit consent* and *accepted standards*' (Williams and Orrom 1954: 15). A convention is, on the one hand, simply an agreed on standard or method of performance. An audience will willingly suspend its disbelief and accept that an actor can put on a grey cloak and become 'invisible', though in reality he continues to be seen. Spectators agree to believe that they can 'overhear' a soliloquy, even at the back of the auditorium, while it goes unnoticed by any other actors on stage. The second sense of convention as tacit − not fully conscious − agreement comes through most clearly when the usual conventions are disturbed:

> We will agree that a murderer may hide behind a door (where we can still see him), and that he may look down, with an expression of agony, at his hands (which we at once agree are stained with innocent blood); but if he should come forward to the front of the stage, and in twenty lines of verse, or in recitative or song, or in dance, express (if more fully and intensely) the same emotion, we at once, or many of us, feel uneasy, and are likely to say afterwards that it was 'unreal'.
>
> (Williams and Orrom 1954: 18)

In this second sense, conventions refer to the tacit agreement, likely to be unconscious, which yet forms and grounds social consciousness. Thus the very existence of dramatic conventions as methods always indicates at the same time the existence of a level of tacit consent to and understanding of them amongst the audience. The question is then how and why do changes in convention take place?

For Williams, the answer is that such changes in convention as dramatic method must in some sense reflect or articulate some degree of change in the grounds of social consciousness itself. According to Williams, it seems likely that 'the effective changes took place when there was already a latent willingness to accept them, at least among certain groups in society, from whom the artist drew his support' (1954: 20). And it is precisely this 'latent willingness' which most interests Williams. For potentially at least, it gives a place for the contemporary artist or critic to create something new:

It may be possible, eventually, so to understand the relation of particular conventions to the life of the time in which they flourished, that a reasonable prediction of what is necessary in a present situation may be made and argued. I do not think that any such understanding at present exists, but certain points seem to me to be sufficiently grounded to be put forward as tentative argument.

(1954: 21)

Williams returns here to the starting point of Communist Party criticism, that a position exists from which 'a reasonable prediction of what is necessary in a present situation may be made and argued'. But – doubtless bearing in mind the criticisms he had received from Tillyard on just this point – he writes with considerable circumspection. No such position or understanding exists at present; all that Williams can put forward is a 'tentative argument', though one he thinks is reasonably well grounded. What follows is the elaboration of the idea of structure of feeling, his recasting or supersession of the Marxist idea of structure and superstructure, in the crucial paragraph from which Williams makes his selective quotation in 1979.

The paragraph in fact begins with a strong statement which can only be understood as being written against the Marxist structure and superstructure argument. 'In principle,' writes Williams:

it seems clear that the dramatic conventions of any given period are fundamentally related to the structure of feeling in that period. I use the phrase *structure of feeling* because it seems to me more accurate, in this context, than *ideas* or *general life*. All the products of a community in a given period are, we now commonly believe, essentially related, although in practice, in detail, this is not always easy to see.

(1954: 21)

When Williams writes that the phrase 'structure of feeling' seems 'more accurate' than '*ideas* or *general life*', he is arguing against the Marxist structure and superstructure paradigm in which: 'The mode of production in material life determines the general character of the social, political and spiritual processes of life' (in Marx's words, as cited in *Culture and Society* (Williams 1958a: 266)). By eliding the topic sentence of the whole paragraph, Williams distorts the thrust of his argument in 1954. Without these qualifying sentences, the first sentence which he quotes in 1979 reads as a partial endorsement of the usual structure and superstructure analysis (as it is translated in *Culture and Society*):

In the study of a period, we may be able to reconstruct, with more or less accuracy, the material life, the social organization, and, to a large extent, the dominant ideas. It is not necessary to discuss here which, if any, of these aspects is, in the whole complex, determining; an important institu-

tion like the drama will, in all probability, take its colour in varying degrees
from them all...

(cited in Williams 1979: 159; Williams and Orrom 1954: 21)

But read in context, the 'may' has a negative rather than a positive sense; the
orthodox Marxist analysis is belittled rather than endorsed. In orthodox Marxist
analysis, dramatic or literary conventions of any kind would be 'fundamentally
related' to the economic base, not to Williams's 'structure of feeling'. In *Politics
and Letters*, three more sentences are then cut from the original version, and
their excision also has the effect of blunting the force and address of the original
argument. They read:

> But while we may, in the study of a past period, separate out particular
> aspects of life, and treat them as if they were self-contained, it is obvious
> that this is only how they may be studied, not how they were experienced.
> We examine each element as a precipitate, but in the living experience of
> the time every element was in solution, an inseparable part of a complex
> whole. And it seems to be true, from the nature of art, that it is from such a
> totality that the artist draws; it is in art, primarily, that the effect of the
> totality, the dominant structure of feeling, is expressed and embodied.
>
> (Williams and Orrom 1954: 21)

This is no mere practice of textual analysis; what is at work in Williams's idea of
the structure of feeling is a statement of the fundamental claims of literary
criticism, its insistence that 'it is in art, primarily, that the effect of the totality,
the dominant structure of feeling, is expressed and embodied' – and, or
because, if in art, then in criticism. The function of the structure of feeling is
then much more important than it appears if the final sentences are quoted
alone:

> To relate a work of art to any part of that observed totality may, in varying
> degrees, be useful; but it is a common experience, in analysis, to realize that
> when one has measured the work against the separable parts, there yet
> remains some element for which there is no external counterpart. This
> element, I believe, is what I have named the *structure of feeling* of a period,
> and it is only realizable through experience of the work of art itself, as a
> whole.
>
> (1954: 21–2)

Williams's original claims, in 1954, for the 'structure of feeling' are far
stronger than he represents them in 1979. Structure of feeling needs to be
recognised for what it was: a concept deployed as a conscious alternative and
direct challenge to the available Marxist formula. Indeed, this comes through,
though obliquely, a little later in the discussion in *Politics and Letters*, where
Williams remembers the criticisms of a friend or colleague: 'I know what you

are really doing', he was told, 'you are writing a socialist history of culture, but whenever you see a socialist term coming up you omit it and put in another term': structure of feeling for structure and superstructure. When he admits that 'my language was very different from that in which I would have written between '39 and '41' (1979: 156), we should remember that what he was arguing against was the Marxist criticism he had espoused as an undergraduate, but which he had turned away from under the pressure of the discursive constraints of the discipline in general and the unanswerable criticisms of Tillyard in particular.

If we examine the actual emergence of the term 'structure of feeling', we soon see that it is best understood as Williams's most significant attempt so far to preserve and yet to go beyond the Marxist arguments concerning literary and cultural reproduction which had been so thoroughly criticised within the new literary criticism of Cambridge English. The means of this supersession is to be the idea of 'structure of feeling'. Its task is then twofold: first, to explain the nature of major shifts in dramatic convention, but second, to explain these shifts without recourse to the clumsy Marxist metaphor of 'base and superstructure'. As Williams himself put it, though referring to the composition of *The Long Revolution*:

> the kind of 'relating' I was thinking of...was the idea that, say, because there was an industrial revolution there must have been industrial poetry .... It would seem to be a reasonable deduction from a very simple version of economic determination, that since the decisive phenomenon was the advent of capitalism, there should be capitalist poetry. When I was writing *The Long Revolution* I was probably over-preoccupied by these one-dimensional sorts of explanation and relation.
>
> (Williams 1979: 144)

This was just the kind of one-dimensional thinking he had found at work – as we discussed in Chapter 1 – in writers such as Christopher Caudwell in his chapters on the English poets in *Illusion and Reality*.[23]

Conclusion

Those critics who have had something to say about Williams's early writings on drama have tended to restrict themselves to the repetition of a point first made in a review of *Drama from Ibsen to Eliot* in 1953. J.R. Williams saw a certain 'extremism' at work, 'the kind that says drama consists entirely of words', and went so far as to accuse Williams of 'fanatical overstatement'.[24] Jan Gorak turns this observation into yet another instance of Williams's fundamental 'alienation'. 'Williams alienates himself from the very canon he seeks to re-examine', he writes: 'Unable to free himself from the limiting assumptions that language provides all dramatic life, his commentaries often ignore the substance of the action, focusing instead on the inadequacies of the playwright's words'

(Gorak 1988: 23–4). Following Gorak, in what is surely the best single essay on Williams's writings on drama to date, Bernard Sharrat articulates the same point around a central issue of theory: the emphasis which Williams places on the artist's instrumental relation to language. Sharratt refers to Williams's empiricism as one which invites us:

> to think in terms of a simple empiricist notion, of an elementary encounter with some recalcitrant particular, some inner 'I' forging a shape for its own localizable and specific 'experience' prior to the secondary act of writing this down in a formal dramatic mode, and subsequently releasing that shaped whole for inevitable partial realization in an essentially inadequate theatrical performance.
>
> (Sharrat 1989: 132)

Similarly, Graham Holderness, in his fine introduction to the new edition of *Drama in Performance*, writes:

> The emphasis on the primacy of the text can lead towards too rigid and mechanistic a conception of the control exercised by text over performance. If the dramatic text is a completely written exposition of all the play's potentialities of performance, as Williams seems to affirm, then each 'correct' performance should be identical to every other.
>
> (Holderness 1991: 10)

Just as, in *Preface to Film*, Williams had found the 'performance' of cinema to be. In other words, these critics are correct in stating that he had an overriding interest, in these early works on drama, in the idea of what he called 'total expression', the iterability of performance. But what they neglect to ask is the significance of this interest. If Williams was treating drama as a 'kind of reader', what kind of reader was he? The answer – at least as regards the structure of feeling – is less as a Leavisite and more as the non-Marxist Marxist that he had set himself the task of becoming.

For the significance of the dramatic text was in the end subordinated to the structure of feeling it could – even if only partially – express. As Williams put it in *Preface to Film*:

> naturalism was a response to changes in the structure of feeling, which, in the event, it could not wholly express. The structure of feeling, as I have been calling it, lies deeply embedded in our lives; it cannot be merely extracted and summarized; it is perhaps only in art – and this is the importance of art – that it can be realized, and communicated, as a whole experience.
>
> (Williams and Orrom 1954: 54)

In the end, the most serious charge that the *New Left Review* interviewers put to Williams with regard to the idea of structure of feeling is, in fact, its very *raison d'être*, the ways in which it assures the literary or dramatic critic access to a social consciousness somehow behind the available evidence. As they put it, isn't Williams guilty of:

> a silent elision from the texts of the period as privileged evidence of the structure of feeling to the structure of feeling as privileged evidence of the social structure or historical epoch as such? The concept then tends to become an epistemology for gaining a comprehension of a whole society.
>
> (Williams 1979: 164)

In fact, that was precisely what English studies meant to Williams in this early period: an epistemology for gaining a privileged insight into the history of the social totality. And this is why the study of drama – properly understood – is central and not peripheral to his work as a whole. Indeed – as with his reply to this question – we can see that a part of the progress from this early point onwards lies precisely in the relinquishing of this totalising claim. Nonetheless, it remains a part of his work through to the end, as even a quick glance at his inaugural lecture as Professor of Drama reveals.

'People have often asked me why,' said Williams, 'trained in literature and expressly in drama, making an ordinary career in writing and teaching dramatic history and analysis, I turned – *turned* – to what they would call sociology if they were quite sure I wouldn't be offended' (Williams 1974e: 19). As the emphasis and repetition make clear, what the ordinary professional critic might see as some intrusive element, as some eccentric or peripheral concern on Williams's part in his writings on drama was its 'sociological' bent – the Cambridge codeword for anything resembling a Marxist analysis of literature. But the 'sociological' was central. In a telling aside, which works to locate Williams in the very tradition of social criticism he had delineated in *Culture and Society*, he refers to the example of John Ruskin. 'Ruskin didn't turn from architecture to society' he notes; 'he saw society in its architecture', and because of this was able to 'learn to read both architecture and society in new ways' (1974e: 19–20). For Williams, the study of drama has worked in much the same way as Ruskin's architecture. 'I learned something from analysing drama' he writes:

> something which seemed to me effective not only as a way of seeing certain aspects of society but as a way of getting through to some of the funda- mental conventions which we group as society itself. These, in their turn, make some of the problems of drama quite newly active. It was by looking both ways, at a stage and a text, and at a society active, enacted, in them, that I thought I saw the significance of the enclosed room – the room on the stage, with its new metaphor of the fourth wall lifted – as at once a dramatic and a social fact.
>
> (Williams 1974e: 20)

In the end, this insistence on 'looking both ways' can serve to correct both orthodox literary analysis, and the orthodox social analysis of Marxist economism. To be able to understand the significance of the lifted fourth wall of the naturalist theatre means understanding both the history of the conventions of drama, but also the deeper conventions underlying that narrowly academic history. It is to see through to 'the fundamental conventions which we group as society itself', what Williams refers to as 'a structure of feeling in a precise contemporary world' (Williams 1974e: 21). The analysis and interpretation of dramatic form cannot take place outside the understanding of the basic structures of a social order. It is then that this analysis can help to understand the fundamental conventions of the social order itself. Where techniques become methods, 'significant general modes' of consciousness, then the analysis of dramatic forms questions and corrects both orthodox literary studies and orthodox Marxist thinking. This is then the major line of theoretical continuity – however revised, improved and elaborated – between Williams's earliest work on drama and his final positions on cultural materialism.[25]

3   Culture and communication
1950–62

Culture and Society 1780–1950 was first published in September 1958, and reprinted four months later in January 1959. Since then it has hardly been out of print; it is Williams's best-seller. By 1979, it was reckoned to have sold some 160,000 copies worldwide, and had been translated into Catalan, Japanese, German and Italian. For critics and scholars of Williams's work, *Culture and Society* is regarded as 'one of the most widely read texts of cultural history ever written', one of the 'founding texts of cultural studies', 'probably the most formative socialist work of the period', 'a lifechanger for youngish readers in 1960', 'foundational', 'probably his most famous' book. As one advertisement put it in the 1960s, 'Not to know about...*Culture and Society* is to brand oneself the intellectual equivalent of a square.' *Culture and Society* is Williams's classic; and, perhaps like all classics, its original circumstances and address have been forgotten.[1]

Culture and Society is that rare thing in academic writing, a crossover work, one read by at least two generations of liberal and leftist academics, and by an extraordinary number of non-academics. Most commentators have tended to divide into two camps. For the first, the book represents a masterpiece of disinterested academic commentary, while the second see it as exemplifying the worst of Williams's theoretical and political failings. The *New Left Review* interviewers, for instance, remark on its 'striking tone of equanimity and authority' (Williams 1979: 98), while J.P. Ward applauds the 'level reasonableness of the writing' (Ward 1981: 17). But for the Althusserian theorist of the 1970s, the book seemed 'an idealist and academicist project', too deeply rooted in the 'empiricist' problematic; while from the post-structuralist position of the late 1980s, it – and Williams's related works – demonstrated a commitment to a dated and unrealisable 'Enlightenment ideal of culture'.[2] By the late 1970s, in the *New Left Review* interviews, Williams himself seemed tired of discussing the book. *Culture and Society* appeared too deeply marked by his 'disgusted withdrawal' from all forms of collaboration, as well as by the 'intense disappointment that they were not available' (Williams 1979: 106).

What tends to disappear in such readings – including, at moments, Williams's own – is any sense of the impact of *Culture and Society* on contemporaries. The polemical edge of *Culture and Society* is forgotten as the context of its production and the circumstances of its address disappear over the horizon of the present. In this chapter, I seek to revive some of the central lines of argument in *Culture and Society* and the related work, *The Long Revolution*, and argue that these two books – which represent a significant defining phase in Williams's work – are best understood when placed in the broad context of the cultural politics of the time, and, particularly when brought into relation with the debates in and around adult education through the late 1940s and into and across the 1950s. Williams's work in this period constitutes what Edward W. Said described as a 'beginning' when he wrote, in his influential study *Beginnings: Intention and Method*, of how in retrospect 'we can regard a beginning as the point at which, in a given work, the writer departs from all other works; a beginning already establishes relationships with works already existing, relationships of either continuity or antagonism or some mixture of both' (Said 1975: 3). *Culture and Society* embodies just such a set of antagonistic and yet continuous relations.

The starting point of this massively popular work was insistently local and emphatically conjunctural; but it belonged in many ways more to the late 1940s than the late 1950s. In the foreword to the study, Williams acknowledges that the origins of the project go back to the 1940s, and to the initiative of the journal *Politics and Letters*: 'Our object then was to enquire into and where possible reinterpret this tradition which the word 'culture' describes in terms of the experience of our own generation' (1958a: vii). 'Our generation': in retrospect, that of the Angry Young Men, the Scholarship Boys and, ultimately, the New Left. Perhaps most strikingly, the 1950s sees the first appearance of distinctively working-class voices on the cultural scene of the new welfare state:[3] in drama, John Osborne and Arnold Wesker; in fiction, John Wain and Kingsley Amis; and in the new form of cultural criticism, Richard Hoggart and Williams himself. 'I knew perfectly well who I was writing against', remembered Williams in 1979, 'Eliot, Leavis and the whole of the cultural conservatism that had formed around them – the people who had pre-empted the culture and literature of this country' (Williams 1979: 112). With the publication of *The Long Revolution* in 1961, and the later study *Communications* (1962), Williams became the spokesperson of the New Left, and perhaps even the first public intellectual of the British working class.[4]

Williams's final results in the English Tripos Examinations were outstanding, and Trinity College immediately offered him a scholarship to stay on as a graduate student.[5] This was usually the first step on a relatively easy climb – in that period – to tenure as a lecturer in the University. But Williams turned away. Like a significant number of other leftist intellectuals, he preferred to move away from the academy to work in what was perceived as the more politically charged and more politically positive environment of adult education.[6] He worked as a staff tutor for the Oxford Delegacy for Extra-Mural Studies, organising and teaching classes in collaboration with the Workers' Education Association from 1946 until his appointment as Lecturer in Drama and return to Cambridge in 1961.[7]

Despite his academic achievements, and the material security afforded by the new job, Williams was still troubled intellectually. After the closure of *Politics and Letters* in 1948 (a year which had also seen the failure of a projected documentary film with Paul Rotha), he felt a sense of depression and isolation settle on him. 'The collapse of the journal', he later related:

> was a personal crisis.... So many other initiatives, like the film, had also been blocked or failed. The experience confirmed the pattern of feeling I had found in Ibsen. For a period I was in such a state of failure and withdrawal that I stopped reading the papers or listening to the news. At that point, apart from going on with the adult education teaching, I felt I could only write myself out of this in a non-collaborative way. I pulled back to do my own work. For the next ten years I wrote in nearly complete isolation.
>
> (Williams 1979: 77)

We need to distinguish here between what Williams experienced or remembered as a sense of intellectual isolation – the fact that he felt no one was thinking on the same lines as himself – and the real resources of sociality, friendship and professional support he was able to draw on from his group of colleagues and friends. After all, as John McIlroy has charted, with exemplary precision, Williams had good relations and debates with many colleagues and friends in the adult education movement and beyond.[8] The real sense of isolation lay rather in the hostile consensus of conservative opinion which he faced and argued against in *Culture and Society* and *The Long Revolution*. The task of this chapter is to recover something of this context of argument and debate. We can better understand that sense of intellectual isolation if we see just how different the central and related ideas of *Culture and Society* – culture and the masses – were in the dominant discourses of the period. And we can get some idea of what lay behind this by examining some of the first responses to *Culture and Society* by contemporary reviewers, particularly from those who were hostile to the very nature of Williams's arguments.

Reviews and reviewers

An early review of *Culture and Society* by Frank Kermode was one of the few to take issue with its literary history as such.[9] In 'From Burke to Orwell', Kermode found the book to be of 'quite radical importance' (Kermode 1959: 86), but found Williams guilty of misrepresenting the history of the figure of the Romantic Artist, 'perhaps in order to be over-generous to working-class culture' (1959: 87). For many other reviewers (and this became clearer still in responses to *The Long Revolution* in 1961), the political agenda which Kermode read in the margins of the work became the central focus of attention and argument. Indeed, aside from Kermode's essay, most contemporary reviews of the two works saw them less as academic contributions to literary and cultural history, and more as political polemics. The reviews then fell into two broad categories: those which welcomed the books as expressions of the 'New Left' sensibility; and those which rejected them on just that account. The debate on *Culture and Society* in the pages of Bateson's journal, *Essays in Criticism*, may serve as an exemplary instance for our analysis of their contemporary impact and resonance.[10]

Richard Hoggart's review prompted the debate between Williams and some opponents in the Critical Forum section of the journal. Hoggart, despite a history of differences with Williams, welcomed the book as both 'a cogent study' of the culture and society tradition and as 'a substantial contribution to it' (Hoggart 1959: 171). He singled out its final chapter for particular praise. *Culture and Society* was 'the most solidly based and intelligent' piece of work to come from the 'New Left'; it captured 'the extraordinary sense of social change in the air' (1959: 171). This review – from a fellow tutor in the WEA and the author of *The Uses of Literacy* (1957) – was the occasion for a Critical Forum debate in which Ian Gregor, Malcolm Pittock and Williams himself took part (Gregor *et al.* 1959).

For Ian Gregor and Malcolm Pittock, it was precisely that sense of social change which posed the main problem, and their negative responses may help us grasp the political challenge represented by Williams's work. A striking feature of their accounts is a certain rhetorical ploy in which the political motivations of Williams's arguments are ruled out of court for contravening the apparent rules of objective academic criticism, while the political motivations of their own arguments are held to be irreproachable.

Both Gregor and Pittock single out the Conclusion to *Culture and Society* as the focal point for their disagreements. Gregor goes straight to the point and accuses Williams of being guilty of a 'sleight-of-hand' in arguing for a definition of culture as a 'whole way of life', and consequently as one which can include both 'conscious art' and the creation of democratic institutions by the working class as cultural achievements. He therefore rejects any definition of culture which might claim that 'the National Union of Mineworkers is a creative achievement of the same kind as *Sons and Lovers*' (Gregor *et al.* 1959: 428). Since such a definition is unthinkable in the terms given by Leavisite cultural analysis, it is unthinkable *tout court,* Williams is guilty of advancing arguments 'in general terms' when 'they are in fact politically weighed' (1959: 425). In a word, Gregor disagrees with Williams's cultural politics, but prefers to attribute that disagreement not to the fact of Williams holding different political views to his own, but in a daze of conservative blindness, to his holding political views at all!

Similarly, Malcolm Pittock claims he does not want Williams 'to show his political colours', only 'to give his ideas a sharper definition' (Gregor *et al.* 1959: 431), but he then goes on to offer a series of criticisms which, though they are presented as if they were simply neutral, common-sense or even logical, are clearly derived from his own sense of political identity. His concluding remark, with its insulting condescension to working-class intelligence, does much to explain Williams's later ire in recalling the debate. The review closes by quoting from the final chapter of *Culture and Society* the phrase: 'The human crisis is always a crisis of understanding: what we genuinely understand we can do' (Williams 1958a: 338), and then querying: 'What we genuinely understand we can do...But what happens if most of us are incapable of understanding?' (1959: 432). Such a remark embodies the conservative consciousness which is the very target of the arguments in *Culture and Society*. Gregor and Pittock clearly belong to that group of people who, in Williams's terms, 'had pre-empted the culture and literature of this country' (Williams 1979: 112).

A later review of *The Long Revolution*, also in *Essays in Criticism*, offers striking confirmation of the reactionary nature of Pittock's own conservative agenda (Pittock 1962). Here, in a general complaint about the book's 'omissions' and 'wishful thinking', Pittock argues that Williams 'converts what is really only a theory of change into a theory of progress' (Pittock 1962: 88), and asserts his conservative pessimism against Williams's socialist optimism:

> The power over our environment offered by the revolution in technology and communications is inseparable from power over ourselves: as in the most extreme instance we can use this power just as easily to destroy human society as to develop it....Mr. Williams has, in short, the optimism about human possibility which usually goes with a political commitment to Socialism.
>
> (1962: 90)

It is perhaps difficult now to imagine the depth of opposition to these arguments. Another telling account is the essay which greeted Williams on his arrival in Cambridge in 1961. Maurice Cowling, conservative historian and Fellow of Peterhouse College, was the author of the lead article 'Mr Raymond Williams', which appeared in the university's major humanities journal, *The Cambridge Review* of May 27.[11] Never in the history of the university had a new lecturer been treated to such an unwelcoming welcome.

In this essay, Cowling gives an extraordinarily dismissive and yet indignant description of the 'central place' held by Williams amongst a whole 'group of English radicals, lapsed Stalinists, academic Socialists and intellectual Trotsky-ites...with others from the extra-mural boards, the community centres and certain Northern universities' (Cowling 1961: 546). We can see at work here what we may call the rhetoric of the centre. What most disturbs Cowling is that someone so determinedly, in Cowling's terms, from the periphery of British cultural and academic life should come to occupy a central position in national cultural life. 'In this movement,' writes Cowling, the movement we now know as the New Left:

> Mr Williams has a central place – not just because of what he is saying, but because he covers his Leavite [sic] refurbishing of Marx's and Rousseau's political slogans with an academic solemnity which in England the liberal mind can seldom resist.
>
> (Cowling 1961: 547)

Cowling's review, and its appearance in the *Cambridge Review* at the very moment of Williams's return to Cambridge, signals some of the real vehemence with which 'the Establishment' responded both to Williams and to the issues raised by the New Left. In particular, Cowling remarked on one central aspect of Williams's enterprise, rejecting with disdain the very motivation of his work: 'It should not be imagined', he sniffs in conclusion, 'that it is the function of an English scholar to engage in social criticism.' (1961: 548). With this pronouncement, Cowling sought to confine literary studies to the very dimension of apolitical professionalism from which Williams was trying to free it.

Cowling was not alone in seeing *Culture and Society* as one of the first books to articulate the concerns of the New Left. 1956 is usually seen as the crucial year. The vicious crushing of the Hungarian revolt by Soviet tanks brought an end to hopes of the internal transformation of socialism in the East, despite Stalin's death in 1953 and Krushchev's Twentieth Congress criticisms of him; while the British and French invasion of the Suez canal zone similarly tore through any illusions concerning the equally implacable rapaciousness of Western capitalist interests, despite the much touted 'end of imperialism' and the partial gains, in Britain, of the welfare state. Within a year, the Communist Party of Great Britain had lost a third of its membership and many people on the left felt the need for a new direction, one which could reject both the tired dogma of the Communist Party and the new liberal rhetoric.[12]

The founding of *Universities and Left Review* and *The New Reasoner* and the publication of Norman Mackenzie's *Conviction* revealed the need for a new socialist alignment, one which could challenge and go beyond the Stalinist heritage, and at the same time question the complacency induced by the new welfare state policies and the extraordinary period of near full employment and zero inflation. A new attempt at synthesis was provided by the focus on the centre of Williams's concerns since the late 1940s: the idea of culture. In a recent retrospective account, Stuart Hall offers three motives for this particular intellectual and political investment by the New Left in culture:

> First, because it was in the cultural and ideological domain that social change appeared to be making itself most dramatically visible. Second, because the cultural dimension seemed to us not a secondary, but a constitutive dimension of society. (This reflects part of the New Left's long-standing quarrel with the reductionism and economism of the base–superstructure metaphor.) Third, because the discourse of culture seemed to us fundamentally necessary to any language in which socialism could be redescribed. The New Left therefore took the first faltering steps of putting questions of cultural analysis and cultural politics at the centre of its politics.
>
> (Hall 1989: 25–6)

Not surprisingly, Hall picks out Williams as the trailbreaker: 'No one expressed the fundamental and constitutive character of this argument for and within the New Left more profoundly than Raymond Williams' (1989: 27).[13]

Nor is this simply a view afforded by hindsight. The publication – and attendant public attention and acclaim – of *Culture and Society 1780–1950* in 1958, followed by the related essays of *The Long Revolution* in 1961 and of *Communications* in 1962, brought an end to at least one dimension of Williams's isolation. From that point onwards, Williams was not only a central figure for Britain's New Left, but also that rare figure in British intellectual life: a public intellectual, enjoying a wide measure of respect from and access to Britain's mass media, writing for daily newspapers and broadcasting for the radio. For Labour politician Richard Crossman, *The Long Revolution* was 'the first theoretical exposition of the new socialism'; not to have read *Culture and Society* was to brand oneself 'the intellectual equivalent of a square'.[14]

The great debate

But if *Culture and Society* should certainly be recognised as a manifesto for the New Left, and situated as a key work of the post 1956 realignment, it is still necessary to go a step further, and to remember that the book itself began as a project as far back as the late 1940s. *Culture and Society* needs to be read both in terms of the continuity of Williams's intellectual development, his ongoing struggle with literary studies and Marxist analysis, and his response to specific debates. If the New Left found much of interest in his idea of culture, we must not forget that this idea was itself the product of Williams's own particular interests. One dimension of assessment which has been largely neglected is that provided by the general conservative backlash against the extension of working-class education heralded by the Beveridge Report of 1942 and inaugurated by the Education Act of 1944.

According to the terms of this Act, secondary education was now extended to cover all children up to the age of fifteen, and each child had a chance of going to grammar school and then on to university if they passed the crucial hurdle of a general examination at the age of eleven. The results of these changes were, in fact, to be only a marginal increase in the number of working-class children at universities. Nonetheless, the very possibility of increased access to higher education was perceived by some as threatening.

T.S. Eliot, the unlikely hero of *Drama from Ibsen to Eliot*, was quick to respond to what he and others perceived as a major threat to the *status quo*. In a series of essays and lectures composed between 1943 and 1948, Eliot weighed in against the egalitarian impulse of the Beveridge Report and the new Education Act.[15] Equality of education, wrote Eliot, is 'Jacobinism in education'; and went on to argue:

the ideal of a uniform system such that no one capable of receiving higher education could fail to get it, leads imperceptibly to the education of too many people, and consequently to the lowering of standards to whatever this swollen number of candidates is able to reach.

(Eliot 1948: 100–1)

The reactionary panic is clear from the confusion of Eliot's language. The initial idea is that those 'capable of receiving higher education' should have a right to it; but somehow these capable students suddenly mutate into 'a swollen number of candidates'. Though he is forced to qualify that this ugly swelling takes place 'imperceptibly', he insists that this unperceivable and unjustified swelling must necessarily lead to a 'lowering of standards'. With arguments such as these at work, it is hardly surprising that *Notes towards the Definition of Culture* figures as the work which provided the 'initial impetus' for *Culture and Society*. Williams saw it as one of the first to articulate the reactionary appropriation of the idea of culture as the Cold War settled in (Williams 1979: 97).

Williams's careful response to Eliot is fully documented in *Culture and Society* – and, less visibly but more acutely, in the silent revisions in his studies of drama, with their removal of Eliot and promotion of Brecht. At the same time, and of particular concern to Williams as a tutor in the WEA, were the arguments in and around the related notions of adult and workers' education in the post-war period, known by its participants as the 'Great Debate'.[16]

The extraordinary shift in social sensibility as Britain recovered from the rigours of the Second World War, moved towards almost full employment and zero inflation, and began to feel the effects of the implementation of welfare state policy, had the paradoxical effect of diluting progressive political thought. J.F.C. Harrison, examining the social forces at work in the shifts in WEA policy, hit the nail bang on the head:

> The problem for the WEA comes primarily not from within but from without – from a new social environment and from new developments in the world of adult education. Without suggesting that we are now living in a new world, it is nevertheless clear that a full employment welfare state has begun to create new social attitudes which make obsolete many approaches based on pre-war suppositions and data.
>
> (Harrison, in Raybould 1959: 10)

In other words, any concern with the politics of class was seen as inappropriate in the 'full employment welfare state'. For Harrison, as for others, the very centre of the WEA movement – the figure of the working adult seeking a politically stimulating education – was no longer a valid one: 'the whole concept of the manual worker,' he argued, and 'the whole approach implied in the idea of the working-class movement no longer means what they once did. They are part of a world which is passing away' (Harrison, in Raybould 1959: 16).[17]

S.G. Raybould, Director of Extra Mural Studies at Leeds University and Vice-Principal of the WEA from 1949 to 1957, was a key figure in the whole debate. In a series of works published between 1947 and 1951 Raybould argued – against figures such as G.D.H. Cole and Robert Peers – that the crucial question for adult education was not that of offering a general cultural and political education, but the attainment of 'university standards' in adult education classes.[18] A central feature of Raybould's own arguments for raising the standard of adult education to university level was the same apparent disappearance of the worker as Harrison had noted. In *The English Universities and Adult Education*, Raybould argued that there was:

> urgent need for fresh thinking about the nature and purpose of adult education.... It [the impulse to form the WEA] was an impulse born of the situation, educational, political, and economic, of working-class people at the beginning of the century, and was expressed in the phrase 'education for social and industrial emancipation'. That impulse has not spent its force, but it is less compelling than it was.
>
> (Raybould 1951: 41)

Certainly it was less compelling enough for Raybould to argue for the redefinition of adult education away from the extra-mural classes for working-class students, and towards the provision of university education for the middle classes.

It is then in these debates in and around adult education that one of Williams's central interests – in what has come to be known as 'historical semantics', which is so central to the whole method and intention of *Culture and Society* – first began to take shape as he made his own contributions to the 'Great Debate' about the future of adult education in a number of essays for *The Highway*. For Williams and others the adult education movement had seemed an important opportunity for providing working-class people with the elements of a broadly political education. In this, they were following the original impetus of the movement. Albert Mansbridge, in the inaugural speech of the Institute for Adult Education, had, on 28 May 1921, asserted that:

> by the foundation of the Institute it is hoped to create a widespread public opinion which shall ultimately win for adult education its rightful place in the national system...essentially it will be an instrument of research and propaganda.
>
> (Cited in Hutchinson 1971: 10)

Similarly, R.H. Tawney in his address to the WEA, published in *The Highway* in 1934, had argued:

It is to serve the working class movement in the way proper to an educational body, not by propaganda, but by offering its members the educational opportunities which are one condition of its progress, and by creating a climate of public opinion impatient of educational privilege and determined to end it.

(Tawney 1934: 69)

It was a harsh historical irony for Williams and at least some of his fellows that just at the moment when this climate came into existence – with the postwar Labour government and the boom in adult education numbers – that the directly political aims of the movement were to be successfully challenged by Raybould and others in the name of standards.[19] Raybould's reforms threatened to remove the very *raison d'être* for socialists to work at all in adult education rather than in the university system. As Williams recollected in his Tony Maclean Memorial lecture of 1983:

the impulse to Adult Education was not only a matter of remedying deficit, making up for inadequate educational resources in the wider society, nor only a case of meeting new needs of the society, though these things contributed. The deepest impulse was the desire to make learning part of the process of social change itself.

(Williams 1983f: 158)

Nothing better illustrates that impulse than the central arguments in, and structure of, *Culture and Society* itself, and the related studies of *The Long Revolution*.

In *Politics and Letters*, he noted the ways in which he was able to move away from traditional canonical concerns of the university in his WEA classes. 'There seemed little point in teaching the writing of essays' he recollected; 'I taught the writing of reports, minutes, memoranda, and committee speaking and oral reports – skills relevant to their work' (Williams 1979: 78). But more important than this simple question of relevant skills was the challenge to the founding notions of culture implicit in the usual ideas of the curriculum as a whole. In an important essay, 'The Teaching of Public Expression', he issued the following challenge:

Does one impose on a social class that is growing in power the syllabus of an older culture; or does one seek means of releasing and enriching the life-experience which the rising class brings with it? If the latter, as I choose, then the WEA has a lot of its thinking in front of it.

(Williams 1953b: 248)

Culture and Society sought both to examine that 'syllabus of an older culture' and the 'life-experience' of the 'rising class' in an all-out attack on the reactionary appropriation of the idea of culture as it was being defined by the forces for a 'minority civilisation' in the institution of academic literary studies, and in the new definitions of adult education promulgated by Raybould and his followers.

In Eagleton's judgement, *Culture and Society* is an 'idealist and academicist project' (1976b: 25); but it is important to recognise that this is a political judgement held from a distinctive Althusserian position on the meaning of intellectual activism. In Williams's terms, *Culture and Society* was certainly not to be seen as merely an academic history of cultural thought. *Culture and Society* was a strategic response, written from within the imperatives of the adult education movement, to the pressing debates in what he was beginning to understand not just as the politics of culture and education, but as cultural politics *tout court*. This politics took place at the very level of meaning and was embodied in the debates about the continued relevance of words such as 'worker' and 'manual worker', as well as in the very idea of culture itself.

The idea of culture

Though *Culture and Society* appealed because of its apparently effortless contemporaneity, and its articulation of the central concerns of the New Left, we need also to recognise the fact that it represented the culmination of work begun in the 1940s: it represented a breakout from the tight place of Williams's intellectual and political predicament. The preliminary work for the book was done in the adult education classes which Williams taught on the idea of culture from 1949, and this was prompted in the first instance by the publication of Eliot's *Notes Towards the Definition of Culture* in 1948. The first writers under discussion were Eliot, Leavis, Clive Bell and Matthew Arnold, with Bell's *Civilization* – just republished in 1947 – perhaps serving as a particular source of aggravation.[20]

By 1953, he had amassed enough material to publish 'The Idea of Culture' in F.W. Bateson's new journal *Essays in Criticism*. Under Bateson's editorship, the journal sought to integrate more cogently than *Scrutiny* had been able historical with practical critical analysis. This essay, with its attention to and insistence on 'the intimate and complex relations between ideas and the other products of man's life in society', clearly fitted this general rubric, and Williams's concern to argue against the ahistorical abstraction associated with the *Scrutiny* approach, would have been particularly welcome: 'we need a more than ordinary awareness of that pressure of active and general life which is misrepresented entirely by description as "background". There are no backgrounds in society; there are only relations of acts and forces' (Williams 1953a: 245). The focus is not, as it had been *ad nauseam* since Eliot's famous pronouncement of 1921, the 'dissociation of sensibility' which had somehow 'set in' during the seventeenth century; but the industrial revolution of the nineteenth (Eliot 1921: 287–8).

To this end, Williams argues that the word culture takes on an important new sense during this period. More neutral than civilization, it comes to refer to the 'whole way of life' of a society and corresponds to 'the strong tendency to wish to study societies as wholes' which is characteristic of both Marxism and anthropology. At the same time, the fact that this idea of culture is a response to, and not just a reflection of, change, was crucial to Williams's attempt at distancing himself from what he understood as the cruder models of Marxist interpretation familiar from his undergraduate years. In this developing model of an active, reactive and finally proactive culture, the key idea is that of tradition, and tradition is deeply bound up with the living language. 'The history of a word' he writes:

> is in the series of meanings which a dictionary defines; the relevance of a word in common language. The dictionary indicates a contemporary scheme of the past; the active word, in speech or in writing, indicates all that has become present. To distinguish the interaction is to distinguish a tradition – a mode of history; and then in experience we set a value on the tradition – a mode of criticism. The continuing process, and the consequent decisions, are then the matter of action in society.
>
> (Williams 1953a: 242)

Language was inherently political, the very stuff of ideology, and the promised book was to be a composite work which brought together the two modes of history and criticism in order to make an ideological response, to participate in that 'action in society'. To write in this composite mode is necessarily to participate in the tradition of which one writes, to add oneself to the list, to speak for one's own generation. For Williams, such a study promised to unite the professional and the political impulses whose sundering had so troubled him throughout the *Politics and Letters* period. With *Culture and Society* he at last managed to break out of the tight place of the 1940s, and it is not surprising that he later recorded the sense of relief with which he completed the project in 1956:

> I have never known a book which more completely seemed to close itself with the last page that was written. I had the strongest sense I have ever experienced that now it was done, I was in a quite new position and could move on.
>
> (Williams 1979: 109)

In this sense, we may wish to read Williams's magisterial and even-handed tone as more than the expression of the liberal ideal of academic objectivity; it works as a part of the necessary machinery for generating the academic authority with which he wished to strengthen his oppositional political objectives, his response to the right-wing appropriation of the idea of culture. *Culture and Society* is best seen as the polemical and oppositional work which it is, the first major expression of his long and defining struggle with 'official English culture' (Williams 1979: 316). Its very success in founding the 'culture and society tradition' has necessarily blinded us to its own real achievements, while opening the way to many criticisms of the gaps in the book's idea of the 'tradition'.[21]

The tradition

Williams's success lies first of all in the establishment of the existence of a culture and society tradition, a distinctively British discourse on culture which broadly opposed the tendencies of the new industrial society. The conclusion to the book states the case with some force:

> The development of the idea of culture has, throughout, been a criticism of what has been called the bourgeois idea of society. The contributors to its meaning have started from widely different positions, and have reached widely various attachments and loyalties. But they have been alike in this, that they have been unable to think of society as a merely neutral area, or as an abstract regulating mechanism. The stress has fallen on the positive function of society, on the fact that the values of individual men are rooted in society, and on the need to think and feel in these common terms. This was, indeed, a profound and necessary response to the disintegrating pressures which were faced.
>
> (Williams 1958a: 328)

This authority is turned to good account in the positive arguments put forward in the conclusion. But before we examine these, let us briefly examine the basic line of argument which the book as a whole puts forward.

With a casual disdain for the usual divisions of cultural political analysis, Williams establishes the beginnings of the major nineteenth-century tradition in the work of two figures whose work usually represents the oppositions between conservative and radical thinking: Edmund Burke, vociferous opponent of the French Revolution, and William Cobbett, champion of the labouring classes.[22] It was they who started 'traditions of criticism of the new democracy and the new industrialism...traditions which in the middle of the twentieth century are still active and important' (1958a: 4). This same tradition continued through the writings of Robert Southey, Robert Owen and the Romantic poets, with Wordsworth providing one of the seminal statements of the new idea of culture as the ' "embodied spirit of a People", the true standard of excellence...the court of appeal in which real values were determined, usually in opposition to the "factitious" values thrown up by the market and similar operations of society' (1958a: 34).

Following Wordsworth, Coleridge, in his *On the Constitution of Church and State* (1830), 'worked out this idea of Culture, the court of appeal to which all social arrangements must submit' (1958a: 61). Mill, Bentham, Carlyle, Newman, Arnold and the novelists of the 1840s all made their own contributions to the tradition; and Pugin, Ruskin and Morris all wrote persuasively in support of the central idea that 'the art of a period is closely and necessarily related to the generally prevalent "way of life", and further that, in consequence, aesthetic, moral and social judgements are closely interrelated' (1958a: 130).

Williams found little of interest in the second phase of the tradition (from around 1880 through to 1914). He prefaces Part II of the book with the admission that 'we shall not find in [the major writers of the period]...anything very new: a working-out, rather, of unfinished lines; a tentative redirection' (1958a: 161–2). Consequently he offers only the briefest outlines of work by W.H. Mallock; Whistler, Wilde and Pater; or even of Gissing and Shaw. Part II closes with a brief assessment of the work of T.E. Hulme, whose work 'challenged the tradition at its roots' (1958a: 190), but whose main importance Williams assigns as Hulme's influence on T.S. Eliot. Critics of *Culture and Society* are surely right to see this as the weakest part of the book as a whole (it is clearly the part where Williams himself is least engaged, least interested and least knowledgeable), and point rightly to the implications of this blindness to what was, after all, the main period of Victorian imperial expansion.[23]

Part III of the study focuses on the real origins of the project as it began in 1946. It examines the work of D.H. Lawrence, R.H. Tawney, T.S. Eliot, George Orwell, I.A. Richards and F.R. Leavis, as well as the British Marxist writers of the 1930s. We can see at work just what the project as a whole owed to the tradition of literary criticism, as well as to the particular debates at work within adult education. A great deal of the internal drama of the book is Williams's attempt to draw some support for his arguments from the leading figures of a discipline which in so many ways was actively hostile to the idea of the participatory democracy which he invoked in the name of furthering a 'common culture' – itself a phrase used by Eliot to describe an antithetical cultural and political order. The constitutive tension of the book is its turning of the tradition against some of its own preconceptions.[24] As we shall see, the pivot of the argument can be found in the idea of the masses.

It is this tension which explains what otherwise seems an oddly unmotivated set of remarks concerning literacy. Williams writes with disdain of the 'ready-made historical thesis' (1958a: 306) which argues that the 1870 Education Act brought a new mass-reading public into being, and that this public was 'literate but untrained in reading, low in taste and habit'. This public was then the harbinger of the new crude popular culture of the twentieth century, the culture of radio, movies and the gutter press. Against this, the founding rhetoric of Cambridge English, Williams argues long and hard. The new institutions of popular culture were never produced, he insists, 'by the working people themselves', and to identify them with the actual wishes and desires of the working class is deeply mistaken. What needs to be identified instead are the motives and ideology of the producers of the new mass media. In any case, he writes, 'the contemporary historians of popular culture have tended to concentrate on what is bad and to neglect what is good' (1958a: 308). This selectivity is in turn reinforced by a certain *déformation professionelle*. He argues that in 'judging a culture, it is not enough to concentrate on habits which coincide with those of the observer':

> To the highly literate observer there is always a temptation to assume that reading plays as large a part in the lives of most people as it does in his own....To the degree that he acquires a substantial proportion of his ideas and feelings from what he reads he will assume, again wrongly, that the ideas and feelings of the majority will be similarly conditioned. But, for good or ill, the majority of people do not yet give reading this importance in their lives; their ideas and feelings are, to a large extent, still moulded by a wider and more complex pattern of social and family life. There is an evident danger of delusion, to the highly literate person, if he supposes that he can judge the quality of general living by primary reference to the reading artifacts.
>
> (1958a: 308–9)

He notes and rejects the contempt which the highly literate tend to have for other intelligent creative activities, general skills such as gardening, metalwork and carpentry, and active politics. 'The contempt for many of these activities, which is always latent in the highly literate, is a mark of the observer's limits, not those of the activities themselves' he insists (1958a: 309).

It is in these arguments that Williams reveals both his deep connection to literary criticism, and the distance he wishes to take from it. For at the very moment when he is arguing for the relevance of the culture and society tradition to contemporary arguments in favour of democracy, he was arguing against the general case put forward by the literary critics, and in particular by I.A. Richards and F.R. Leavis, the two literary critics covered in the book, and rightly seen as the formative figures in the discipline of English studies in Britain; and against, in particular, the implications of Q.D. Leavis's study, *Fiction and the Reading Public*, the most sustained attempt to put historical flesh on the bones of Leavis's assertions.[25]

The masses

Central to the urgency of much literary critical thought, was a certain representation of 'the masses' which Williams turns to in the conclusion to the book.[26] Here he argues that all the connotations of 'mob' are to be found at work in most compounds of masses:

> masses was a new word for mob, and the traditional characteristics of the mob were retained in its significance: gullibility, fickleness, herd-prejudice, lowness of taste and habit. The masses, on this evidence, formed the perpetual threat to culture. Mass-thinking, mass-suggestion, mass-prejudice would threaten to swamp considered individual thinking and feeling. Even democracy, which had both a classical and a liberal reputation, would lose its savour in becoming mass-democracy.
>
> (1958a: 298)

He takes a hard line here, and points out that the term mass democracy can either be used as 'an observation or a prejudice' (1958a: 298). As an observation, it may refer to the fact that the complex reality of twentieth-century democracy in Britain is very different from what its nineteenth-century partisans could have imagined, and that the new mass media do have a powerful shaping effect on that reality. But the everyday use of the term is hardly ever in this sense. Instead, it is used in almost all cases in the deeply prejudicial way which is articulated in the following terms:

> Democracy, as in England we have interpreted it, is majority rule. The means to this, in representation and freedom of expression, are generally approved. But, with universal suffrage, majority rule will, if we believe in the existence of the masses, be mass-rule. Further, if the masses are, essentially, the mob, democracy will be mob-rule. This will hardly be good government, or a good society; it will, rather, be the rule of lowness or mediocrity. At this point, which it is evidently very satisfying to some thinkers to reach, it is necessary to ask again: who are the masses?
>
> (1958a: 298–9)

For Williams, the real answer to this question is that the masses are the working people of England:

> But if this is so, it is clear that what is in question is not only gullibility, or lowness of taste and habit. It is also, from the open record, the declared intention of the working people to alter society, in many of its aspects, in ways which those to whom the franchise was formerly restricted deeply disapprove. It seems to me, when this is considered, that what is being questioned is not mass-democracy, but democracy. If a majority can be achieved in favour of these changes, the democratic criterion is satisfied. But if you disapprove of the changes you can, it seems, avoid open opposition to democracy as such by inventing a new category, mass-democracy, which is not such a good thing at all.
>
> (1958a: 299)

'The submerged opposite', he argues 'is class-democracy, where democracy will merely describe the processes by which a ruling class conducts its business of ruling' (1958a: 299).

It is from this discussion – the pivotal argument of the whole book – that Williams goes on to make his most celebrated and most contentious point: the difficulty he has with 'the whole concept of masses'. 'We have to return the meanings to experience', he argues in a characteristic formulation:

> Our normal public conception of an individual person, for example, is 'the man in the street'. But nobody feels himself to be only the man in the street; we all know much more about ourselves than that. The man in the

street is a collective image, but we know, all the time, our own difference from him. It is the same with 'the public', which includes us, but yet is not us. 'Masses' is a little more complicated, yet similar. I do not think of my relatives, friends, neighbours, colleagues, acquaintances, as masses; we none of us can or do. The masses are always the others, whom we don't know, and can't know. Yet now, in our kind of society, we see these others regularly, in their myriad variations; stand, physically, beside them. They are here, and we are here with them. And that we are with them is of course the whole point. To other people, we also are masses. Masses are other people.

(Williams 1958a: 299–300)

'There are in fact no masses' he asserts; 'there are only ways of seeing people as masses' (1958a: 300). And it is just these ways of seeing, the formulae by which we may conveniently interpret others, 'for the purposes of cultural or political exploitation' that we need to consider in analysis. His central point can be understood as the urging of a critical literacy which will untie the knots of representation through which the empirical data of the facts of the world are put forward for social action. With this central point, Williams deconstructed, if we may use one of the senses of Derrida's labile term, the dominant system of representation which had emerged, perhaps most vividly in the 1930s.[27] The isolation experienced by Williams was not a social one, but an intellectual one – one described best, perhaps, in Althusser's phrase, as a 'theoretical solitude'.[28] And it is this which comes through most strongly in the turn he gives to the idea of working-class culture.

Williams writes against both Marxist and reactionary conceptions of culture, which consider it either as 'the inheritance of the rising class', or call for its defence 'against new and destructive forces' (1958a: 319). Working class culture has nothing to do with 'the small amount of 'proletarian' writing and art which exists' (1958a: 320). It needs to be understood in terms of the implications of the idea of culture as a 'whole way of life'. It then refers not only to intellectual and imaginative work, or even to housing, dress, and modes of leisure. 'Industrial production tends to produce uniformity in such matters,' he writes 'but the vital distinction lies at another level....The crucial distinction is between alternative ideas of the nature of social relationship' (1958a: 325). First, there is the bourgeois understanding of social relationship as individualism: 'an idea of society as a neutral area within which each individual is free to pursue his own development and his own advantage as a natural right', though this idea is modified in practice by idea of service to the community. The working class idea and practice of social relationship is different. It is above all 'an idea which, whether it is called communism, socialism or cooperation, regards society neither as a neutral area nor as protective, but as a positive means for all kinds of development, including individual development' (1958a: 326).

Once this is grasped, it becomes easier to see that working class culture is not a matter of proletarian art, but rather the practice of 'the collective idea' itself (1958a: 327). It is the idea of solidarity versus the idea of service which, argues Williams, always serves in practice 'to maintain the status quo' (1958a: 330). 'We may now see what is properly meant by 'working-class culture', he writes:

> It is not proletarian art, or council houses, or a particular use of languages; it is, rather, the basic collective idea, and the institutions, manners, habits of thought and intentions which proceed from this....The working class, because of its position, has not, since the Industrial Revolution, produced a culture in the narrower sense. The culture which it has produced, and which it is important to recognize, is the collective democratic institution, whether in the trade unions, the cooperative movement or a political party. Working-class culture, in the stage through which it has been passing, is primarily social (in that it has created institutions) rather than individual (in particular intellectual or imaginative work). When it is considered in context, it can be seen as a very remarkable creative achievement.
>
> (1958a: 327)

With this idea of culture as something like a Wittgensteinian 'form of life' and the Marxist idea of ideology, rather than a matter of aesthetic taste, Williams could do little more than to underline the differences which separated him from a Gregor and a Pittock. In fact, there was no common ground between them: *Culture and Society* had deconstructed it. In the end he could only insist that: 'However difficult it may be to understand in detail, art is part of the whole way of life, and the individual artist has behind him and within him an important body of social experience without which he could not even begin' (Gregor *et al.* 1959: 435). And he looks forward to the central arguments of *The Long Revolution* to further substantiate his case:

> Communication as a whole is a creative activity, in the sense that (as the neurologists are now showing) it is by learning to perceive, to describe and to communicate description to others that we create the common reality of our lives. Institutions are best seen as forms of communication, embodying a particular version of reality and a particular response to it. Art is one of the most important of these, and its biological, social and personal functions can be usefully compared with those of other kinds of institution. For there are no 'entirely different order(s), economic, political – what you will'; there is one lived reality, within which we respond and act in varying forms.
>
> (Gregor *et al.* 1959: 435)

Culture and Society – and the related essays of *The Long Revolution* – represented a powerful response to the post-1945 hardening of attitudes in politics and education. To write it, and to make a beginning, Williams had to distance himself from his own early influences, and to subject that orthodoxy of which they were a part to a critical and historical analysis. No one summed up Williams's achievement in doing this better than Edward Thompson in his review of *The Long Revolution*:

> With a compromised tradition at his back, and with a broken vocabulary in his hands, he did the only thing that was left to him; he took over the vocabulary of his opponents, followed them into the heart of their own arguments, and fought them to a standstill in their own terms.[29]
>
> (Thompson 1961: 27)

This argument with 'official English culture' was to continue in the next phase of Williams's work on his return to Cambridge as a university lecturer in 1961.

4 Cambridge criticism 1962–73

The turbulent decade of the 1960s was an extremely active one for Williams, both as a public intellectual and as a professional academic. He gave his support to various activist groups – the Campaign for Nuclear Disarmament, the Cambridge Left Forum, the Vietnam Solidarity Campaign, the National Convention of the Left and the consequent writing of the *May Day Manifesto*, the defence of Rudi Dutschke, and even participation in the Arts Council and canvassing for the Labour Party. At the same time, he continued his non-academic writing with the completion of his novel *Second Generation* in 1962, and the beginning of *The Fight for Manod* (published in 1979), plus the writing of three plays: *Koba*, never performed, but published as the third section of *Modern Tragedy* in 1966, *A Letter from the Country* (1966), and *Public Enquiry* (1967), both of which were shown on the BBC. There was also a constant flow of journalism, reviews and a regular column on television for *The Listener*.[1] He continued his usual process of self-correction, making significant revisions to his view of the history of drama with the revision and republication of *Drama in Performance* and the retitled *Drama from Ibsen to Brecht*, both in 1968, writing an important reassessment of the appeal and limitations of the work of George Orwell (1971), and editing Volume 2 of *The Pelican Book of English Prose: From 1780 to the Present Day* (1969).[2] For the sake of this study, it is necessary to narrow the focus of attention and assessment. This chapter examines the renewal of Williams's contact with Cambridge English and its particular, and particularly productive, frictions, as well as the continuation of his troubled dialogue with Marxism as he sought to respond to the telling criticisms made of *Culture and Society* and *The Long Revolution* by Victor Kiernan and E.P. Thompson.

In Williams's recollection of the events, it was on a spring morning in 1961 that he opened a letter from the University of Cambridge to find that he had been appointed to a lectureship in the English Faculty.[3] Over the next two days other letters arrived explaining the situation and asking him whether he would accept such an appointment were it to be offered. Tired of the losing battles in adult education, he was glad to accept, and after the obligatory ordeal-by-dinner at High Table, was given a Fellowship at Jesus College which he took up in the summer of 1961. He was to remain a fellow of the college until his death in 1988, though he had formally retired from the post of Professor of Drama in 1983.

In the first of his two formal retirement lectures on 25 April 1983, Williams reviewed the history of his relations with Cambridge English. He closed the lecture with an emphasis on what he termed his own distance from it:

> many friends have told me that I have never distanced myself enough, but they are wrong. The distance is entire, the intellectual conflicts absolute. My only community and inheritance in Cambridge is with some of the questions then posed and with the campaigning energy and seriousness that were brought to them.
>
> (Williams 1983g: 190)

But distance and conflict both presuppose some common ground, some site of contested perspective. This was to be found in 'some of the questions then asked'. What were these questions, what were the terms of his renewed professional contact with Cambridge English? In *Politics and Letters*, he had claimed 'If you look at the implied relationships of nearly all the books I have written, I have been arguing with what I take to be official English culture' (Williams 1979: 316). For this we can read 'official English culture', or in large part at least, English culture as it was defined and disseminated by the Cambridge English faculty.[4] For, as Williams goes on to say, his *Modern Tragedy* (1966) was a reply to George Steiner's *The Death of Tragedy* (1961); *The English Novel from Dickens to Lawrence* (1970) his riposte to Leavis's seminal *The Great Tradition* (1948); while *The Country and the City* (1973) started life as a sharp reaction to a Special Paper in Part Two of the English Tripos on the Country House poem.[5]

At the same time, Williams's work continued, though somewhat obliquely, in its critical dialogue with Marxism. In response to a question concerning that indirectness, he replied:

> Why do I discuss a minor eighteenth-century poet in more detail than I do Marx? Because this is where a really reactionary social consciousness is being continually reproduced, and to till your own alternative garden to it is not enough. In fact, it would be a trap for me. There would be a good many people in English cultural circles who would be delighted if I spent the rest of my time clearing up some questions of Marxist literary theory. I don't propose to give them the satisfaction.
>
> (Williams 1979: 317)

Nonetheless, despite this sidelong response to Eagleton's criticisms and the probings of the *New Left Review* team, the writings of this period continually interact with problems in Marxist theory, and *Marxism and Literature*, published in 1977, is nothing if not a thorough attempt at settling accounts. In this chapter, we shall focus on both the oblique oppositional dialogue with Marxism as well as with the more direct critique of Cambridge English.

To be sure, Williams had already formulated some important objections to the methodology of Cambridge English, both in the early *Reading and Criticism*, where he criticised the foundations of Leavisite 'evaluation' through close reading by attending to the pre-selective nature of passage selection, and again, in *Culture and Society*, where he developed this line of argument in relation to I.A. Richards.

He sums up the main elements of Richards's positions as follows: 'The experience of literature is thus a kind of training for general experience: a training, essentially, in that capacity for organization which is man's only profitable response to his altered and dangerous condition' (Williams 1958a: 249). This is the new and dangerous condition of mass society and mass culture. Above all, he is critical of what he sees as the essential passivity inherent in Richards's definition of the reading experience. 'Great literature is indeed enriching, liberating and refining', he writes:

> but man is always and everywhere more than a reader, has indeed to be a great deal else before he can even become an adequate reader; unless indeed he can persuade himself that literature, as an ideal sphere of heightened living, will under certain cultural circumstances operate as a substitute. 'We shall then be thrown back...upon poetry. It is capable of saving us.' The very form of these sentences indicates the essential passivity which I find disquieting.
>
> (1958a: 251)

In conclusion, he argues that: 'All that Richards has taught us about language and communication, and for which we acknowledge our debt, has to be reviewed.' For in the end, Richards remained a captive to the image of 'Aesthetic Man' which Richards had unknowingly inherited from his own opponents and predecessors: 'alone in a hostile environment, receiving and organizing his experience' (1958a: 252). He was to argue against just this image of both reader and writer as passive and isolated in this next stage of writing. In particular, he was to question the embodiment of these tendencies in the figure of the observer, as exemplified in Orwell's work as 'the plain man who bumps into experience in an unmediated way and is simply telling us the truth about it' (Williams 1979: 385).[6]

Tragedy, revolution and the modern world

Williams sums up the agenda of *Modern Tragedy* in the following terms: 'We are not looking for a new universal meaning of tragedy. We are looking for the structure of tragedy in our own culture' (Williams 1966: 62). This was, in fact, to be a double task: the criticism both of that 'official English culture', and its relentless search for universal meanings in literature, but also a thinking through of the idea of political revolution itself. The two came powerfully together in the ways in which Cold War values were embodied in the official view of the 'universal' values of Tragedy.

Modern Tragedy grew out of the lectures Williams gave for the final-year course on Tragedy. 'It was never a book I had foreseen writing' he averred; rather it was:

> a response to the shock of returning to Cambridge and encountering the course on tragedy there in a much more ideological form than it had been when I was a student.... It was as if I went into the lecture room with the text of a chapter from *Drama from Ibsen to Eliot* in front of me, and came out with the text of a chapter from *Modern Tragedy*.
>
> (Williams 1979: 211)

The main difference between the two lay in the shift from the relatively technical address of the earlier work, its focus on dramatic conventions and dramatic performance, to something which was 'closer to ideological criticism'. *Modern Tragedy* was above all a polemical work, addressed to the dominant ideology which he saw as produced and reproduced in the Cambridge English Tragedy paper, and as it was epitomised in George Steiner's successful *The Death of Tragedy.*[7]

Death of tragedy

Steiner's study has all the hallmarks of his peculiar talents. Wide-ranging, multi-lingual, enthusiastic and erudite, it is not afraid to use a wide range of reading of primary texts as the basis to argue a grand thesis. Written in a passionate and enthusiastic style, it easily gained a wide readership, while pernickety scholars were grieved at its lack of secondary scholarship, and saw its grand argument achieved at the expense of fine detail. The main thesis of the book is easily stated. Tragedy has been in decline since the moment of the Greeks; and though the causes of this decline are multiple and multi-causal, in essence they can be reduced to the fact that real tragedy fits neither the Christian worldview nor (and here Steiner joins the ranks of Cold War polemicists) the Marxist ideology.

First, and most important, Steiner saw the history of tragedy as the history of the decline of a form which had achieved its moment of unparalleled perfection with the Greeks. The idea of tragedy, 'and the vision of man which it implies are Greek. And nearly till the moment of their decline, the tragic forms are Hellenic' (Steiner 1961: 3). The death of tragedy 'is inseparably related to the decline of the organic world view and its attendant context of mythological, symbolic and ritual reference. It was on this context that Greek drama was founded, and the Elizabethans were still able to give it imaginative adherence' (1961: 292). The history of tragedy is the history of this decline, with dramatists like Racine able to rekindle some of the fire of the ancient form from the half-extinguished embers of the present. Others were not so fortunate. Ibsen cannot be regarded as a tragic dramatist: in his work there is, properly speaking, 'no tragedy at all, but dramatic rhetoric summoning us to action in the conviction that truth of conduct can be defined and that it will liberate society' (1961: 291). Yeats's work only confirms the general case: his 'failure to construct a mythology for the age is part of that larger failure or withdrawal from imaginative commitment which occurs after the seventeenth century. Greek tragedy moved against the background of rich, explicit myth' (1961: 319).

But for all the impressionistic passion of its local readings, the argument is in the end unable to generate the level of conceptual consistency necessary to sustain his thesis. In the last chapter, Steiner offers his final conclusion. It is significant that this is argued from anecdotal evidence, as commentary on a medieval parable overheard in Poland. 'Tragedy is that form of art which requires the intolerable burden of God's presence', asserts Steiner, and after the seventeenth century, God is simply not there: 'I would suppose that He turned away during the seventeenth century' (1961: 353).

As a whole, the book embodies a distinctive anti-Marxist stance. Steiner identified three main elements in the death of modern tragedy. First, there was the impossibility of reviving the original Greek forms themselves; second, the ways in which Christianity, with its belief in redemption, spread antipathy to the harshness of Greek tragic values; and finally, there was the denial of tragedy by a Marxism which he sees as the twentieth-century heir to the wilful delusions of Christian belief. For Steiner, Marxism is the twentieth-century mythology:

> For we have before us now the startling fact of a mythology created at a specific time by a particular group of men, yet imposed upon the lives of millions. It is that explicit myth of the human condition and of the goals of history which we call Marxism. Marxism is the third principal mythology to have taken root in Western consciousness.
>
> (Steiner 1961: 323)

Steiner repeatedly refers to Marx on necessity as if that term were synonymous with the Greek concept of Ananke; and to Lunacharsky, first Soviet commissar of education, and his view 'that one of the defining qualities of a communist society would be the absence of tragic drama....In a communist state, tragedy is not only bad art; it is treason calculated to subvert the morale of the front lines' (1961: 343, 344–5).[8]

Against this, what did Williams have to argue? In the first instance, he was able to deploy his growing armoury of concepts against traditional literary criticism. The most powerful of these was his developing sense of 'semantic history', the history of cultural struggle in and through language. Tragedy, like culture, like industry, like so many other keywords is admittedly 'a single and powerful word' (Williams 1966: 16), but it is above all a word with a history. And this history is not only open to interpretation, but is itself the embodiment of a history of interpretation through the mechanisms of the 'selective tradition'. It is all too easy, writes Williams, 'to see this tradition as a continuity...so many of the later writers and thinkers have been conscious of the earlier, and have seen themselves as contributing to a common idea or form' (1966: 15); but for the cultural historian any tradition 'is not the past, but an interpretation of the past: a selection and valuation' (1966: 16).

That interpretation is shown first of all in the primacy given to Greek tragedy, and the many 'attempts to systematise a Greek tragic philosophy, and to transmit it as absolute' (1966: 17). The valuation then lies in the essentialisation of Greek tragedy as a form, along with the consequent view of later tragic drama – exemplified in Steiner's study – as a falling away from the Greek achievement, a gradual fading of the form through the ages to its eventual demise in the modern world. This essentialising attitude is then responsible for a refusal to see and understand the later forms of tragedy in and on their own terms. The usual under-valuation of medieval tragedy is a case in point: 'Only an extraordinary powerful attachment to an absolute meaning of tragedy could force us to overlook the use of the word, in a quite specific sense, in a major historical period' (1966: 19). In an almost Wittgensteinian way, Williams urges us to seek for the meaning of tragedy in the word's use at a particular moment, a useage embodied in social convention and (to borrow Wittgenstein's term) in 'forms of life'. Against essence, Williams poses history.[9]

What is necessary is a fully historical understanding of tragedy, a history of its forms, and the different social conventions underlying those forms. For Williams, the specific differences in the idea of tragedy correspond to shifts in the basic structures of social organisation. The medieval emphasis on 'the fall of princes' is comprehensible in a feudal period, while Dryden's idea of the necessity for 'decorum' is 'an aristocratic rather than a feudal conception' (1966: 25). The ahistorical idea of tragedy relies above all on the notion of 'an unchanging human nature' (1966: 46), and only if we reject this assumption can we see that tragedy:

> is not then a single and permanent kind of fact, but a series of experiences and conventions and institutions. It is not a case of interpreting this series by reference to a permanent and unchanging human nature. Rather, the varieties of tragic experience are to be interpreted by reference to the changing conventions and institutions.
>
> (1966: 45–6)

Central to this historical view is the emphasis placed on the historicity of contemporary tragic theory itself. 'The most striking fact' he writes, 'about modern tragic theory is that it is rooted in very much the same structure of ideas as modern tragedy itself, yet one of its paradoxical effects is its denial that modern tragedy is possible, after almost a century of important and continuous tragic art' (1966: 46). In particular, he argues, the 'real key, to the modern separation of tragedy from "mere suffering", is the separation of ethical control and, more critically, human agency, from our understanding of social and political life' (1966: 48–9).

Williams isolates three distinctive elements in this mode. First, there is the contemporary emphasis on the destruction of the hero, and related to this, the focus on the hero at the expense of an understanding of the tragic action as a whole (1966: 54–5). Second, there are the ways in which death is represented as a singular and solitary event, 'as a proof of the loss of connection' when it is rather 'a theoretical formulation of liberal tragedy, rather than any kind of universal principle' (1966: 58). Third, there is the assumption of a 'transcendent evil' (1966: 58). Together, these form the ideological assumptions informing both modern tragedy, and the interpretation of the history of tragedy. 'The most common interpretation of tragedy' he writes, 'is that it is an action in which the hero is destroyed' (1966: 54), but this focus solely on the hero marginalises the tragic action as a whole: 'we are taking a part for the whole, a hero for an action. We think of tragedy as what happens to the hero, but the ordinary tragic action is what happens through the hero' (1966: 55). Similarly, the real universality of death is shifted, in the interpretation of liberal tragedy, to the singular loneliness of death. Since death 'is universal...the meaning tied to it quickly claims universality' (1966: 56).

To move beyond this ideology, Williams argues that we have to make an effort to reconnect our academic thinking and intellectual experience with an analysis and understanding of broader realities. 'If we find', he writes:

> a particular idea of tragedy, in our time, we find also a way of interpreting a very wide area of our own experience; relevant certainly to literary criticism but relevant also to very much else.... We must try also, positively, to understand and describe not only the tragic theory but also the tragic experience of our own time
>
> (1966: 61)

This tragic experience is located in the experience of revolution, and particularly in the history of the Russian Revolution. The fourth section of Part I of the book, 'Tragedy and Revolution', turns to examine these powerful connections and ideas.

Tragedy and revolution

The concluding section of Part I attempts to counter and to question the leading ideas of both liberalism and Stalinism. For Williams, the most complex effect of any powerful ideology, such as that informing the contemporary idea of tragedy, is 'that it directs us, even when we think we have rejected it, to the same kind of fact' (1966: 61–2). We find in the present the same forms and structures of tragic experience which we have already and unknowingly read into the past. A central feature of this constitutive blindness has been the elision of the social and political dimensions of tragedy: 'That kind of interest is commonly relegated to politics, or, to use the cant word, sociology. Tragedy, we say, belongs to deeper and closer experience, to man not to society' (1966: 62). The major aim is therefore to refuse such a division and to reintegrate our thinking about tragedy, and modern tragedy in particular. For modern tragedy is above all a response to the human experience of revolution, an experience which is necessarily at once personal and political, public and private. Here, the links between the two divided realms of experience posited by the bourgeois theory of tragedy are in reality 'inescapable and urgent' (1966: 74).

To this end, we have to go beyond the usual alternatives of either turning a blind eye to the reality of revolutionary violence, or the insistence on seeing only the forces of violence and terror at work in revolution, and then wishing to forego revolution altogether. 'Revolution' he argues 'asserted the possibility of man altering his condition, tragedy showed its impossibility, and the consequent spiritual effects' (1966: 68). We need to get beyond the 'contemporary reflex', which we have seen at work in a liberal thinker like Steiner, and which maintains that 'the taking of rational control over social destiny is defeated or at best deeply stained by our inevitable irrationality, and by the violence and cruelty that are so quickly released when habitual forms are broken down' (1966: 74); but we must also question a number of blind spots in the Marxist tradition itself.

Characteristically, Williams challenges a 'main current' of thinking to be found in Marxism, one 'which though Marx may at times have opposed it is also profoundly mechanical, in its determinism, in its social materialism, and in its characteristic abstraction of social classes from human beings' (Williams 1966: 75). It is from such a perspective, he fears, that it is possible 'to interpret revolution not only as constructive and liberating', and not to see or to accept or to question its violence, its dehumanisation and consequent liquidation of its enemies:

> Real suffering is then at once non-human: is a class swept away by history, is an error in the working of the machine, or is the blood that is not and never can be rosewater. The more general and abstract, the more truly mechanical, the process of human liberation is ordinarily conceived to be, the less any actual suffering really counts, until even death is a paper currency.
>
> (1966: 75)

He urges a constant resistance to the dehumanising abstraction related in most people's minds to the excesses of Stalinism, and emphasises that the tragic essence of revolution is to be found above all in the simple fact that revolution is a struggle not only 'against mere institutions and social forms, but against other men' (Williams 1966: 77). At the same time, he also questions the usual liberal response, first by situating it as a product of the 'long revolution' in the West, and second by calling attention to everyone's involvement in violence. He argues against the ways in which we commonly narrow down the meaning of revolution to a moment of violence and terror, rather than accepting revolution as a moment of violence in a whole history of violence and terror.

The essential point is that violence and disorder are institutions as well as acts. When a revolutionary change has been lived through, we can usually see this quite clearly. The old institutions, now dead, take on their real quality as systematic violence and disorder; in that quality, the source of the revolutionary action is seen. But while such institutions are still effective, they can seem, to an extraordinary extent, both settled and innocent. Indeed, they constitute, commonly, an order against which the very protest of the injured and oppressed seems the source of disturbance and violence (1966: 66).

It is all too easy from the perspective of a Western democracy, committed to the principles of what Williams called the 'long revolution', to denounce the obvious violence of other situations while enjoying the fruits of an invisible structural violence in the comfort of home. What is finally necessary is the recognition of our own involvement in such structural violence, and to see that this must be faced as itself a kind of disorder: 'From the experience of this disorder, and through its specific action, order is recreated. The process of this action is at times remarkably similar to the real action of revolution' (1966: 66). He locates this as the contradictions engaging 'the identification between a permanent order and a social system' (1966: 67). 'I am writing', he notes, to sharpen his general point, 'on a day when British military power is being used against "dissident tribesmen" in South Arabia' (1966: 79).

Part II of *Modern Tragedy*, 'Modern Tragic Literature', consists of seven essays which may be taken as evidence to support the general positions advanced in the first part of the study. The works and authors discussed illustrate various constituents of the modern structure of tragic feeling. Ibsen anticipates Arthur Miller in the way his protagonists are no longer heroes but victims, caught and defined in a conflict with a social world beyond their control. Lawrence's novel *Women in Love* represents a crucial turning away from the social dimension, and the attempt 'to create the individual person without *any* relationships' (1966: 138), and Williams contrasts this turning away with Tolstoy's emphasis on the social understanding of characters in his novel *Anna Karenina*.[10] The drama of Pirandello, Ionesco and Becket re-interprets and remoulds the substance of Chekhov's drama, moving it away from his emplacement in nineteenth-century realism and its assumption of a 'total world' (1966: 139) to the twentieth-century emphasis on the 'general consciousness of illusion' (1966: 141). In each essay, Williams pushes his central point – that the 'deepest crisis' in modern thinking 'is the division of experience into social and personal categories' (1966: 121). This division mars the work of even those dramatists like Camus who wish to try and face the difficult relations between tragedy and revolt. Only Bertolt Brecht, in Williams's view, has some partial success with his 'recovery of history as a dimension for tragedy' (1966: 202), and his full recognition of the tragic nature of revolution as 'the known harshness of the revolutionary struggle' (1966: 203).[11]

Contemporary reviews of the book were unable to make or accept this connection.[12] Two instances can serve as example. The first is by Frank Kermode; the second is anonymous but is likely, from the focus of its own interests and knowledge, to have been written by George Steiner. Kermode comments on the 'oddness of the book'; its structure 'seems finally to be self-indulgent, however strangely the general tone of sullen, incorrigible intelligence may seem to tell against such a judgement' (Kermode 1966: 83). While Kermode praises the intentions of the author to make the book about 'the connections, in modern tragedy, between event and experience and idea, and its form which is designed at once to explore and to emphasise these radical connections' (Williams 1966: 9); he insists that 'I doubt if it will feel like a work of such ambitious unity to anyone but the author' (Kermode 1966: 84). For Kermode, the best are the opening pages where some of those connections are made through the writing: 'only here is the word "I", though heavily muffled, allowed to make its necessary appearance' (Kermode 1966: 84). On the potted history of tragic ideas, and the supporting essays, Kermode is unaggressive: 'the surprising thing is not that it is unconvincing but that it is never ridiculous' (1966: 84). In the end, he would be happy to follow Williams's advice about choosing which parts of the book to read – but to read none of it: 'there are still those earlier works to learn from, books in which the equations to be solved were of more general interest, less a personally satisfying "structure of feeling" ' (1966: 85).

The anonymous reviewer in the *Times Literary Supplement* rejects the central argument of the book ('the category of Tragedy is no longer very useful...drama after Chekhov and Samuel Becket is a mixed open form' (*Times Literary Supplement* 1966: 717)); praises it as a 'deeply honest book' and sees 'Koba' as evidence of 'the depth of his [Williams's] imaginative involvement' (1966: 718); but, in the end, judges the book negatively: 'a book on modern tragedy which does not touch on the sociology of the audience and of the literary act, which hardly alludes to the interactions between stage drama and other modes of dramatic performance, must inevitably appear somewhat anachronistic and donnish in bias' (1966: 718). Finally, it is an 'honest, often moving, yet disappointing book' (1966: 718).

But perhaps what counts most – and certainly what counted most to Williams – is what is most occluded in these responses: the terms of the opposition to the dominant ideology of tragedy at work within 'Cambridge English'. In a sense, the substance of the book is to be found in its address, its situatedness. It is this which gives this 'donnish book' the paradoxically anti-academic force registered by at least one reader, who recorded how *Modern Tragedy* 'changed my life in a way few books have'.[13]

The novel and the question of form

Modern Tragedy sought to contest the versions of Cold War ideology at work in the Cambridge English Tragedy Paper. In part, this consciously anti-Marxist discourse had relied for its arguments on a massive repression of the historicity of tragic forms. In the place of the study and analysis of this real formal historicity, a critic like Steiner had promoted the idea of a single tragic essence as the measure of all tragic forms, and argued from that basis that the modern period was one in which the death of tragedy had been accomplished. For Steiner, real tragedy was just not possible in an age of secular values and mass democracy.[14]

In large measure, something of that same ahistorical or even anti-historical impulse had long been characteristic of the Cambridge English approach to the novel. E.M. Forster, eminent novelist and Fellow of King's College from 1946 until his death in 1970, had struck the decisive note in his Clarke lectures at Cambridge in 1927, published as *Aspects of the Novel* in the same year. 'Time', he stressed, 'is to be our enemy' (Forster 1927: 16), and he took the slogan 'History develops, Art stands still' as the 'crude motto' of the study which was to stress what he saw as the timeless problems of the novelist's craft, the universal struggle with recalcitrant form. 'All through history', he asserts, in accents strengthened by his own natural authority as novelist:

> writers while writing have felt more or less the same. They have entered a common state which it is convenient to call inspiration, and, having regard to that state, we may say that History develops, Art stands still.
>
> (Forster 1927: 28)

Forster's concern is with the novelist's craft, his technique, and in this sense with the novel as form; and these concerns are articulated around T.S. Eliot's idea of tradition:

> We are to visualize the English novelists not as floating down that stream which bears all its sons away if they are not careful, but as seated together in a room, a circular room, a sort of British Museum reading room – all writing their novels simultaneously.[15]
>
> (1927: 16)

When novels and novelists are seen in this light, the critic – the new critic in the Cambridge English mould – will be able to avoid the dangers of pseudo-scholarship characteristic of older forms of literary studies. He or she will become purely and more actively a reader:

> The reader must sit down alone and struggle with the writer, and this the pseudo-scholar will not do. He would rather relate a book to the history of its time, to events in the life of the author, to the events it describes, above all to some tendency.
>
> (1927: 21)

A part of the task of *The English Novel from Dickens to Lawrence* will be to break out of this circular room, and to reconnect the writer's problems with form to the world outside the British Museum, to that threatening flow of experience of which Forster urges the novelist and the critic to beware. Although Williams's central antagonist is F.R. Leavis, and his seminal *The Great Tradition* (1948), it is as well to remember that Leavis had taken Forster at his word, and had elevated the critic to the position of judge over that 'common state' of inspiration.

The Great Tradition

Structurally, *The English Novel from Dickens to Lawrence* is the 'symmetrical inversion' of Leavis's *The Great Tradition* (Williams 1979: 244). Both books begin with Jane Austen, but soon part company: Leavis marginalises Dickens, who is central for Williams; Leavis prefers George Eliot's later novels, and the Lawrence of *Women in Love*, while Williams's preference is for both early Eliot and early Lawrence; and while Hardy is a negligible figure for Leavis, for Williams he is central to the tradition as a whole.

But beyond the mere facts of this inversion, at times 'quite deliberate' as Williams informs us, and which has led some to see no more than a principle of alternative selection at work in *The English Novel*, there is in fact a more fundamental disagreement being worked out in the book. This concerns the central idea of form. Properly considered, *The English Novel from Dickens to Lawrence* does not merely offer an alternative canon; it is a challenge, through the idea of form, to the principles of canonical selection itself, and ultimately, to the very idea of criticism at work in Leavis's study.[16]

'What,' asks Leavis, 'is the "form" from which a "picture of life" derives its value?' His answer comes through in a series of largely rhetorical questions:

> Is there any great novelist whose preoccupation with 'form' is not a matter of his responsibility towards a rich human interest, or complexity of inter-ests, profoundly realized? – a responsibility involving, of its very nature, imaginative sympathy, moral discrimination, and judgement of relative human value?
>
> (Leavis 1948: 41)

At work here is the inextricable link, for Leavis, between formal and moral criteria. Indeed, the link between the two is strong enough to be counted as causal and therefore diagnostic: formal failure is always the symptom of moral failing. When Eliot, or Conrad or James, is writing well, they write with that key but conceptually elusive quality, 'maturity'; and when badly, it is always because that 'maturity' has somehow failed. Leavis's discussion of George Eliot exemplifies the deep connections between formal success and moral maturity which form the basis of Leavis's critical judgements.

In Eliot's writing, Leavis notes 'an alternation between the poised impersonal insight of a finely tempered wisdom and something like the emotional confusions and self-importances of adolescence' (1948: 92). The presentation of Maggie Tulliver in *The Mill on the Floss* is exemplary. Her character is figured 'too purely from the inside': in the end, Eliot herself suffers from the same immaturity as the character she identifies with so strongly:

> Maggie's emotional and spiritual stresses...exhibit, naturally, all the marks of immaturity...they belong to a stage of development at which the capacity to make some essential distinctions has not yet been arrived at – at which the poised impersonality that is one of the conditions of being able to make them can't be achieved.
>
> (1948: 55–6)

Since it is that 'poised impersonality' which is the *sine qua non* of the novelist's art, it is George Eliot's own impersonality which has failed her through an over-identification with the character. For Leavis, Maggie Tulliver 'represents an immaturity that George Eliot can never leave safely behind her' (1948: 56); and it even returns to mar the almost perfect achievement of *Middlemarch* in the character of Dorothea, which Leavis reads as similarly betraying a failure of impersonality on Eliot's part, an emotional flaw in the formal structure of the novel. Thus, in his final summing up of *Middlemarch*, Leavis argues that 'the emotional fullness represented by Dorothea depends for its exalting potency on an abeyance of intelligence and self-knowledge'. Eliot's own emotional maturity has failed her, and consequently we find that in the novel:

> the situations offered by way of 'objective correlative' have the day-dream relation to experience; they are generated by a need to soar above the indocile facts and conditions of the real world. They don't, indeed, strike us as real in any sense; they have no objectivity, no vigour of illusion. In this kind of indulgence, complaisantly as she abandons herself to the current that is loosed, George Eliot's creative vitality has no part.
>
> (1948: 96)

This failure can be measured against what Leavis sees at work in Eliot's writing at its best, when:

> her sensibility is directed outward, and she responds from deep within. At this level, 'emotion' is a disinterested response defined by its object, and hardly distinguishable from the play of intelligence and self-knowledge that gave it impersonality.
>
> (1948: 96)

Such are the key terms of Leavis's mode of evaluation. It is not only that great art is mature and impersonal; it is that the one is the condition for the other. There can be no great art without maturity. The maturity of the author and the formal excellence of the novel come together in what might be called the practice of impersonality. As far as writing is concerned, this is a state of mind which allows the object to be seen exactly for what it is; and this state of mind is only accessible to the truly mature for it is the 'play of intelligence and self-knowledge' which constitutes emotional maturity. This circle of certitude makes it impossible for Leavis to spell out any 'theoretical' (a hated word) position: everything necessary is embodied in the concrete evaluations.[17]

So it is that, despite Leavis's claims to the contrary, actual novels are valued and judged in relation to some ideal type or model of the novel as he himself understands it: the novel as 'a dramatic poem in prose', novels in which the writer sees 'clearly and understandingly, sees with a judging vision that relates everything to her profoundest moral experience: [Eliot's] full living sense of value is engaged, and sensitively responsive' (Leavis 1948: 6). In the ideal novel, a mature judgement of life is fully embodied in the visionary textuality of the writing. The task of the critic is to assess how far particular novels are able to go in realising these ideals, and to offer criticism and correction where necessary. Thus, even the novelists of the 'great tradition', though they may enjoy all the necessary attributes of the great novelist, might not manage to write the great novel. Though all the ingredients may be there in the *oeuvre* as a whole, there is no guarantee that they will come together in a single text. Hence Leavis's final judgement of *Middlemarch*: 'only one book can, as a whole (though not without qualification), be said to represent her mature genius. That is, of course, *Middlemarch*' (1948: 76). In reality, as Mulhern observes, the definitive Eliot novel would in some sense comprise the sub-plot of *Felix Holt*, the 'good half' of *Daniel Deronda* and only then almost all of *Middlemarch* (Mulhern 1979: 259)!

And as with Forster, time, or rather history, is the enemy if any such account of the novel is to be sustained. The aim of the critic, in this mode of evaluation, is to discern the line of the 'great tradition'; but this means in turn, to go back to T.S. Eliot's formulation, to attempt to see the history of the novel 'not as consecrated by time, but to see it beyond time' (Eliot, in Forster 1927: 30). And if, ideally, this means imagining the world's authors 'all writing their novels at once' (1927: 21), then this implies that the critic is able to oversee them, can 'look over their shoulders for a moment' (1927: 21) and either chide them gently, as Forster does, or speak to them a little more harshly, as is Leavis's tendency.

Commentators have been only partly right in seeing Williams's study as merely offering some alternative points of interest on the same map of the novel. *The English Novel from Dickens to Lawrence* is in the end less concerned with the pronouncement of local judgements regarding the inclusion or exclusion of particular novelists, and more interested in challenging both the principles of evaluation at work in the novelistic canon, and in the idea of criticism underlying these principles. As Stuart Hall astutely remarked, the main interest of the book lies in 'the manner in which the term "form" is deployed'

(Hall 1980: 63). This comes through most strongly in the assessments of Dickens, Eliot and Hardy.

Form and structure in the novel

'By the standards of one kind of novel', writes Williams 'which has been emphasised in England as the great tradition, Dickens's faults – what are seen as his faults – are so many and so central as to produce embarrassment' (Williams 1970: 31). He mentions Forster's criticism in *Aspects of the Novel*, regarding the 'flatness' of Dickens's characters, and the Leavisite critique of Dickens's use of the language of direct persuasion rather than as the medium of Jamesian analysis and introspection, acknowledging that in Dickens's writing: 'Significance is not enacted in mainly tacit and intricate ways but is often directly presented in moral address and indeed exhortation' (1970: 31). But while Williams allows that according to the criteria of 'the fiction of an educated minority', Dickens is easily criticised, he insists that 'we get nowhere – critically nowhere – if we apply the standards of this kind of fiction to another and very different kind' (1970: 31). To get somewhere, the first step to take is to examine the situatedness of Dickens's writing, the social context to which his form – or even his apparent lack of form – was the embodied response.

The formal criteria for canonisation in the great tradition are ahistorical and ignore the real situatedness of the author who uses form, or who experiences, through formal problems, the disturbances of social history. To resolutely adopt only formal criteria would lead in the end to patently absurd conclusions, as Williams spells out in an imagined formal comparison between Trollope and Eliot:

> To read *Doctor Thorne* beside *Felix Holt* is not only to find ease in Trollope, where there is disturbance in George Eliot…. It is also, quite evidently, to see the source of these differences in a real social history. And I think we have to remember this when we are asked by several kinds of critic to abstract 'construction', 'organisation', 'thematic unity', 'unity of tone' and even 'good writing' and judge novels by these canons. On these abstract criteria – and especially those of unity – we should have to find Trollope a better novelist than George Eliot.
>
> (1970: 84–5)

While this is a move which Leavis explicitly rejects, the main point certainly holds. Leavis is, in fact, as constant as Williams in his insistence on the importance of the novel as an almost cognitive representation of a social order, but his understanding of form is classically liberal, and individualistic to the point of asociality. Formal failure can only and always ever be a symptom of failed maturity, of individual moral consciousness. Though the novelist may well write about society, the novelist at his or her best stands – like the critic – somehow outside it, divorced (and this is the very sign of Leavis's idea of maturity) from the social reality which he or she is then judging. For Williams, it is just this idea of the novelist's – and the critic's – ideal position of objective 'outsiderness' that is most troubling, since to understand the constitutive tensions of form, it is above all necessary to understand the inescapable positionality of the author or critic.

This comes through most clearly in the consideration of those formal or technical problems which Leavis had seen as evidence of immaturity or moral failing. Since mature writing implied impersonality, anything which detracted from that impersonality led to formal failure. Leavis writes of 'the supremely mature mind of *Middlemarch*' (Leavis 1948: 52); but even *Middlemarch* suffers from George Eliot's inherently dangerous tendency towards autobiographic identification. It was precisely this tendency which was responsible for the failure of *The Mill on the Floss*.

Like Leavis, Williams finds something of a new consciousness at work in *Middlemarch*; but, unlike him, he cannot recommend it. He too finds 'elements of Maggie Tulliver' in Dorothea; but insists, against Leavis, that 'she is now at arm's length being looked at'. This, certainly, represents a new 'signifying consciousness' in Eliot's work; but it is not one he can endorse:

> It is a consciousness, a fictional method, that has been widely recommended. It is referred back to the cool 'impersonality' of Jane Austen; forward to the wrought observation of Henry James and thence to what is often called, in a sweeping indeed overbearing dimension, maturity...it is a method that when abstracted is a cold placing, a critic's fiction. Indeed, more than that, it is a social mode in which the observer, the signifier, is not himself at stake but is refined into a fictional process, indeed into a fiction.
>
> (Williams 1970: 90–1)

For Williams, this mode of analysis – the method of Leavis's *The Great Tradition* – has both general and highly specific components. Generally, it is 'the mode of an anxious society – an anxious class preoccupied with placing, grading, defining'. And more specifically, it is the critical mode of Cambridge English itself, as he emphasises:

> As you'll have gathered, I don't really find it particularly mature, though when it bears down on you in a whole place – in a university for example – it has an apparent poise that takes some time to live through: a mode in which we are all signifiers, all critics and judges, and can somehow afford to be because life – given life, creating life – goes on where it is supposed to, elsewhere.
>
> (1970: 91)

There is a false confidence to such maturity, which is only ever the brittle maturity of the outsider: to this Williams prefers the real uneasiness of the 'participant who is also an observer' (1970: 110).

The novelist who exemplifies this position of participant-observer is Thomas Hardy, the most unjustly neglected author of Leavis's account. Leavis can find no better words for Hardy than Henry James, in a disparaging moment, found for him: the 'good little Thomas Hardy' whose *Tess of the D'Urbervilles* is 'chock-full of faults and falsity, and yet has a singular charm' (cited in Leavis 1948: 34). In comparison with George Eliot, Hardy 'decent as he is', is no more than 'a provincial manufacturer of gauche and heavy fictions that sometimes have corresponding virtues' (1948: 146). For Williams, this evaluation, made on the apparently formal grounds of technique, though in fact on technique confounded with maturity, is unwarranted and unhelpful. The real criteria for any meaningful assessment lie elsewhere: in the writer's engagement with 'a real social history', in and through the materiality of form. 'What we have to emphasise,' writes Williams, bringing both Hardy and Eliot together, is:

> the creative disturbance which is exactly George Eliot's importance: the disturbance we shall see also in Hardy. That is where the life is, in that disturbed and unprecedented time. And those who responded most deeply, who saw most, had no unified form, no unity of tone and language, no controlling conventions, that really answered their purposes. Their novels are the records of struggle and difficulty, as was the life they wrote about.
>
> (Williams 1970: 85)

For Williams, in terms which anticipate his reading of Vološinov, the formal problem of expression faced by such writers are not the product of some aspect of a private subjectivity – a question of self-knowledge or maturity. It is a problem of social subjectivity, or what he refers to as 'the recurring problem of the social consciousness of the writer' (1970: 77). Hardy is an exemplary case, since he was:

> neither owner nor tenant, dealer nor labourer, but an observer and a chronicler, often again with an uncertainty about his actual relation. Moreover his is not writing for them, but about them, to a mainly metropolitan and unconnected literary public.
>
> (1970: 101)

Thus the most significant problem with Hardy's writing is the product of that key situation: he was a 'participant who is also an observer' (1970: 110). The phrase provided the key to some of the central arguments of *The Country and the City*, as we shall see below.

Williams links Leavis's casual disparagement of Hardy to a much wider field of force, out of which a British Council critic could write of Eliot, Hardy and

Lawrence as 'our three great autodidacts' – meaning, as is pointed out, only that they happened not to have been educated at a public school and then at an Oxbridge college. The conflict between 'customary and educated life' – itself so central to Hardy's own work – continues in and through the continuing assessments of Hardy in academia.[18]

Alive in Williams's assessment of Hardy, and at work in the very high value he places on him (he is 'our flesh and grass'), is the very heart of the whole argument, his conception of the novel. If, for Leavis, the novel at its best was the 'poem in prose' he had outlined as early as 1933, what was it for Williams? The novel was, of course, 'a major form in English literature'; but it was also much more than a literary genre. We may better grasp the force of Williams's idea of the novel in terms of what we may now call the general practice of representation.

The key to this is given in the Conclusion to *The English Novel*, where Williams discusses the 'particular bearing' of his study, the idea of the 'knowable community'. He writes:

> When I say that the problems including the formal problems of the novel are in the end mainly problems of relationships I am pointing to an area where it is still difficult to relate, a continuing and more general experience of the educated and the customary.
>
> (1970: 188)

He takes Virginia Woolf's writing as an example of how deeply this problem has entered the question of form itself. He quotes from her famous essay on 'Modern Fiction', and turns to its representation of the 'ordinary mind on the ordinary day' and argues:

> that 'the ordinary mind on the ordinary day' is social, and that it relates us necessarily to others, and that consciousness, real consciousness, doesn't come passively like that, a receiving of impressions, but is what we learn, what we make, in our real relationships, including with fathers and mothers and shops.
>
> (1970: 189)

Woolf's brilliant description of the tasks of the new modernist and anti-realist novel falls too easily into an overemphasis on the private life in the bourgeois division of life into public and private aspects, and ignores the real problems to be faced by the novel, 'the problems of knowable community'; that is, the acceptance of the real indissociability of public and private life, not to mention the divisions of class once Woolf's public/private split is accepted.[19]

In the end, the very existence of such a deep division of experience is itself a symptom of a complex social history. The history of the novel testifies to an 'important split' which takes place between 'knowable relationships and an unknown, overwhelming society' (1970: 15). This whole history, this whole process is exemplifed in James Joyce's *Ulysses*, which Williams reads as being about 'the loss of a city, the loss of relationships' and where the only 'knowable community' exists in 'the need, the desire, of a racing separated consciousness' (1970: 167). This is the task and the burden of the novel, the problem of the knowable community in the new urban society. The case is summed up in the introduction to the book:

> The problem of the knowable community, with its deep implications for the novelist, is then clearly a part of the social history of early nineteenth-century England and of the imaginative penetration and recoil which was the creative response. But what is knowable is not only a function of objects – of what is there to be known. It is also a function of subjects, of observers – of what is desired and what needs to be known. A knowable community, that is to say, is a matter of consciousness as well as of evident fact. Indeed it is just this problem of knowing a community – of finding a position, a position convincingly experienced, from which community can begin to be known – that one of the major phases in the development of the novel must be related.
>
> (1970: 17)

In the end, this is a question of representation. The novel may seek to provide a representation of society, in the usual sense of a realist representation, the use of language to reflect an external world; but what Williams draws constant attention to is the sense of representation in its social-political sense, that writing is always a writing from a position, a matter of the subject and of consciousness, and not only of the object, of the external world. In this sense of representation, the role of language in writing is constitutive, and not merely instrumental; the writer is always participant and not only an observer, marked by the language he or she adopts at the same time as they try to get beyond that language, in the move which denies any authority not only to the Leavisite formalist model of the novel, but also to any Marxist theory of literature as reflection, 'tendency' or simple product of base and superstructure dynamics. As he puts it in the conclusion to the book:

> Much ordinary social experience is of course directly reflected, represented, in what is indeed an ideology, what can be called a superstructure. But in any society at all like our own, and especially in this one in the last hundred and fifty years, there's a very vital area of social experience – *social* experience – that doesn't get incorporated: that's neglected, ignored, certainly at times repressed; that even when it's taken up, to be processed or to function as an official consciousness, is resistant, lively, still goes on its way, and eventually steps on its shadow – steps, I mean, in such a way that we can see which is shadow and which is substance. It is from this vital area, from this structure of feeling that is lived and experienced but not quite yet

arranged as institutions and ideas, from this common and inalienable life that I think all art is made.

(1970: 192)

The English Novel closes with this challenge to overly mechanical and overly reductionist accounts of the relations between culture and society, between art and economy, and anticipates Williams's later formulations of dominant, residual and emergent energies which were later to be picked up by critics who wished to challenge any too reductive formulations of ideology or power.[20]

The Country and the City

Early reviewers were divided in their responses to what is now commonly regarded as Williams's greatest oppositional text, *The Country and the City*, published in 1973. H. Coombes, for example, could only conclude that Williams's '*idée fixe* [the critique of the organic community] inhibits the use of any literary critical powers he may have possessed' (Coombes 1973: 71), and Evan Watkins seemed to agree, writing in 1978, that *The Country and the City* was 'deeply flawed...too immersed in the analysis of historical detail...too immediately personal' (Watkins 1978: 141), while Christopher Ricks found 'there is such bullyingness and deadness in the prose' (cited in Inglis 1995: 237). Roger Scruton, in his conservative study, *Thinkers of the New Left*, asserted in 1985 that it was 'one of the most two-dimensional surveys of English literature ever to have retained the lineaments of academic respectability' (1985: 61). Others had more positive responses. Lawrence Lerner, in *Encounter*, wrote approvingly that he doubted 'if it is possible...ever again to read the country house poems in the same way' (Lerner 1973: 63), and Marshall Berman, in what became the standard judgement, wrote that in *The Country and the City*, 'the intellectual power and the ideological passion and the personal integrity come together more convincingly than ever before' (Berman 1973: 1). *The Country and the City* is Williams's *magnum opus*, his 'richest book', 'his greatest book', 'one of the most brilliant and seminal he has produced', his 'necessary book'.[21]

The Country and the City begins with a characteristic discussion of the varied historical meanings of 'country' and 'city' as keywords – 'powerful words', writes Williams, and not surprisingly so 'when we remember how much they seem to stand for in the experience of human communities' (Williams 1973a: 9) – and moves – long before this kind of situated writing was to become a standard ploy in academic identity politics – from this 'general problem' to its location as a 'personal issue'.[22] Williams had not only read the available 'descriptions and interpretations' of moving from country to city, he had in a sense lived them through in the move from Wales to England, from Pandy to Cambridge, and lived and thought through them 'as a problem'. The study is the attempt to resolve that problem, and to better understand the relations between the country and the city, so that the study, 'though it often and necessarily follows impersonal procedures, in description and analysis, there is behind it, all the time, this personal pressure and commitment' (Williams 1973a: 11).

The Country and the City is a magisterial work, and in a strong and particular sense. It generates its air of massive authority not only through academic knowledge and the deployment of its protocols, but through the power and appeal of the autobiographical. Surveying with professional expertise and personal experience the images of the country and the city available across a very broad (though mainly English) range of writing, *The Country and the City* is by far the most successful realisation of the ideal of committed academic writing which Williams had learned as a youth. For purposes of discussion, we can divide the book into two main sections dealing respectively with the country and then with the city, and then a two-part conclusion in which he discusses first a selection of the available present writing on country and city followed by – in the two final chapters – the wider political implications of the argument as a whole.

The first section deals primarily with the history of pastoral writing. Chapters 1–14 focus on images of country life, mainly in poetry, from Hesiod's *Works and Days* through Theocritus and Virgil to Carew and Jonson, across Pope and Crabbe, up to and as far as Clare and Wordsworth. The second section, Chapters 14–20, concentrates on representations of the city and of city life, borrowing and at times adapting material from the previously published *The English Novel from Dickens to Lawrence* (1970). It examines the development of ways of seeing and representing the city from the eighteenth century, across Dickens, Eliot and Hardy and through Virginia Woolf to James Joyce, whose *Ulysses* Williams sees as the 'climax' of the tradition, just as *Finnegan's Wake* represents its 'crisis' (1973a: 294). Chapters 21–3 examine twentieth-century 'country' writing, including Meredith, Lawrence and Grassic Gibbon, the journal *The Countryman*, and some science fiction. The two final chapters – 'The New Metropolis' and 'Cities and Countries' – examine the troping of the country and city figure into the contemporary world of imperialism and post-imperialism, concluding, through an analytic twist which annoyed many non-Marxist readers, with a final transformation of the country and city opposition into the very idea of capitalism itself:

> capitalism, as a mode of production, is the basic process of most of what we know as the history of country and city. Its abstracted economic desires, its fundamental priorities in social relations, its criteria of growth and of profit and loss, have over several centuries altered our country and created our kinds of city. In its final forms of imperialism it has altered our world.
>
> (1973a: 363)

There is no space here for a thorough consideration of the many analyses and arguments put forward in this rich and varied study. I shall rather examine the ways in which the book as a whole represented a response to two currents of thought and analysis, and how these came together to give *The Country and the City* its distinctive place in his work as a whole. The first of these is the continued opposition to the ways in which Cambridge English constructed its version of literary history, in this instance, around the tradition of the country house poem; and second, as a way of replying to some of the substantial criticisms put to his earlier work by two Marxist historians, Edward Thompson and Victor Kiernan. These came together in an emphasis on the politics of all acts of representation in and through the idea of the embodied observer. Let us first examine some of the key terms in leftist criticisms of Williams's earlier work.

Disembodied voices

As we saw in Chapter 3, *Culture and Society* and *The Long Revolution* were greeted with some hostility and opposition by conservative critics. But these two works were also the focus of some challenging and incisive criticisms from the left, and in particular from two socialist historians, Victor Kiernan and Edward Thompson, who wrote perhaps the two most thoughtful reviews. Kiernan's review of *Culture and Society* appeared in the summer 1959 issue of *The New Reasoner*, and Thompson's assessment of *The Long Revolution* ran across two issues of the *New Left Review* in 1961.

While Kiernan accepts that Williams has written a 'fascinating and important book', his final judgement is that the study lacks the essential credentials of a properly Marxist study of culture and society. For Kiernan, the 'prime requisite for any study of cultural history is a firm framework of historical fact – economic, social, political...the one great deficiency of the book is the lack of just this' (Kiernan 1959: 75–6). In particular, he criticises Williams for failing to define any precise sense for the term 'Industrial Revolution', and for neglecting the crucial importance of class in the ideological debates which he analyses. He is also guilty of neglect with regard to what Kiernan identifies as the three absolutely essential components of any historically based survey of nineteenth-century culture, the forces of religion, nationalism and imperialism; while the final chapter, Williams's own 'tract for the times', omits any discussion of the crucial role of the state as an actor essential to any account of the political and ideological conflicts involved in the book's arguments.

Kiernan attributes these failures of analysis to Williams's entrapment in the discipline and accompanying ideology of literary studies themselves. 'To be seen in the round, and understood in its real bearings,' he argues:

> a pattern of ideas must be seen taking shape in the minds of members of a determinate social group in a specific epoch. Mr Williams's method in this book has been to take a number of individual publicists of each generation in turn, extract passages from their works, and add his comments...a procession of individuals does not add up to a class...As a result these writers

have somewhat the style of disembodied intelligences, spirit-voices addressing us through the lips of a medium.

(Kiernan 1959: 78)

In other words, Kiernan argued that Williams's prediliction for the formalism of textual analysis hindered or pre-empted the possibility of real historical and social analysis afforded by the concept of class.

Thompson's review was in broad agreement with many of Kiernan's points, and he too located Williams's failings in his training in the discipline of English studies. His lengthy review appeared in two consecutive issues of the *New Left Review* and it constitutes one of the major engagements with Williams's work from a left-wing perspective. Thompson is more than willing to acknowledge the importance of Williams's work – 'so far as we can speak of a New Left – he is our best man' (Thompson 1961: 24) – but he too was disturbed by the ways in which he saw some of Williams's project undermined by Williams's own entanglement in the presuppositions of English studies. He took issue, in the first instance, with what many came to regard as one of the strengths of Williams's style. J.P. Ward later described this well as the:

level reasonableness of the writing, the suggestion that wholeness and unity were available in a class-divided society and the suggestion that it was not just an intellectual's abstraction but a cultural discovery, there ready and waiting to use, were unquestionably the main reasons for the book's huge success and appeal.

(Ward 1981: 17)

But for Thompson, the problem was that this 'reasonableness' itself represented what he called a 'concealed preference – in the name of genuine communication – for the language of the academy' (Thompson 1961: 25). The real violence and the real stakes of the whole argument lay concealed and obscured within this academic reasonableness, and he criticised the ways in which, as he put it, a 'sense of extreme fastidiousness enters whenever logic prompts us to identify those "patterns", "systems" and "forms" with precise social forces and particular thinkers' (1961: 25). How can T.S. Eliot be placed in something called the same 'tradition' as D.H. Lawrence and William Morris, when Eliot writes in opposition to everything they stood for? We cannot do so, writes Thompson:

unless we are using 'tradition' in the sense in which we describe both Calvin and Ignatius Loyola as belonging to a common 'Christian tradition'. But once we include both Reformation and Counter-Reformation within one common tradition, we must recognise that we are in danger of becoming so aloof that the energies of the disputants cannot be seen through the haze.

(1961: 25–6)

In fact, a fatal weakness of the whole account is the absence of the primary conceptual tool of the historian: the idea and understanding of context, and implicit in the historian's sense of social context, the idea and understanding of ideological conflict. The final judgement is damning: 'There are no good or bad men in Mr Williams's history, only dominant and subordinate 'structures of feeling' (1961: 29). What the book's narrative finally has to offer is no more than 'a procession of disembodied voices – Burke, Carlyle, Mill, Arnold – their meanings wrested out of their whole social context' (1961: 24–5), and consequently, a version of history which lacks any properly developed idea of ideological struggle: 'What Mr Williams has never come to terms with is the problem of *ideology*' (1961: 35). Thompson reads Williams's emphasis on communication as value – perhaps the central theme of *The Long Revolution* – as the crucial index of this general theoretical failing:

> It is this confusion [value-making communication] which enables him to lose sight of power: and it is only when the systems of communication are replaced in the context of power-relationships that we can see the problem as it is. And it is the problem of ideology.
>
> (1961: 37)

With characteristic adroitness, Thompson insists that Williams is wrong to represent culture as a 'whole way of life'; culture if anything represents a 'whole way of *conflict*' (1961: 33). Anything less than this is to depart from 'the main line of the socialist tradition' (1961: 34). In the end, judged Thompson, the:

> aspiration for a common culture in Raymond Williams's sense ('common meanings, common values') is admirable: but the more this aspiration is nourished, the more outrageous the real divisions of interest and power in our society will appear. The attempt to create a common culture, like that to effect common ownership and to build a co-operative community, must be content with fragmented success so long as it is contained within capitalist society.
>
> (1961: 36)

Disembodied intelligences; disembodied voices; an incoherent account of tradition; a mistaken aspiration for a common culture. There is no doubt that Williams felt the force of these criticisms, even if it seemed for quite some time that he could only do his best to deflect rather than confront them. Awareness of them still pricked his thinking enough for him to begin his response to the many points raised about his work at the Slant Symposium with a response, if not a reply, to one of Thompson's points: 'I would therefore agree that in this sense the problem of a common culture is the problem of revolutionary politics' (Williams 1968c: 297).[23] But it was only with *The Country and the City* that he sought to refute the criticisms, though this is not a dimension of the study that Williams ever foregrounded, or that, to my knowledge, has been remarked on by other critics. Yet it is essential to understanding the argument of the book as a whole.

The country house ideology

Critics have followed Williams in emphasising the institutional context of *The Country and the City*. Like *Modern Tragedy*, it was 'a very antagonistic book' (Williams 1979: 304), and one whose starting-point – the 'much discussed question of how to read the English country-house poems' (1979: 303) – was grounded firmly in Cambridge English. The 'Country House Poem' was the topic of one of the optional examinations that could be taken in Part Two of the English Tripos, and the germs of the book as a whole can be found in the lectures he gave on this topic as early as 1967 (Williams 1967a, 1967b). We can take G.R. Hibbard's 1956 essay, 'The Country House Poem of the Seventeenth Century', as an exemplary instance of the 'particular literary orthodoxy' the book set out to challenge (Williams 1979: 304).[24]

Hibbard constructed his argument in terms of the orthodox idea of literary history as the formal history of literary genres and traditions. The 'country house poem' forms a 'thin but clearly defined tradition' in English literature, a tradition of poems which are written in praise of 'the English country house and of a whole way of life of which the country house was the centre'. This 'homogeneous body of poetry' (Hibbard 1956: 159) extends from Ben Jonson through Andrew Marvell, and stretches as far as Pope's writing. While there is no doubt that this poetry owes a 'considerable debt to Latin poetry', Hibbard is confident that it is a poetry best described in the particular sense of Augustan that literary criticism has given to seventeenth- and eighteenth-century English writing. 'It is truly Augustan', writes Hibbard:

> in the sense that it voices and defines the value of a society conscious of its own achievement of a civilized way of living, and conscious also of the forces that threatened to undermine and overthrow that achievement. The function of the poet in this society was to make it aware of itself; and because the poet had a function the relation between poet and patron in these poems is sound and wholesome.
>
> (Hibbard 1956: 159)

In this way, the essay repeats and exemplifies the founding claims for literature and for literary criticism of the Cambridge English project. Leavis had earlier expressed something of this same stress on the image of an achieved society with his own view of the Common Reader of the eighteenth century. In *Education and the University* (1943), he argued that:

> The acquiring of taste is probably more difficult today than it ever was before. Consider for contrast the eighteenth century. Not only were there fewer books to read, fewer topics and fewer distractions; the century

enjoyed the advantages of a homogeneous – a real – culture. So Johnson
could defer to the ultimate authority of the Common Reader.... [Today]
there is no Common Reader: the tradition is dead.

(Leavis 1943: 106–7)

Leavis here represents the eighteenth century as the age of the common
reader, the age of a homogeneous, a real, culture. Such a representation of the
eighteenth century necessarily involves the elision of social and cultural divisions
in the name of an impossible homogeneity, whose passing is regretted only in
the name of seeking to bring it about again. There is no Common Reader: the
tradition is dead – but long live the tradition, let us revive the common reader,
that is, let us revive the culture of criticism which can create critics in the image
of common readers. For the literary critic of the 1920s and 1930s, and beyond,
the eighteenth century represented an image of a stable, orderly and harmoni-
ous society to set against the fragmented world of modern commercial culture,
of Leavis's 'techno-Benthamite' civilization.

Williams set himself clearly against any such idea of tradition, and any such
consequent system of representation. 'When I first went to Cambridge', he
remarked in 1967, in a lecture which outlines the main arguments of the book:

I was offered the interpretation I am now rejecting: a convention of rural
order, of Old England, against industrial disorder and the modern world. I
had the strongest personal reasons for doubting it, but it has taken me
many years to reach the point where I can try to say, intellectually, where it
was wrong.

(Williams 1967a: 632)

Such a 'convention of rural order' structured Leavis's arguments about
Augustan culture as it did his broader opposition between minority culture and
mass civilization; and it also comes through very strongly in Hibbard's whole
argument, with its casual assumption of the 'sound and wholesome relation'
between poet and patron.

As truth will paint it

Ben Jonson's poem 'Penshurst' presents a useful site for some elaboration of
Williams's critical relation to orthodox readings of rural writing. First published
in 1616, the poem is written in praise of the great house where Sidney had once
lived, and in which he had begun to write his *Arcadia* in 1580. In Hibbard's
reading, Jonson's poem 'represents the norm, slightly idealized, but still the
norm' (Hibbard 1956: 159) of the relations between poet and patron,
landowner and peasant in the seventeenth century. The country house of
Penshurst is the 'embodiment of a natural bond between lord and tenant'
(1956: 164), and a poem such as this exemplifies a social and moral order

which we, in the mass democracy and mass culture of the twentieth century, have lost.

But to an alert reader, Hibbard's phrase 'slightly idealized' gives away the game. Such a reading of the poem is actually a refusal to read it. As Williams notes, the first thing to notice about a poem like Jonson's 'Penshurst' (or, for that matter, Carew's 'To Saxham' (1638)), is that this particular country house is not given to represent the norm of available hospitality; it is rather treated as the exception to a general practice of meanness and deprivation. He pays particular attention to the role of negative identification in the poems: Penshurst and Saxham are in fact defined against unmentioned other houses and hospitalities. 'The morality is not, when we look into it, the fruit of the economy; it is a local stand and standard against it', he argues (Williams 1973a: 42), and sums up:

> Any mystification, however, requires effort. The world of Penshurst or of Saxham can be seen as a moral economy only by conscious selection and emphasis. And this is just what we get: not only in the critical reading I have referred to, but in Jonson's and Carew's actual poems. There were of course social reasons for that way of seeing: the identification of the writers, as guests, with the social position of their hosts, consuming what other men had produced. But a traditional image, already becoming complicated, was an indispensable poetic support.
>
> (1973a: 44)

It is precisely the effort involved in mystification which gives literary writing its defining textual density. This textual density prevents literary writing from holding any secure place in any simple category of reflection or presentation, and similarly withholds from it any status as direct evidence in historical inquiry. Literature belongs in the category of representation, and as such, any description which literary writing has to offer always needs to be understood in relation to the fact of address, and the consequent idealisations and mystifications which are likely to accompany this. With his analysis of pastoral writing, Williams anticipates the theoretical point he was to find expressed with such force and clarity in the writings of Vološinov, and which he was to insist on as a central component of his own theory of cultural materialism, as we shall see in the following chapter.

A central component of this general mystification – and one that has since become the common starting point for a whole generation of critics – is quite simply the removal or displacement of the fact of labour from the poems in question.[25] Williams writes of the 'magical extraction of the curse of labour' from the world of the poems, and how this is often achieved by 'a simple extraction of the existence of labourers' (1973a: 45). Against this way of seeing, or better, this refusal to see, he quotes the poet-labourer Stephen Duck on 'the cheat' of the whole thing, and sums up:

It is this way of seeing that really counts. Jonson looks out over the fields of Penshurst and sees, not work, but a land yielding of itself....To call this a natural order is then an abuse of language. It is what the poems are: not country life but social compliment; the familiar hyperboles of the aristocracy and its attendants.

(1973a: 46)

The Rev. George Crabbe – in many ways the point of reference and identification for Williams's own account – was right.[26] He opens Chapter 3 with a couplet taken from the second book of Crabbe's poem *The Village*, originally published in May 1783:

No longer truth, though shown in verse, disdain,
But own the Village Life a life of pain.

(Crabbe 1851: 118)

Crabbe's work is crucial to any assessment of the pastoral tradition, including the Country House poems, because it sets out to position itself against the mediating power of existing conventions, and refuses to simply repeat the 'Mechanic echoes of Mantuan song' (1851: 114). It thus raises the central question: the conflict and opportunity afforded by the inevitable discrepancies between 'experience' and 'conventional seeing', the question of 'perspective'. For in order to 'own' – to own up to, to be willing to admit, and, crucially, to articulate – that the Village Life was, in reality, a 'life of pain' meant challenging the poetic conventions which had done their best to disown and disavow that fact. Crabbe takes the first and necessary step in grasping the existence and force of literary convention. And Williams pursues the second – to see that any convention is itself grounded in questions of social positioning and social understanding – just the questions of 'mystification' (Williams's preferred term) which the book as a whole then goes on to examine.

The chapter closes – in a pointed alternative to Hibbard's reading of Herrick – with an analysis of 'The Hock-Cart'. Here, the reality of labour is acknowledged in the 'rough hands' which perform the 'tough labours'. But the centre of the poem lies less with the peasant workers than in the recipient of its formal address – the Right Honourable Lord Mildmaye, Earl of Westmorland. As Williams observes, Herrick 'places himself between the lord and the labourers to make explicit (what in Jonson and Carew had been implicit and mystified) the governing social relations' (1973a: 47). While the labourers are allowed the brief respite and pleasure of drinking the lord's health, it is only to refresh themselves for a moment and then, as Herrick emphasises, to get back to work. 'It is perhaps not surprising' notes Williams:

that *The Hock-Cart* is less often quoted, as an example of a natural and moral economy, than *To Penshurst* or *To Saxham*. Yet all that is in question is the degree of consciousness of real processes. What Herrick embarrassingly intones is what Jonson and Carew mediate. It is a social order, and a consequent way of seeing, which we are not now likely to forget.

(1973a: 47)

In many ways, these comments can serve to sum up the whole impetus of *The Country and the City*. At stake is the question of 'the degree of conscious-ness of real processes'. Williams argues against readings like Hibbard's, which, in representing the eighteenth century (or any other) as the time of a 'homogeneous – a real – culture', fail to engage with these processes, and are blind to just the kind of social conflicts which Williams's own critics had charged him with being blind to. In the chapters which follow, he deepens and extends his general argument, urging the need to understand the historical processes to which the literary texts are in part a response, and therefore to grasp the ideological force of literary convention.

The observer embodied

Drawing extensively on the arguments and material of *The English Novel from Dickens to Lawrence*, Chapters 14, 'Change in the City', through to Chapter 20, 'The Figure in the City', examine the dynamics, continuities and shifts in the representation of London from the early eighteenth century up to the twentieth century. Williams rejects any too-easy contrast between 'the fiction of the city and the fiction of the country' in which 'in the city kind, experience and community would be essentially opaque; in the country kind, essentially transparent', arguing that 'in realizing the new fact of the city, we must be careful not to idealize the old and new facts of the country' (1973a: 202). The key point concerns the positionality of the writing subject:

> For what is knowable is not only a function of objects – of what is there to be known. It is also a function of subjects, of observers – of what is desired and what needs to be known. And what we then have to see, as through-out, in the country writing, is not only the reality of the rural community; it is the observer's position in and towards it; a position which is part of the community being known.
>
> (1973a: 202–3)

In other words, in the village 'as in the city there is division of labour, there is the contrast of social position, and then necessarily there are alternate points of view' (1973a: 203). Williams illustrates this through a fine comparison between the work of Jane Austen and George Eliot, starting with a characteristically wry observation that, for Jane Austen, neighbours 'are not the people actually living nearby; they are the people living a little less nearby who, in social recognition, can be visited' (1973a: 203). With George Eliot, the matter stands differently. The 'knowable community' of Austen's novelistic world is, as Williams notes, 'socially selected'; but 'what it then lacks in full social reference it gains in an available unity of language' (1973a: 206–7). It is just this unity which is lacking in Eliot. 'There is a new kind of break in the texture of the novel,' writes Williams, 'an evident failure of continuity between the necessary language of the novelist and the recorded language of many of the characters' (1973a: 207) and this, he argues, can be attributed to the 'very recognition of conflict, of the existence of classes, of divisions and contrasts of feeling and speaking [which] makes a unity of idiom impossible' (1973a: 207).

With these and similar observations, Williams sought to distance himself from the criticisms of a Thompson or a Kiernan. By trying to show and assert the importance of the social positionality of the subject, and how this comes through in problems of narrative texture and discursive idiom, he demonstrated the ways in which a reading and analysis of literary tradition could demonstrate the existence, functioning and consequences of a conflictual and class-differentiated culture. This same positionality of the subject, and the related question of the observer's perspective is similarly crucial to representations of the city.

Williams draws out some of its implications through an analysis of marginal and non-canonical writers such as Alexander Somerville, Joseph Archer and Richard Jefferies ('no neutral observer...[if] at times the committed writer...at times the class reporter or even the party hack' (1973a: 235)), as well as the better known work of novelists such as Dickens, Hardy and Gissing. What is decisive, though, is the development he sketches in Chapter 20, 'The Figure in the City', where he argues that: 'Perception of the new qualities of the modern city had been associated, from the beginning, with a man walking, as if alone, in its streets' (1973a: 280).

In Blake, in Wordsworth, in Dickens and Gaskell, through Baudelaire, Balzac and Dostoievsky, we read of this common figure. Williams's main focus is on the question raised by his phrase 'as if alone', for the city experience can always be read, he affirms, in either of two ways, as 'an affirmation of common humanity, past the barriers of crowded strangeness; or into an emphasis of isolation, of mystery – an ordinary feeling become a terror' (1973a: 281). Though the nineteenth-century writers explore both alternatives, it is the latter which becomes dominant. As this happens, the representation of the city tends to lose the firmness and solidity of its empirical and referential qualities, and to assume the implications of the symbolic. James Thomson's two poems, 'The Doom of the City' (1857) and the more famous 'The City of Dreadful Night' (1870–3), exemplify a shift in which:

> Struggle, indifference, loss of purpose, loss of meaning – features of nine-teenth-century social experience and of a common interpretation of the new scientific world-view – have found, in the City, a habitation and a name. For the city is not only, in this vision, a form of modern life; it is the physical embodiment of a decisive modern consciousness.
>
> (1973a: 287)

This modern consciousness is traced through Eliot's poetry, and across the atomised subjectivities of Virginia Woolf and James Joyce.[27] In the end, writes Williams, the choice is between this atomised subjectivity, which tends to take refuge in myth, and the development of a more fully collective consciousness, the consciousness which can power social improvement and ultimately revolution. 'Out of the cities' he concludes:

> came these two great and transforming modern ideas: myth, in its variable forms; revolution, in its variable forms. But they are better seen as alternative responses, for in a thousand cities, they are in sharp, direct and necessary conflict.
>
> (1973a: 296)

Framed in this way, 'the images of country and city' examined by the book (1973a: 347) amount to no less than a certain history – a literary history – of capitalism itself, since 'capitalism, as a mode of production, is the basic process of most of what we know as the history of country and city' (1973a: 363). With this assertion, Williams seeks to connect the 'limited inquiry' of *The Country and the City* – and even the 'country and the city within a single tradition' (1973a: 368), largely that of Great Britain – with the pressing issues of contemporary politics and the wider forces of imperialism and a now global capitalism.[28] In so doing, he is defending the claims of literary analysis for politics against both his apolitical opponents in English studies, and against his Marxist critics in the discipline of history, who saw his training in literary studies as the source of his conceptual failings (Kiernan 1959: 78; Thompson 1961: 25). But not content with defence alone, he also turns to the attack.

For this same opposition between country and city has also played a role in Marxist theory and analysis. Marxism does not allow an intellectual vantage point or improved perspective outside of the arguments under consideration. It is itself fully caught up in the system of representation he describes, and the role of the structuring opposition between town and country within it has not, he argues, enjoyed sufficient critical attention. In a famous passage in *The Communist Manifesto*, Marx and Engels wrote of how the bourgeoisie:

> has subjected the country to the rule of the town. It has created enormous cities, has greatly increased the urban population as compared with the rural, and has thus rescued a considerable part of the population from the idiocy of rural life. Just as it has made the country dependent on the towns, so it has made barbarian and semi-barbarian countries dependent on the civilized ones, nations of peasants on nations of bourgeois, the East on the West.
>
> (Marx and Engels 1888: 71–2)

Here, Marx and Engels retain the bourgeois opposition between town and country in the contrast between civilization and 'the idiocy of rural life'. This opposition is echoed by Trotsky, who saw the history of capitalism as 'the victory of town over country' (Williams 1973a: 363); and in the end the structure of this opposition enabled 'one of the most terrible phases in the whole history of rural society' (1973a: 364): Stalin's programme of modernization and industrialization, and his self-styled ' "victory" over the peasants' (1973a: 364). Ultimately, argues Williams, this 'major distortion in the history of communism was erected' on just the 'kind of confidence in the singular values of modernization and civilization' that was the yield of the town and country opposition.

And yet, more recently, in the process of the Cuban and Chinese Revolutions, Williams finds that another emphasis is being made, one in which 'the exploited rural and colonial populations became the main sources of continued revolt' (1973a: 365).[29] This emphasis corresponds to 'a formulation which is at once the most exciting, the most relevant and yet the most undeveloped in the whole revolutionary argument' (1973a: 365). Theoretically, in other words, it can be stated in the broad terms of Williams's distinctive version of the New Left project. At its centre is the idea of a common culture as the starting-point and rallying call of contemporary political action as 'not only analytic but programmatic response: on new forms of decision-making, new kinds of education, new definitions and practices of work, new kinds of settlement and land-use' (1973a: 366). In the end, he writes, the:

> division and opposition of city and country, industry and agriculture, in their modern forms, are the critical culmination of the division and specialization of labour which, though it did not begin with capitalism, was developed under it to an extraordinary and transforming degree. Other forms of the same fundamental division are the separation between mental and manual labour, between administration and operation, between politics and social life. The symptoms of this division can be found at every point in what is now our common life: in the idea and practice of social classes; in conventional definitions of work and of education; in the physical distribution of settlements; and in temporal organization of the day, the week, the year, the lifetime. Much of the creative thinking of our time is an attempt to re-examine each of these concepts and practices. It is based on the conviction that the system which generates and is composed by them is intolerable and will not survive.
>
> (1973a: 366)

As the *New Left Review* team note, seen in these terms *The Country and the City* 'represents a progression beyond the characteristic problematic of classical Marxism' (Williams 1979: 315). And yet, at the same time, they are curious as to why this dimension of the book as a 'very powerful, even polemical, corrective to a main tradition of revolutionary socialism' is down-played. Why is there no 'properly extended engagement' with the tradition, why is discussion of it confined to only 'a few paragraphs' (1979: 316)? Williams replies in terms of his particular 'biographical trajectory', and the limitations of his 'curious entry' into Marxist culture as an undergraduate student in the 1940s, a statement which is best understood as at least a partial confession of (situated) ignorance. This, I think, is a partial truth.

Williams does not mention what I believe is crucial to the structuring arguments of *The Country and the City*: the particular ways in which a significant dimension of the book's address is determined by the desire to respond at last to the earlier Marxist criticisms of his work, the criticisms of Kiernan and Thompson. This dimension, his argument with 'official Marxist culture', just as much as his opposition to 'official English culture', is what drives the writing and arguments of *The Country and the City*, though it is characteristic that the former is done so obliquely. Nonetheless, it is important to recognise this dimension of the study which takes the Marxist criticisms levelled at his own earlier work – the charges of analysing literary texts without due regard to conflict and context, of presenting them as the work of 'disembodied intelligences' – and turns them against the orthodox literary historical accounts of rural and metropolitan writing. In so doing, Williams replies implicitly to the criticisms he never responds to explicitly, in a sense insulating himself against these criticisms by projecting them out onto orthodox literary history. And at the same time, not content with this purely defensive measure, he goes on the attack by criticising Marxist tradition itself by placing it within the framework of literary history, the history of representations of the country and the city that the book criticises. Just as he had done earlier by placing Marx's thinking, or the English appropriation of it, within Romanticism, he places Marxism firmly within Literature, and so asserts the force of his own thinking and analysis against his leftist critics.[30]

With these three related works – *Modern Tragedy, The English Novel from Dickens to Lawrence*, and especially with *The Country and the City* – Williams found himself writing a literary criticism which was both professional and personal, academic and political, scholarly and yet committed. E.P. Thompson's warning that *The Country and the City* was 'not a conventional work of scholarship, and whoever reads it this way will end up in disagreement and irritation' was correct, though Thompson's insight can be extended. The book was deliberately not a conventional work of scholarship in two senses. First, it set out to criticise the practice and assumptions of conventional criticism, and did so in a powerful and revealing way which helped to open the way, particularly for an invigorated and more politically and historically aware mode of literary studies in general, and perhaps of eighteenth-century studies in particular.[31] Second, as its detractors noted, it was only in part a conventional work of scholarship: its autobiographical stance challenged the position of neutral observer associated with academic criticism, and, in this sense, Williams's work anticipates – though in a much more historically nuanced mode – some of the contemporary forms of reader response theory.[32] Thus while some readers did end up in 'disagreement and irritation', many more found a strong appeal in what he had described as the intellectual resolution of a conflict between personal experience and academic orthodoxy (1967a: 632). Finally, here was a criticism which was textual and political at one and the same time, fully able to place and argue a political question in the frame of literary history:

> There is only one real question. Where do we stand, with whom do we identify, as we read the complaints of disturbance, as this order in its turn is broken up? Is it with the serfs, the bordars and cotters, the villeins; or with the abstracted order to which, through successive generations, many hundreds of thousands of men were never more than instrumental? And supposing we could make that choice rightly – though the historian who really places himself with the majority of men, and tries to see the world as they were experiencing it, is always improbable – where do we identify, as the order develops into new kinds of order?
>
> (Williams 1973a: 52–3)

Conclusion

Called upon to sum up the theoretical impetus of *The Country and the City*, Williams stressed the idea of representation – a term which does not appear as a term of art in the book itself. 'The emphasis of the book is certainly not on literary texts as records, but as representations of history – including what I am still realist enough to call mis-representations' (Williams 1979: 304). Representation: perhaps the key term in much theoretical and political writing of the 1970s, and yet a term never theorised as such by Williams, despite being the conceptual centre of his arguments against the formalisms of Cambridge English.[33] In this chapter, we have seen how some of the depth and complexity of the new idea is developed through the arguments against the reductive senses of tragedy, against trivialising ideas of form in the novel, and against shallow discussions of the long opposition between town and country. At the centre of this is the theory of the embodied observer, his argument against the literary formalism of Cambridge English, and his response to his Marxist critics. As Stuart Hall later noted, with characteristic insight, *The Country and the City* represented 'a different kind of critical practice' for Williams, perhaps 'the most challenging of Williams's efforts...to put to use his own specialized notions of what is involved in seeing literary form historically' (Hall 1980: 64).

'Seeing literary form historically' meant seeing the subject – that key term of 1970s theory – as embodied in, but not absolutely determined by, the signifying systems through which experience was made into active consciousness. Such was to be the theoretical argument around what Williams specified as the constitutive force of language, which was to be at the centre of his next major work, *Marxism and Literature* – a work in which, as he put it, 'while [it] is almost wholly theoretical, every position in it was developed from the detailed practical work I have previously undertaken' (Williams 1977a: 6). What it is important to stress in retrospect is that this 'practical work' – the development of his anti-formalist case – was never couched simply in the dualistic terms attributed to him by some of his more recent critics.

In the course of the *New Left Review* interviews, for instance, he is questioned about the role and status of 'experience' in his work, and its absence from the first editions of *Keywords* is taken as a significant one, indicating his containment within the Leavisite theoretical paradigm. Does not the term, and his own use of it, 'presuppose a kind of pristine contact between the subject and the reality in which the subject is immersed'? (Williams 1979: 167). Williams denies this, and notes that in current debates, largely conducted in the accents of Althusser, experience has become 'a forbidden word, whereas what we ought to say about it is that it is a limited word, for there are many kinds of knowledge it will never give us, in any of its ordinary senses' (1979: 172). While showing willing to take his interviewer's point that certain kinds of historical process are not immediately experienced and can be described only from a conceptual or scientific discourse, he goes on to emphasise his rejection of the too scientistic a position this may entail. 'Just as I am moving in that direction' he notes:

> I see a kind of appalling parody...beyond me – the claim that all experience is ideology, that the subject is wholly an ideological illusion, which is the last stage of formalism – and I even start to pull back a bit.
>
> (1979: 172)

In fact, as Williams points out, from as far back as *The Long Revolution* he had emphasised the fact that 'there is no natural seeing and therefore cannot be a direct and unmediated contact with reality' (1979: 167).[34] But it looked like something of the same battle would have to be refought and rethought, this time, not on the grounds of literary studies alone, but on the terrain of the new 'critical structuralism'. This emergent discourse – usually associated in Britain with the strengths and weaknesses of Althusserianism – and Williams's understanding of it as a characteristic 'last stage of formalism' would be the focus of his next major work, *Marxism and Literature*.

5 Marxisms: contra Caudwell, against Althusser

Most readers of Williams's work have been struck by its ambivalent relation to Marxism.[1] Certainly, *The Country and the City* (1973) and *Marxism and Literature* (1977) are usually regarded as key works in the Western Marxist tradition of cultural and aesthetic theory.[2] With Georg Lukács and Lucien Goldmann, Williams shared a commitment to teasing out the relations between history and form; alongside Sartre and Gramsci, he explored the ideas of commitment and hegemony; like Benjamin, Brecht and the Frankfurt school, he sought to understand the dynamics of contemporary cultural expression. Throughout his career, he argued for a better understanding of the constitutive force of culture in social reproduction than orthodox Marxist theory appeared to allow, or, to frame his achievement differently (and this is the turning point for Marxist assessments of Williams), he overestimated the force of culture in social reproduction in ways which exemplify the left-idealist tendencies of Western Marxism. Thus, while it is customary to place or claim Williams as a major thinker in the Marxist tradition, it is just as usual to mark out his differences and deviations from it. The person who appears as the 'Communist Professor of Communications' of one description did 'not even seem to be aware of what Marxism is' in another.[3] As McIlroy and Westwood wryly put it, 'Williams remained an original and unconventional swimmer in the contradictory currents of Marxism' (1993: 267).

Unconventional, and certainly disdainful of any orthodoxy but his own, Williams's preferred stance was always an independent one, his preferred mode of thinking, oppositional, as we have seen at length in his relation to the formation he referred to as 'Cambridge English'. With Marxism, the stance remains the same: independent and oppositional. We shall see how this leads, in relation to Marxism, to a particular form of interpretive appropriation, where as Williams seeks to preserve the appearance of an almost absolute intellectual autonomy, he none the less refreshes and revitalises his thinking by a selective – and not always fully acknowledged – appropriation. As he distances himself from any appearance of influence, he incorporates or subsumes the ideas and insights he finds most useful to his own project. It is this mode of distancing and appropriation which makes his relationship to Marxism such a complex and disputed area of his work.

Throughout his career, Williams rejected any taxonomy of the orthodox, appeared to show little interest in the question of how Marxists might classify his work, and consistently argued against the intellectually impoverishing tendency to reduce the force and integrity of actual arguments to a fixed currency of apparently stable and known-in-advance positions: 'Are you a marxist, a revisionist, a bourgeois reformist? Are you a Communist, a left radical, a fellow-traveller? What answer can a man make to that kind of robot questioning?' (Williams 1961b: 129). In 1961, his response was simple and direct: 'Go away'. Similarly, in 1971, with regard to criticisms levelled at Lukács and Goldmann as to whether their work constituted forms of left-Hegelian or left-idealist deviancy, he remarked 'If you're not in a church, you're not worried about heresies' (Williams 1971d: 20).

While the main point – dogmatic objection reduces actual arguments to already-known and rejected positions – can be accepted, we need to beware of a self-defensive strategy which would seek, consciously or unconsciously, to represent even reasoned objections as dogmatic, precisely as a means of avoiding them. For all the force and mass of Williams's immense *oeuvre*, for all the apparent confidence of its usually Olympian and reasoned tone, there are moments when it is difficult to decide whether it is a justified or measured show of indifference, an arrogance or a self-protective evasiveness, which is at the root of his notorious reluctance to name directly the opponents he is either engaging or to whom he is responding. The unprepared reader is often left in the dark as to the identity of these opponents and the sources of the positions which Williams confronts, actively and yet somehow evasively. For that reason, I shall try and indicate my own sense of Williams's opponents and antagonists in his dealings with Marxism, and show some of the complexity of his relations to figures such as Caudwell and Althusser. I concentrate on the accounts offered in *Culture and Society* and *Marxism and Literature*.

Marxism and culture

Chapters 1 and 2 showed how his rejection of the available forms of Marxist literary criticism presented a major intellectual crisis for the young Williams, yet at the same time provided a significant starting point for his work as a whole. Chapter 3 argued that *Culture and Society*, published in 1958, was in part his response to that crisis, and seemed to him – along with *The Long Revolution*, which followed in 1961 – to provide a sense of what forms of politically progressive work might be done from within literary studies. 'Marxism and Culture' – Chapter 5 in Part III of *Culture and Society* – represents his first systematic attempt to articulate both the limits and the possibilities of Marxist theory. Williams's developing sense of culture was the pivotal point from which this articulation was made.

One thing was clear to Williams from the start: Marx was never the practitioner of 'what we would now know as Marxist literary criticism' (Williams 1958a: 265). At the same time, he stresses how Marx had 'outlined, but never fully developed a cultural theory' (1958a: 265). Citing Marx's seminal discussion of what became known as base and superstructure theory in his *Critique of Political Economy* (1859), and his later, equally famous discussion in *The Eighteenth Brumaire*, Williams deploys the basic skills of textual analysis. While Marx refers to 'the economic structure' as the 'real foundation, on which rise legal and political superstructures and to which correspond definite forms of social consciousness' (cited in Williams 1958a: 266) in the *Critique*, and writes of how 'a whole superstructure is reared of various and peculiarly shaped feelings, illusions, habits of thought, and conceptions of life' from the 'several forms of property [and] the social conditions of existence' (cited in 1958a: 266), he notes that the formula of structure and superstructure may best be understood as provocative analogy, rather than the fully worked-out concept it often appears to be to orthodox Marxists. Against these, he turns to Friedrich Engels's later clarification of the matter in a letter to Joseph Bloch in 1890. Engels stresses that though 'the determining element in history is ultimately the production and reproduction in real life', the various elements of the super-structure 'also exercise their influence upon the course of the historical struggles' (cited in 1958a: 267). Here, suggests Williams, there is a 'lessening of the usefulness of the formula which Marx used': 'Structure and superstructure, as terms of an analogy, express at once an absolute and a fixed relationship. But the reality which Marx and Engels recognize is both less absolute and less clear' (cited in 1958a: 267–8).

Once this conclusion – the need for a 'less absolute' version of base and superstructure argument – is accepted, then it can be no easy matter to discover what can be taken, in cultural criticism, 'as finally and authentically Marxist' (1958a: 284). Nothing better illustrated this difficulty than the debate in Marxist circles over the work of Christopher Caudwell in the early 1950s. We shall see that Williams's ambivalent relations to Caudwell perfectly mirrored his complex relations to Marxist cultural theory as a whole.

Contra Caudwell

Most commentators on Williams's work have been struck only by his hostile reaction to Caudwell's work. Caudwell at first appears as the exemplar of the worst failings of English Marxist criticism, in a notorious discussion which represents one of the few moments when the balanced and even-handed tone of *Culture and Society* breaks down. Caudwell 'has little to say, of actual literature, that is even interesting' (Williams 1958a: 277); his work is 'not even specific enough to be wrong' (1958a: 277).[4] In fact, this attitude was complicated by elements of a far more positive appreciation, and, though this came through most strongly in *The Long Revolution*, it was already present in the earlier work.

Williams's focus on 'actual literature' is inherited from the *Scrutiny* reservations about Marxist literary criticism in general, and perhaps those regarding Caudwell in particular. As Mulhern puts it, quoting Leavis, 'Marxist criticism...became a byword in *Scrutiny* for its "shamelessly uncritical use of vague abstractions and verbal counters" ' (Mulhern 1979: 159).[5] H.A. Mason's caustic review of *Illusion and Reality* in 1938 was typical of the *Scrutiny* stance. Mason found a 'surprising staleness and tameness in their [the Marxist] approach to literature' (Mason 1938: 429). Books like Caudwell's were 'essentially amateur works and consequently the proportion of unrelated generalisation is high...the book [*Illusion and Reality*] does not get anywhere' (1938: 429, 433).

Williams's critical rejection of Marxist literary criticism is generated from within this circle of professional literary critical judgement:

> What many of *us* have felt about Marxist cultural interpretation is that it seems committed, by Marx's formula, to a rigid methodology, so that if one wishes to study, say, a national literature, one must begin with the economic history with which the literature co-exists, and then put the literature to it, to be interpreted in its light.
>
> (Williams 1958a: 281; my emphasis)

And though he refers more widely to Alick West's *Crisis and Criticism* (1937), Ralph Fox's *The Novel and the People* (1937), and the collection of essays edited by the poet Cecil Day-Lewis, *The Mind in Chains* (1937), it is Caudwell's work which is singled out for particular discussion.[6] *Illusion and Reality* (1937), *Studies in a Dying Culture* (1938) and *Further Studies in a Dying Culture* (1949) are all marked for Williams by the inevitable reductionism of too rigid and mechanical an application of Marx's base and superstructure formula.[7]

Caudwell's *Illusion and Reality* has chapters on 'The Development of Modern Poetry' and 'The Future of Poetry'. These sketch the phases of the history of English poetry from the period of 'primitive accumulation', through the industrial revolution, to the present 'decline of capitalism'. The chapter 'English Poets' closes with a table which, in Williams's phrase, 'puts' the literature to the economic history, 'to be interpreted in its light' (Williams 1958a: 281), and it charts the main phases of Britain's economy alongside first the 'General Characteristics', and then the 'Technical Characteristics' of poetry. When the economy in Britain was at the stage of primitive accumulation, the 'dynamic force of individuality...is expressed in poetry' generally, and this comes through as technique in the prevalence of an 'iambic rhythm' which expresses 'the heroic nature of the bourgeois illusion' and so 'is allowed to flower luxuriantly and naturally; it indicates the free and boundless development of the personal will' (Caudwell 1937: 117).[8]

For Williams, undoubtedly remembering the objections posed to such assertions by Tillyard in their undergraduate tutorials together, this kind of sketch is little more than fantasy. While Caudwell asserts that the history of drama in Britain was driven by the emergence of individuation as the effect of an increasing division of labour, he is unable to produce the detailed readings necessary to support this assertion. He asserts but cannot demonstrate that Elizabethan tragedy emerges as the result of the alliance of the monarchy with the bourgeois class: 'the mystery moves to court and becomes the Elizabethan tragedy' (1937: 257). This mechanical and impressionistic account of the drama is matched by the principles and practice of his textual analysis. What is striking is not so much the sheer clumsiness of Caudwell's paraphrase of Shakespeare's line – 'Sleep, that knots up the ravelled sleeve of care' becomes 'Slumber, that unties worry, which is like a piece of tangled knitting' – but rather the explanation that goes with it. For Caudwell, in a reductive adaption of Freud's distinction between manifest and latent content in *The Interpretation of Dreams*, this paraphrase

> carries over most of the manifest content, but the affective tones which lurked in the associations of the words used have vanished. It is like a conjuring trick. The poet holds up a piece of the world and we see it glowing with a strange emotional fire. If we analyse it 'rationally', we find no fire. Yet none the less, for ever afterwards, that piece of reality still keeps an afterglow about it, is still fragrant with emotional life. So poetry enriches external reality for us.
>
> (1937: 214)

This impressionistic enthusiasm recalls the examples of bad critical writing which I.A. Richards demolished with glee in his *Practical Criticism* (1929). For the literary critic trained in the practical criticism of a Richards, an Empsom or a Leavis, the semiotic charge of poetry certainly did not resemble a 'conjuring trick', and the whole premise of the new practical criticism was that poetry could be analysed 'rationally'. Caudwell's impressionistic style of description – 'glowing with a strange emotional fire', 'fragrant with emotional life', 'afterglow' – was anathema to the careful semantic analysis of practical criticism. As Richards famously put it: 'The corrective [to such impressionistic criticism] is equally obvious – exercise in analysis and cultivation of the habit of regarding poetry as capable of explanation' (Richards 1929: 216). Caudwell's literary analysis, like that of the other English Marxists, was unprofessional, unable to fit into the rules and structures of analysis and evidence provided by the paradigm of Cambridge English studies.

Any dogmatic application of the structure and superstructural model, he argues, 'leads very quickly to abstraction and unreality' (Williams 1958a: 281). He derides Caudwell's description of poetry since the fifteen century as modern poetry, and modern poetry as capitalist poetry, 'the superstructure of the bourgeois revolution in production' in Caudwell's phrase (Caudwell 1937: 55). 'To describe English life, thought and imagination in the past three hundred years simply as "bourgeois", to describe English culture now as "dying", is', he writes damningly, 'to surrender reality to a formula' (1958a: 281–2). Such unreal and badly grounded ideas come through even more damagingly in the related Marxist tendencies of prediction and prescription. Confident in the ultimate triumph of the proletariat, it is an easy step for Caudwell and others (though Williams refers only to Alick West, Ralph Fox and Rex Warner, he is undoubtedly recollecting the Zhdanov of the Zoschenko Affair) to predict and then prescribe the nature of 'socialist realism'. This 'authoritative prescription' is just 'the kind of literary criticism which has made Marxism notorious' he notes (1958a: 276); notorious, that is, from the professional perspectives of literary criticism.

A great deal of the acerbity of the tone in dealing with Caudwell comes, no doubt, from the projection on to him of Williams's own humiliation when trying to argue the Marxist line with Tillyard, and failing to convince. 'I was continually found out in ignorance, found out in confusion', recalled Williams (1979: 51). This humiliation is projected outwards, and turned onto Caudwell himself:

> It is not only that it is difficult to have confidence in the literary qualifications of anyone who can give his account of the development of medieval into Elizabethan drama, or who can make his paraphrase of the 'sleep' line from *Macbeth*, but for the most part his discussion is not even specific enough to be wrong.
>
> (Williams 1958a: 277)

Caudwell's clumsy abstractions could not meet the discipline's demands for textual evidence.

Yet it would be a mistake to assume that this stance of critical rejection, the result of Williams's internalisation of the new professional techniques of Cambridge English, provided the only frame for his discussion and assessment of Caudwell, and of the potential interest of Marxist cultural theory. Crucial to Williams in this regard were some of the hotly contested debates around Caudwell's work conducted in the *Modern Quarterly* in 1951 and 1952. For in this debate, Caudwell figures as just the opposite of what we have seen above: not the exponent of a rigid mechanical Marxism, but the purveyor of what E.P. Thompson refers to as a ' "heretical" rejection of reflection-theory' (Thompson 1977: 265).[9]

Pro Caudwell

For Maurice Cornforth, editor of the *Modern Quarterly*, Caudwell's work appeared to challenge the most fundamental tenet of Marxism: the primacy of the material world.[10] Quoting Stalin, he writes that:

> 'the multifold phenomena of the world constitute different forms of matter in motion,' and 'that matter is primary, since it is the source of sensations, ideas, mind, and that mind is secondary, derivative, since it is a reflection of matter, a reflection of being'.
>
> (cited in Thompson 1977: 240)

Caudwell's idea of an 'inner energy', which Williams connects to the Romantic heritage, is, for Cornforth, no more than a form of bourgeois idealism. And it is precisely at this point that Williams finds the strongest connection between his own work and Caudwell's. Caudwell finds that art is valuable because the artist has the power to articulate 'new feelings as yet unformulated', to constitute new adaptions to reality. Artists are explorers, lonely individuals, ahead of their time: 'they are engaged in dragging into the social world realms at present non-social' (cited in Williams 1958a: 278). For orthodox Marxists such as Cornforth, this is an idealist emphasis; it challenges the passive mode of reflective consciousness inherent in the structure and superstructure model. For Williams, this was a good thing. 'In writing of this kind', he writes approvingly, 'it would seem that Marx's basic conception of the relation between "the real foundation" and "consciousness", and hence between structure and super-structure, is being revalued' (1958a: 279). In fact, he argues, this revaluation (a positive key term in the Cambridge English vocabulary) is a valuable aspect of much writing in the English Marxist tradition, both of the 1930s and the 1950s. Williams cites E.P. Thompson's comment on William Morris – 'Morris has not emphasized sufficiently the ideological role of art, its active agency in changing human beings and society as a whole, its agency in man's class-divided history' – to hammer the point home, and notes with some satisfaction that 'it is surely surprising to find a Marxist criticising Morris for seeing 'man's economic and social development always as the master-process', since 'It has normally been assumed that this was precisely what Marx taught, and the position Marxists wished to defend. One had understood that the arts were "dependent upon social change" ' (1958a: 273).

What Williams finds in at least some of the English Marxists, and most explicitly in Caudwell, is a significant debt to Romanticism in their conception of the value of art as an active force in social change. At their best, the English Marxists owe more to the 'culture and society' tradition that is the topic of Williams's own study than to Marx – or at least to Marxism. 'In fact' he writes confidently:

> as we look at the English attempt at a Marxist theory of culture, what we see is an interaction between Romanticism and Marx, between the idea of culture which is the major English tradition and Marx's brilliant revaluation of it. We have to conclude that the interaction is as yet far from complete.
>
> (1958a: 279–80)

This is the substance of Williams' challenge to Marxism. Though the interaction is 'far from complete', Williams has no doubt that his own arguments in *Culture and Society* do mark a serious advance on the general question. When he writes that it 'seems relevant to ask English Marxists who have interested themselves in the arts whether this is not Romanticism absorbing Marx, rather than Marx absorbing Romanticism' (1958a: 274), this suggests nothing less than a fundamental recasting or reframing of the orthodox conceptions of the central object of Marx's works. Most orthodox Marxists would probably identify philosophy, history, politics and economics – but not culture – as the main constituents of Marx's writing, and argue from that point regarding the relative weights of these topics in the causal hierarchy of his thought. Indeed, the history of 'orthodox marxism' lies in precisely these debates, in which Williams's own interpretation of Marx and Marxism participates.[11]

Of course, Williams's recasting is in part supported by the significant emphasis which Marx came to place on political economy. His greatest work, *Capital* (1869), is, after all, subtitled a 'Critique of Political Economy', and political economy is largely regarded as the British contribution to the three dimensions of Marx's project and formation, alongside the German philosophical idealism of Hegel and Feuerbach, and the French socialism of Proudhon. Certainly the response to the great Scottish and English political economists from Adam Smith through to Ricardo and Mill is a concern of many of the figures in Williams's culture and society canon. In this rather limited sense, as a common point or area of reference, some idea of culture as a component of the critique of political economy can indeed be said to be important to both, but this is hardly the substance of Williams's claim.

The claim is far stronger: it is that the 'object' of Marx's thinking, the most appropriate name for the conceptual centre of his life and writings, was the idea of culture, as Williams understood it, and as Williams had represented in *Culture and Society*. Marx's work is subsumed in the *Culture and Society* tradition; Marx's concept of culture is superseded by Williams's own. His interest in the debate around Caudwell is that it exemplifies the limitations of the whole Marxist explanatory paradigm, and what he calls the 'general inadequacy among Marxists, in the use of "culture" as a term' (1958a: 282). 'It normally indicates', he argues, 'the intellectual and imaginative products of society', a useage which corresponds to the 'weak use of superstructure' (1958a: 282). Against this, he insists that 'Marxists should logically use "culture" in the sense of a whole way of life, a general social process' as it is used in *Culture and Society*.

And yet, as Williams came to see, particularly in the writing of *The Long Revolution*, that work had at least one redeeming feature: the emphasis – entirely sympathetic to Williams's developing conception of creativity – on the agency of the creative artist. That this was precisely the emphasis which threatened Caudwell's status as a Marxist was more likely to attract Williams than not, and it is this emphasis which has been insufficiently appreciated. Certainly, for the professional literary critic in Williams, Caudwell was worthless; but for the budding cultural theorist, certain aspects of his work were well worth absorbing.

Critics who have been alerted to the existence of a more positive intellectual relationship between the two have been puzzled not to find it where they expected. R. Sullivan, in his study *Christopher Caudwell*, finds it 'especially disappointing' that the only attention Caudwell receives in *Marxism and Literature* is 'mention in a prefatory note', when his arguments, and particularly those concerning 'the part played by language in the formation of consciousness', considerably anticipate Williams's own, especially so in his use of Vološinov (Sullivan 1988: 122).[12] But Sullivan is looking in the wrong place. It was rather with *The Long Revolution* in 1961, some sixteen years before *Marxism and Literature* and only three years after the caustic comments in *Culture and Society*, that Caudwell's work began to appear to Williams in a much more positive light.[13]

Caudwell's redeeming features came through more strongly as Williams prepared the essays which made up *The Long Revolution*, and found he could 'read with him', rather than, as in *Culture and Society*, 'against him' (Williams 1979: 128). He found ready-made in Caudwell a powerful formulation of the dangers of Freudianism; and, more positively, his emphasis on the creative aspects of human subjectivity were taken up in the important chapter 'The Creative Mind' in *The Long Revolution*.[14]

For despite the orthodox denunciations of a Cornforth, the stress on the culturally constituted nature of human perception which can be found in Caudwell (it is 'impossible for us to assume that there is any reality experienced by man into which man's own observations and interpretations do not enter') is no mere idealism, insists Williams. The 'facts of perception', as figured in Caudwell's work:

> in no way lead us to a late form of idealism; they do not require us to suppose that there is no kind of reality outside the human mind; they point rather to the insistence that all human experience is an interpretation of the non-human reality. But this, again, is not the duality of subject and object – the assumption on which almost all theories of art are based. We have to think, rather, of human experience as both objective and subjective, in one inseparable process.
>
> (Williams 1961a: 36)

One inseparable process; both objective and subjective; not the duality of subject and object. With these phrases, and in this flow of argument, Williams sought to articulate a challenge to the 'naturalist' outlook of much orthodox argument, a perspective from which all disciplines, including those in the human sciences, wrongly seek to emulate the methods and methodologies of the natural sciences, often with crippling conceptual consequences.[15]

Caudwell's essay 'Consciousness: A Study in Bourgeois Psychology' proved especially useful, and, in 1961, helped to anticipate some of the central arguments of what was to become, post-1968, the 'crisis of the subject'. Bourgeois psychology is wrong to separate consciousness from the world; consciousness changes 'as the world changes, not with it or separately from it but in mutually determining interaction with it' (Caudwell 1949: 208–9, cited in Williams 1961a: 37). He then reiterates this in his own terms:

We cannot refer science to the object and art to the subject, for the view of human activity we are seeking to grasp rejects this duality of subject and object: the consciousness is part of the reality, and the reality is part of the consciousness, in the whole process of our living organization.

(cited in Williams 1961a: 39)

That this central statement of Williams's epistemology owes so much to Caudwell reveals something of his importance to the formation of Williams's ideas on culture and communication.

Caudwell's work was Janus-faced for Williams. While one face gloomily confirmed the weakness and self-deception of Marxist literary criticism, the other offered some promise and allure. It presented the consistent interest and appeal which Marxist cultural theory could hold – when it was not too dogmatically Marxist. This double judgement on Caudwell perfectly reflects his judgement on Marxist cultural theory as a whole, and particularly what he sees as its confusions and self-contradictions around the explanatory status of the base and superstructure model. 'In one way or another' he sighs, 'the situation will have to be clarified':

Either the arts are passively dependent on social reality, a proposition which I take to be that of mechanical materialism, or a vulgar interpretation of Marx. Or the arts, as the creators of consciousness, determine social reality, the proposition which the Romantic poets sometimes advanced. Or finally, the arts, while ultimately dependent, with everything else, on the real economic structure, operate in part to reflect this structure and its conse- quent reality, to help *or hinder* the constant business of changing it. I find Marxist theories of culture confused because they seem to me, on different occasions and in different writers, to make use of all these propositions as the need serves.

(Williams 1958a: 274)

The third option, with its emphasis on the ways in which forms of art and artistic representation could 'help or hinder' the political process of changing reality, was and remained the closest to Williams's own position.

In this first settling of accounts, Williams is able to internalise the criticisms he had himself suffered as an undergraduate in an often searing account of the limitations of English Marxism, and especially regarding its deployment of base and superstructure criticism by writers such as Caudwell. And yet, at the same time, he is able to extract with considerable profit some aspects of Caudwell's thought in order to support his own developing sense and theory of the importance of culture in any account and analysis of social, cultural and political reproduction. Indeed, it was the very tension between rejection and incorpora- tion which produced perhaps the greatest statement – in *Culture and Society* and *The Long Revolution* – of the New Left case for a participatory democracy, and at the same time provided something of an authorising and differential backing for that case in the culture and society tradition itself. How this ambivalent stance – fending off, drawing in – continued to characterise his relation to Marxism, and how the theory of cultural materialism grew out of this is the subject of the rest of this chapter.

The alternative tradition

With the benefit of hindsight, it is easy to see that perhaps the most striking feature of Williams's account of Marxist cultural theory in the late 1950s was its extremely limited range of textual and conceptual reference.[16] For the Williams of *Culture and Society*, Marxist cultural theory is the English Marxism he knew as a Cambridge undergraduate: no Korsch, no Lukács, neither Brecht nor Benjamin, not a trace of Sartre. It was to be over a decade before he began to read more deeply into the wider history of European Marxism, as we can see from the paucity of references to, or discussions of, Marxism in his work until the early 1970s.[17]

As one of the key figures in the New Left revision of Marxist theory, Williams must have felt that with the publication of *Culture and Society*, and particularly its chapter 'Marxism and Culture', and the related essays of *The Long Revolution*, that he had settled his accounts with regard to Marxism. What need was there to say more? Marx, as he put in one essay, had correctly stressed the connection between culture and the economy, but had badly mistaken the nature of that connection. Culture and communication were to be understood as primary and not secondary components of the social totality, constitutive and not reflective in the maintenance and development of a social order. Thus, in 1961, the main constituents of the emerging theory of cultural materialism were stressed as Williams wrote that 'we cannot really think of communication as secondary':

> We cannot think of it as marginal; or as something that happens after reality has occurred. Because it is through the communication systems that the reality of ourselves, the reality of our society, forms and is interpreted.
>
> (Williams 1961c: 22–3)

In 1965, Williams sees the New Left as part of a 'general attack on dogmatism within the Marxist tradition' (Williams 1965: 140). The *May Day Manifesto* of 1968, for all its commitment to the renewal of socialist politics and policies in Britain, and though it had plenty of time for the understanding of totality, found no place to discuss or promote any particular variety of Marxism other than New Left humanism. Even up to the time of the Slant Symposium of 1967 – that strange amalgam of Catholics and socialists, gathered together by Terry Eagleton and Brian Wickers – Williams still found no need to revise his central take on Marxism. In his reply to criticisms of his work raised at the conference and elsewhere, he concludes: 'we reject the idea that literature and thought are secondary, superstructural activities occurring after the creation of social reality' (Williams 1968c: 305). As late as 1967, 'orthodox contemporary marxism' seems to have had nothing to offer.

But by the 1970s all this is changing, and Williams begins to criticise those who, like his earlier self, had, too complacently, given up reading Marxist work. So that when he refers to the 'extraordinary renewal of serious study of Marx' in 'the last ten years' (Williams 1972b: 71), or to Marxism as 'a system of political thought which until 1960 and beyond was very generally regarded as un-English, irrelevant and irremediably out-of-date' (Williams 1976b: 233), he is, in part at least, referring to himself.

It seems that Lucien Goldmann's visit to Cambridge in 1970, only months before his death, had helped to revive Williams's interest in Marxist theory.[18] In a memorial tribute broadcast on Radio Three, he noted:

> In the student generation of the last ten years there has been an active rediscovery of Marxism, but this has been little understood by their elders...in part at least because most of their interested elders already know, or think they know, what Marxism is, from memories of the thirties.
>
> (Williams 1972a: 375)

In fact, the key to Williams's own rediscovery of Marxism is the finding of what he calls its 'alternative tradition', and particularly 'its account of consciousness: a social analysis which seems to me radically different from what most people in Britain understand as Marxist' (1972a: 375), and certainly what he had understood as Marxist in *Culture and Society*. In the work of Goldmann, and behind him, in the powerful figure of Georg Lukács, he finds – characteristically – 'not a matter of influence', but rather a series of affinities between his own work and theirs: Goldmann's idea of the 'transindividual subject' does something like the conceptual work he was trying to achieve with his own idea of the 'structure of feeling', while Lukács's distinction between 'actual' and 'possible' consciousness, fits with his own sense of consciousness as a 'primary activity'. This, he writes approvingly, 'is the central result of this alternative Marxist tradition. But this consciousness is still social, and it is centred in history' (1972a: 376). A primary activity, but still centred in history, and still social: Marxism's 'alternative tradition' seemed to offer, for Williams, something of a parallel confirmation, in a different theoretical vocabulary, of the arguments and insights he had been asserting since the 1950s (though it is striking that the features which interested him were precisely those which more orthodox Marxists were wary of).[19] It seemed to at least call for a reassessment of what Marxism now meant, and just what it had to offer to Williams's own project of cultural and political criticism.

The first step in this reassessment came with the writing up of the memorial lecture on Goldmann that Williams had given in Cambridge in April 1971. 'Literature and Sociology' (reversing the title and emphasis of Leavis's seminal essay, 'Sociology and Literature' (Leavis 1952: 195–203)) asserts that the debate with Marxism, which *Scrutiny* seemed to have won conclusively in the

1930s, is in reality far from over. The work of thinkers such as Goldmann and Lukács can no longer be confined to an 'abandoned battlefield' (Williams 1980a: 19).[20] This was followed, two years later, by the lecture 'Base and Superstructure in Marxist Cultural Theory', an essay regarded by many as Williams's single most important theoretical statement.[21]

Base and superstructure

The essay belongs to 'an active and self-renewing Marxist tradition' (Williams 1973b: 49), one which seeks to both clarify and complicate the apparent certainties of the Marxist base and superstructure model. It is framed as the recovery of an emphasis somehow lost 'in the transition from Marx to Marxism' (1973b: 31). The first and most important of these is the sense of the verb 'to determine'.

In the classic Marxist model, the economic base determines the ideological superstructure. This determination is absolute, the superstructure is understood as – ideally, at least – the wholly predictable event of a known cause, the economic base. Ironically, this sense of 'to determine' has its roots in idealist and theological modes of reasoning which Marx's own use of the term is deliberately meant to counter. Marx places the origin of determination in human activity and in social practice where determination is better understood as the setting of limits to, and the exertion of pressures on, human agency. As a counter to the absolute sense usually at work in the base and superstructure model, Williams emphasises an 'equally central, equally authentic' proposition of Marx's: the idea that 'social being determines consciousness' (1973a: 31).

In fact, most discussions of the idea of the economically determined area of the superstructure do admit some qualification, moving from Engels's notion of time-lags and delays, through to Walter Benjamin's 'mediations' and Lucien Goldmann's 'homologous structures'. More important, Williams calls for a thorough reassessment of 'the received notion of the "base" (Basis, Grundlage)' (1973a: 33). In much Marxist theory, the figure of 'the base', by sleight of phrase, has come to be considered as an object in its own right, as the mode of production in a particular stage of its development. But this loses the quiddity of Marx's own emphasis on the volatile, active and contradictory nature of productive activity itself. To get the real sense of determination at work here, we have to realise that 'when we talk of "the base", we are talking of a process and not a state' (1973a: 34), of the setting of limits and the exertion of pressures rather than 'a predicted, prefigured and controlled content' (1973a: 34). If we return to Marx's emphasis on the volatility of productive forces:

> we look at the whole question of the base differently, and we are less then tempted to dismiss as superstructural, and in that sense as merely secondary, certain vital productive forces, which are in the broad sense, from the beginning, basic.

> (Williams 1973b: 35)

In this idea of the base as process, culture is far from secondary and reflective; it has rather a constitutive force.[22] In this, as in other respects, Williams remains absolutely true to the main emphases of his earlier criticisms of the base and superstructure model in *Culture and Society*. All that is different is that he is now able to turn to other thinkers in Marxism's 'alternative tradition' for conceptual support. He sees Gramsci's notion of hegemony as of vital importance:

> For hegemony supposes the existence of something which is truly total, which is not merely secondary and superstructural, like the weak sense of ideology, but which is lived at such a depth, which saturates the society to such an extent, and which, as Gramsci put it, even constitutes the substance and limits of common sense for most people under its sway, that it corresponds to the reality of social experience very much more clearly than any notions derived from the formula of base and superstructure.
>
> (1973b: 37)

And yet, at the same time, for all its emphasis on saturation and determination, terms which might suggest a total and closed and static state of affairs, hegemony is always and essentially an active and ongoing process. Hegemony is determination at work, in process, and as such, it is a volatile, heterogeneous and mobile system, an economy of experience governed by the interplay of what are referred to as dominant, emergent and residual social forces and social meanings. As is stressed, in an often quoted moment:

> no mode of production, and therefore no dominant society or order of society, and therefore no dominant culture, in reality exhausts the full range of human practice, human energy, human intention...it is fact about the modes of domination that they select from and consequently exclude the full range of actual and possible human practice.
>
> (1973b: 43)

Understood in this way, hegemony expresses that sense of determination as the setting of limits which human agency may always challenge, with neither success or failure written in from the start. The new emphases of Gramsci, Goldmann and Lukács now allow the Marxist cultural theorist to face the challenge of historical analysis with 'a much greater precision and delicacy of analysis' (1973b: 38) than before. Marxist cultural theory need no longer be restricted, as it was in the days of a Christopher Caudwell, to merely epochal analysis, the grand but rather sketchy portraits of classic base and superstructure theory.

In many ways, this essay can serve as a summary of the main themes developed in *Marxism and Literature* as a whole, themes which – despite the insistence of some commentators – have not changed in any conceptually substantial way from the arguments put forward in *Culture and Society*.

Marxism and Literature

Any Marxism, like any Freudianism, is likely to be no more than a selective interpretation which claims to represent the unity of an author's thought through a careful process of selection and elision. What are the main elements of Williams's interpretation of Marx in *Marxism and Literature*?

The central focus of the account is given in the phrase 'the transition from Marx to Marxism': the tale to be told is one of 'bitter irony' (Williams 1977a: 86) as Williams recounts some of the ways in which the selective tradition of orthodox Marxism slowly lost sight of Marx's original and fundamental insights. Such a reading poses Williams's own interpretation as a restorative one, claiming the authority of a return to Marx, while at the same time enabling a rearticulation of Marx's thinking in his own terms. The promise is put forward as a return to the complex unity of Marx's original insight into the 'indissoluble unity' of the 'whole social process', including the creative force of 'practical consciousness'. Properly understood, Marxism represents the 'most important intellectual advance in all modern thought' (1977a: 19). Marxism:

> offered the possibility of overcoming the dichotomy between 'society' and 'nature', and of discovering new constitutive relationships between 'society' and 'economy'. As a specification of the basic element of the social process of culture it was a recovery of the wholeness of history.
>
> (1977a: 19)

It is no accident that Williams echoes here one of the most striking of Marx's formulations in the *1844 Manuscripts*, his assertion that 'Communism is the solution to the riddle of history, and knows itself to be the solution' (Marx 1844: 348): striking because this statement is usually taken as expressing an idealistic and insufficiently analytical moment in his thought. For Williams, the problem – perhaps as for Marx at this early stage of his thinking – the discovery of the 'wholeness of history' clouds the difficulties of any absolute 'recovery' of it. If the 'social process' is indeed 'indissoluble', then that poses major problems for any analysis of it, and particularly for any causal analysis of the movement of history. Williams's insistence on 'indissoluble social process' is recognized as a major conceptual problem by many of his Marxist critics.[23]

A key area of this 'constitutive' relationship between economy and society is to be found in one of the most enduring, and enduringly controversial, of Marx's concepts: the concept of ideology.

Ideology

The Marxist theory of ideology has a long and internally diverse history.[24] Marx's theory is recognised as marking a significant advance on Enlightenment discussions which saw the ideological in positivist terms of faulty but adjustable

cognition. For Marx, the ideological was better understood by locating the grounds of such miscognition or misrecognition (as it became in Althusser's later
theoretical recasting) in the social positioning of the subject, and by insisting on
the existence of a causal connection between cognition and position, between
the epistemological and the political. Within the interpretation of Marx's own
work, there is considerable debate regarding the continuity of his own thought
on this question; and later recastings, appropriations and developments of his
work also offer a range of divergent emphases and articulations, ranging from
Lukács's bold emphasis on 'reification', through Gramsci's focus on hegemony,
to Althusser's idea of Ideological State Apparatuses. Indeed, such is the diversity
of argument and interpretation that it is misleading to speak of any single
concept of ideology, either in Marx's own work, or in the work of his interpret-
ers, and it would perhaps be better to speak of a family of related ideas,
comprising a number of distinct though connected branches.

Williams identifies three broad versions of the concept: ideology as the system
of beliefs characteristic of a particular class or group; as a system of illusory
beliefs – false ideas or false consciousness – which can be contrasted with true or
scientific knowledge; and as 'the general process of the production of meanings
and ideas' (1977a: 55). He offers a polemical history of these different uses of
the term in ways which highlight some of the problems he finds with its
contemporary Althu-sserian deployment.

Many of the current problems with the concept of ideology were present
from the start. Antoine Destutt de Tracy, one of the leading figures in the new
Institut de France, charged with the task of revitalising France's entire
education system on the new revolutionary principles of the 1790s, coined the
term in his *Eléments d'Idéologie* of 1801. Here it refers to the 'science of ideas'
which, traced back from Condillac through to Locke, he argued could be the
basis of a whole new approach to education, learning and scientific progress.
The 'natural history of ideas' meant that psychology could now be analysed in
the truly scientific terms of biology, totally replacing the old reliance on
religion as the source for moral, social and political theory.

This essentially Enlightenment project was immediately challenged by
conservative and religious opponents. Williams cites one such opponent – the
Vicomte de Bonald – in order to make a theoretical point. De Bonald, turning to
Rousseau rather   than to Locke for his language theory, drew attention to the
passive elements in de Tracy's theory, 'its preoccupation', as Williams puts it, 'with
"signs and their influence on thought" ' (1977a: 56). De Bonald's critique
prefigures the theoretical problems associated with Althusser's 'structuralist'
theory. 'The rejection of metaphysics', he writes:

> was a characteristic gain, confirmed by the development of precise and
> systematic empirical enquiry. At the same time the effective exclusion of any
> social dimension – both the practical exclusion of social relationships
> implied in the model of 'man' and 'the world', and the characteristic
> displacement of necessary social relationships to a formal system, whether

the 'laws of psychology' or language as a 'system of signs' – was a deep and apparently irrecoverable loss and distortion.

(1977a: 57)

De Bonald's criticisms put into philosophical form Napoleon's political rejection of the ideologues. Though an initial member of the Institut, and a supporter of its aims in the 1790s, Napoleon turned against them in the early 1800s. In 1802, Chautreaubriand signalled the changing political climate by dedicating the first edition of his *Le génie du christianisme* to Napoleon; in 1803 Napoleon abolished the most directly challenging section of the Institut, that dealing with moral and political studies. By 1812 he was ready to tell the State Council that:

> It is to the doctrine of the ideologues – to this diffuse metaphysics, which in a contrived manner seeks to find the primary causes and on this foundation would erect the legislation of peoples, instead of adapting the laws to a knowledge of the human heart and of the lessons of history – to which one must attribute all the misfortunes which have befallen our beautiful France.
>
> (cited in Williams 1977a: 57)

For Napoleon, ideology became a 'nickname...used to distinguish every species of theory' (1977a: 57) which did not rest on the solid grounds of self-interest.

Marx, who had also criticised the Institut members, though from a different perspective, took over these now pejorative connotations of the term in the very title of his and Engels's critique of the Young Hegelians, *The German Ideology* (1846). More importantly, in addition to this polemical and pejorative sense, ideology began to take on a new theoretical distinctness for Marxism in this important text. Williams compares passages from *The German Ideology* and from the first volume of *Capital* in order to illustrate and exemplify some of the tensions between this new theory and its polemical context.

The first is taken from Marx and Engels's *The German Ideology*, generally held to be the first work in which the essentials of historical materialism first make their appearance in the Marxist oeuvre in a concerted critique of left-Hegelians such as Ludwig Feuerbach, Max Stirner and Bruno Bauer. Marx – originally a member of the *Doktorklub* in Berlin where the Young Hegelians met and argued, a friend and correspondent of Bruno Bauer, and deeply impressed by the work of Ludwig Feuerbach – had learned much from them. His turn away from them marks a decisive moment in his own intellectual development. Williams quotes a passage from early in the mammoth study:

> We do not set out from what men say, imagine, conceive, nor from men as narrated, thought of, imagined, conceived, in order to arrive at men in the flesh. We set out from real, active men, and on the basis of their real life-processes we demonstrate the development of the ideological reflexes and echoes of this life-process. The phantoms formed in the human brain are

also, necessarily, sublimates of their material life-process, which is empiri-
cally verifiable and bound to material premisses [sic]. Morality, religion,
metaphysics, all the rest of ideology and their corresponding forms of
consciousness, thus no longer retain the semblance of independence.

(cited in Williams 1977a: 59)

He finds two different emphases at work in the passage, as through the book
as a whole. First, there is the important theoretical point that thinking always
take place in a specific material and ideological context; it can have no
'semblance of independence': this is judged 'entirely reasonable'. A great deal of
The German Ideology is devoted to showing the ways in which the idealist
arguments of the Young Hegelians – what they took to be the solutions to
Germany's social and political problems – were in fact no more than the very
symptoms of those problems. For all their idealist ferocity, the Young Hegelians
were never going to be in a position to lead a social revolution.[25]

At the same time, Williams is dismayed – just as he had been in *Culture and
Society* – by the implications of the recourse to a pseudo-scientific vocabulary in
the passage:

the language of 'reflexes', 'echoes', 'phantoms', and 'sublimates' is simplis-
tic, and has in repetition been disastrous. It belongs to the naive dualism of
'mechanical materialism', in which the idealist separation of 'ideas' and
'material reality' has been repeated, but with its priorities reversed. The
emphasis on consciousness as inseparable from conscious existence, and
then on conscious existence as inseparable from material social processes, is
in effect lost in the use of this deliberately degrading vocabulary.

(1977a: 59)

While this 'deliberately degrading' vocabulary answers a polemical need, this
same polemical emphasis comes to threaten the essential balance of the
argument as a whole. The vocabulary of an essentially passive human response –
used to highlight the failings of the left-Hegelians – is in contradiction with the
philosophy of revolutionary practice or praxis which is the centre of *The
German Ideology*, and which many argue is the main new element in Marx's
thinking in this period.[26]

Against this over-emphasis on human passivity, Williams poses a paragraph
from Chapter 7 of *Capital*, 'The Labour Process and the Valorization Process',
in which the distinctively creative character of human labour is figured through
a bold comparison:

What distinguishes the worst architect from the best of bees is this, that the
architect raises his structure in imagination before he erects it in reality. At
the end of every labour-process, we get a result that already existed in the
imagination of the labourer at its commencement.

(cited in Williams 1977a: 59)

Here consciousness is correctly seen 'as part of the human material social process' (1977a: 59); and, he emphasises:

> its products in 'ideas' are then as much a part of this process as material products themselves. This, centrally, was the thrust of Marx's whole argument, but the point was lost.... What they were centrally arguing was a new way of seeing the total relationships.... In a polemical response to the abstract history of ideas or of consciousness they made their main point but in one decisive area lost it again. This confusion is the source of the naive reduction, in much subsequent Marxist thinking, of consciousness, imagination, art, and ideas to 'reflexes', 'echoes', 'phantoms', and 'sublimates', and then of a profound confusion in the concept of 'ideology'.
>
> (1977a: 59–60)

Centrally, 'the point was lost', and it is the task of Williams's interpretation to recover it. This 'loss', this 'profound confusion' comes through in the restricted sense of ideology as false consciousness, and the implied model of human subjectivity as passive, static, receptive only: for many, the main weakness of Althusser's own theory.[27] In these terms, if ideology is 'false consciousness', then a properly scientific Marxism may be the only possible source of 'true consciousness'. But this is to mistake the relevant idea of science.

For Marxism, argues Williams, science is best understood as closer to the original German sense of any systematic knowledge or organized learning: Marx's work is best understood as 'critical and historical' (1977a: 63), rather than in the polemical sense of science as natural science which Williams attributes to Engels as merely a 'polemical catchword' (1977a: 63). This supposedly 'strong' sense of science is dangerous to Marxism, since it implies the '*a priori* assumption of a "positive" method', one which is not itself subject to self-scrutiny or self-criticism. All too easily, this ends up as 'either a circular demonstration or a familiar partisan claim that others are biased but that, by definition, we are not' (1977a: 64). For Williams, this is simply 'the fool's way out' of genuinely difficult problems. Only in the 'weaker' sense of scientific enquiry as any detailed and connected knowledge, methodically applied to the world, can science lead to the challenging of received assumptions and points of view.[28]

Of course, insists Williams, this does not mean foregoing the first principle of any genuine ideological enquiry of the kind which cultural materialism proposes. There is always the need to examine the organising assumptions, concepts and points of view which organise any body of knowledge. When this is properly done, we are led away from the over-general and dogmatic 'epochal' analysis of a Christopher Caudwell to a genuinely historical analysis, one in which ideology:

reverts to a specific and practical dimension: the complicated processes within which men 'become' (are) conscious of their interests and their conflicts. The categorical short-cut to an (abstract) distinction between 'true' and 'false' consciousness is then effectively abandoned, as in all practice it has to be.

(1977a: 68)

Playing a major role in these 'complicated processes' is human language itself. Here, Williams's accidental discovery of the writings of the Soviet philosopher Vološinov was crucial.[29] *Marxism and the Philosophy of Language* (1929) gave precisely the right emphasis to the understanding of the ideological as 'the process of the production of meaning through signs', and in its insistence on signification 'as a central social process' (1977a:).

This focus on language as central to social process is, to some extent, new to Williams. The first draft, delivered as a series of lectures to the English Faculty at Cambridge, contained no specific consideration of language, while the book has a whole chapter devoted to the topic. In discussion with *Red Shift*, soon after publication, he enthused about his new take on language. 'Marxism does not have a theory of language', he notes, and because of this 'it goes wrong again and again': 'I've found, I believe, a way of showing that language is primary because it is material....I believe that language is the material process of sociality' (Williams 1977b: 15–16). In other ways, the focus on language simply repeats in different terms the emphasis on the centrality of communication to social reproduction which had been a part of Williams's position from the beginning. Vološinov and Vygotsky are new and certainly different points of reference to Caudwell and J.Z. Young, but their writing is called upon to do essentially the same explanatory work. Though Williams's points of reference are somewhat different, the intellectual and political stance of *Marxism and Literature* has not significantly altered from what it was in *Culture and Society* and *The Long Revolution*.

All that has really shifted is the oppositional focus of the arguments. This is now provided, as Williams usefully glossed, by the 'newly dominant mode of critical structuralism...[which] was being taken as Marxist literary theory all over Western Europe and North America' (Williams 1979: 339). The central term and key concept of this new mode was surely that of the 'subject', a term belonging to both grammar and political philosophy which stresses the subordination of the human agent to linguistic and political structures external to it. In an extraordinary diversity of fields, from structural linguistics to structural anthropology, from Lacanian psychoanalysis to Foucauldian power, from literature to cinema, from fashion to the entire system of Western philosophy, the apparent transparency of consciousness and agency was false: the subject was constituted by language, self-consciousness no more than an effect of language. Language itself was fascist, as Barthes declared in his inaugural lecture at the Collège de France, just a few months before the publication of *Marxism and Literature* (Barthes 1978: 14).

For Williams, Althusser's theory of ideology, with its emphasis on the structural determination of human subjectivity, exemplified the dangers of the new critical structuralism. And just as a great deal turned, in classic base and superstructure arguments, on the precise sense of 'determination', so in the theories of language and subjectivity, everything depended on the precise meaning of the constitutive (1977a: 20).

In the brief chapter, 'Language', he offered a brilliant and suggestive analysis of the history of language theory. Following Vološinov's arguments in *Marxism and the Philosophy of Language*, Williams argued that an unconscious determinant on the formation of theories of language had been the circumstances of their formation. In other words the colonialist situation of the observing linguist reinforced the tendency to 'objectivism', and threatened to reduce the idea of language away from its idea as activity towards its definition as a system. 'Language-use', he stresses, 'could then hardly be seen as itself active and constitutive' (1977a: 27). In the development of comparative linguistics:

> Language came to be seen as a fixed, objective, and in these senses 'given' system, which had theoretical and practical priority over what were described as 'utterances' (later as 'performance'). Thus the living speech of human beings in their specific social relationships in the world was theoretically reduced to instances and examples of a system which lay beyond them.
>
> (1977a: 27)

This was Williams's main point *contra* Althusser, and it is no accident that, at this moment in his argument, he looks aside to 'an important and often dominant tendency in Marxism itself': the idea of society as 'a controlling "social" system which is *a priori* inaccessible to "individual" acts of will and intelligence' (1977a: 28). An important component of his argument is therefore to parry representations of language which reduce, or threaten to disable, the positive aspects of the human subject's capacity for agency and activity from within the language-system. This comes through most powerfully in his discussion of what Marxism has to contribute to the understanding of language.

And here there is a difficult intellectual knot. Marxist thinking is 'wholly compatible with the emphasis on language as practical, constitutive activity' (1977a: 29) to be found in Vico; but it also opens up some of major problems regarding the meaning of the key idea of language as 'constitutive'. There is, he writes:

> an obvious danger...of making language 'primary' and 'original', not in the acceptable sense that it is a necessary part of the very act of human self-creation, but in the related and available sense of language as the founding element in humanity: 'in the beginning was the Word'. It is precisely the sense of language as an indissoluble element of human self-creation that gives any acceptable meaning to its description as 'constitutive'. To make it precede all other connected activities is to claim something quite different.
>
> (1977a: 29)

The underlying problem – as Williams indicated with the opening sentence of the chapter – lies in the conception of consciousness and subjectivity at work in such formulations. If, as he had indicated, a 'definition of language is always, implicitly or explicitly, a definition of human beings in the world' (1977a: 21), then there is a difficulty with any language theory which excludes activity and making. The true sense of constitutive is to be found in the work of Vološinov.

Here there is a powerful challenge to the usual opposition between expressive and systematic ideas of language, in which the subject is either seen as all-powerful, or totally subdued, and brings into focus the constant negotiation between system and expression which is the main force of a fully social understanding of language. 'Vološinov argued that meaning was necessarily a social action, dependent on a social relationship', emphasises Williams (1977a: 36), and it is this emphasis on the social relationship which makes his ideas a useful and necessary corrective to the Saussurean insistence on the arbitrariness of the sign. This was the theory of the 'useable sign'. Human beings are born into a language system, but this system is also always an 'active social language'. Although, as structuralist and post-structuralist critics insist, they are shaped by this system, they are also contributors to it. Language always has a creative as well as a systematic character, and language-use is therefore just as much a part of human individuation as it is of human socialisation. These are:

> the connected aspects of a single process which the alternative theories of 'system' and 'expression' had divided and dissociated. We then find not a reified 'language' and 'society' but an active social language. Nor is this language a simple 'reflection' or 'expression' of 'material reality'. What we have, rather, is a grasping of this reality through language, which as practical consciousness is saturated by and saturates all social activity, including productive activity.
>
> (1977a: 37)

In the end, argues Williams, it is 'of and to this experience – the lost middle ground between the abstract entities, "subject" and "object", on which the propositions of idealism and orthodox materialism are erected – that language speaks' (1977a: 37–8).

At this point, Williams has returned to his original arguments in *The Long Revolution*, where, as we saw, he insisted that 'all human experience is an interpretation of a non-human reality...not the duality of subject and object...[but] rather, of human experience as both objective and subjective, in one inseparable process' (1961a: 36). Williams rests his case, though resting it this time on the arguments and authority of Vološinov than on Caudwell.

As we have seen, and as a number of early reviewers remarked, a great deal of what is argued in *Marxism and Literature* is familiar, both as the summary of recent work like the essay 'Base and Superstructure in Marxist Cultural Theory', and beyond that, of the thinking and arguments of *Culture and Society* in the 1950s.[30] Williams's central emphasis remains the same: the insistence on the idea of culture as a way of thinking the social totality, the refusal of cultural production as a secondary effect of the economic base. While it is correct that the range of references to Marxist cultural theory has significantly increased, and that Williams's tone is considerably more welcoming, little has changed in the substance of his own arguments. Though he is now able to refer to a European-wide range of work in what he termed 'Marxism's alternative tradition', what is most notable is the way the arguments of this tradition are seen as supporting Williams's own emphases on the importance of culture to social and political reproduction, with all the strengths and weaknesses of that emphasis.

The fact of this continuity needs to be asserted against those critics, who, sympathetic to both Williams and to Marxism, have been too eager to bring them together. For it has sometimes seemed that one way of resolving the ambivalence which characterise Williams's thinking on Marxism has been to divide it, rather too neatly, into two distinct phases: the first, a moment of hostility towards Marxist theory, and the second, one of greater accommodation to it. In this perspective, 1973 is usually seen as the decisive moment, with the publication of the lecture 'Base and Superstructure in Marxist Cultural Theory' and the study *The Country and the City*. These mark Williams's entry or re-entry into a more fully Marxist mode of intellectual enquiry. Thus Aijaz Ahmad, whose *In Theory* has been one of the most passionate and consistent attempts of recent years to respond, from a Marxist position, to Anglo-American post-structuralist and 'postcolonial' theory, writes of his 'ambiguous relationship...with theoretical Marxism', but has no doubt of his adoption of 'increasingly Marxist perspectives', or the way that his intellect 'kept moving leftward' (Ahmad 1994: 49, 47, 48), and identifies 'the real turn' as coming 'in the mid 1970s' (1994: 49).

Similarly, the editors of *Marxist Literary Theory: A Reader* suggest that 'from a socialist humanist or left-Leavisite approach, Williams's early critical distance from Marxism had, by the 1970s, developed into a more explicit rapprochement with Marxism' (Eagleton and Milne 1996: 242). This in turn echoes Eagleton's own earlier judgement of *The Country and the City* as 'the only one of his texts in which Marxist positions constitute the very terms of debate' (Eagleton 1976b: 41). And this whole general judgement seems to receive confirmation in Williams's own statement, in 1979, that 'now I wouldn't want to write on any question without tracing the history of it in Marxist thought' (Williams 1979: 316).

Or, at least, this view seems confirmed just as long as we do not read the full sentence. 'I wouldn't want to write on any question without tracing the history of it in Marxist thought', but, or as Williams put it, and, 'and then seeing where I stood in relation to that' (1979: 316). Where did he 'stand'? The verb itself is characteristic of that life-long and fierce assertion of critical independence. This trait often made it difficult for readers to identify precisely just who he was writing for, or against, in any particular argument. 'Seeing where I stand': the assumption is that the stance was already there, just waiting to be found, but separate from the Marxist position, his position.

The main response to this by Williams's orthodox Marxist readers has been varied, but often to point out, respectfully enough, though this was not always the case, the problems raised by some of his arguments, and the way certain central problems were often marginalised by his own focus of interest and attention. Where, it has been asked, is Williams's acknowledgement of the importance of the state to his discussions of social change? What is the role and status of class consciousness in his arguments? Where in his work is there any serious consideration of the dynamic of the forces and relations of production? How do his arguments relate to the classical Marxist conceptions of mode of production and social formation? Above all, can his rejection of the base and structure model really be intended to deny the fundamental Marxist emphasis on the determination by the economy of the social totality, in however final an instance?

His lack of attention to these questions – the terms and tenets of orthodox Marxist analysis – led to Perry Anderson's judgement in 1976. While Williams is 'the most distinguished socialist thinker to have come from the ranks of the Western working class', his work 'has not been that of a Marxist' (Anderson 1976: 105). But then, that had never been Williams's aim. Anderson's remark needs to be supplemented, I think, by something like Terry Eagleton's judgement in 1989. 'There are many sterile ways of being correct', he notes, and, troping a phrase of Milton's, concludes that in relation to orthodox Marxism, Williams is best seen as a 'truthteller in heresy'. 'Whatever he has contributed to Marxism' he concludes, 'has been founded, necessarily, on his early break with it' (Eagleton 1989b: 175). Williams's interpretation of Marx was, after all, always an interpretation. His major claim to offer a return to a lost emphasis on the 'indissoluble unity' of the 'whole social process' is an interpretation of Marx's work which offers a valuable correction to extremes of economist or 'mechanical' Marxism. But at the same time, in the process of correction, Williams himself was perhaps guilty of his own overemphases, and something is lost or marginalised in his own interpretation. If the unity of the social process is in reality 'indissoluble', then no causal analysis of it is possible, the flow of social process can never be grasped or articulated.[31]

Conclusion

Can Marxism then be said to be central to Williams's thought? Or marginal? Neither term really fits the nagging constancy with which Marxism provided a point of reference for all his more foregrounded preoccupations with drama, literature and culture. It must never be forgotten that Williams was first and foremost a literary and cultural critic, and that his interest in and interpretation of Marxism was constructed largely from within the discursive boundaries of his profession. Duly considered, this simple fact only makes his theoretical achievement all the more striking: no literary critic before him had ever thought through what Marxism might mean to literary criticism quite so thoroughly, so forcefully, or so originally. Williams's engagement with Marxism was just as oppositional and combative as his relation to orthodox literary criticism. As he put it in 1958, 'I could not have begun this work [the writing of *Culture and Society*] if I had not learned from Marxists and from Leavis; I cannot complete it unless I radically amend some of the ideas which they and others have left us' (Williams 1958b: 14). He was never only the critic of 'official English culture', whose work *contra* Cambridge English we examined in the previous chapter: he was also and always a critic of what he took to be official Marxist culture. The aim was never to be or become a Marxist in any orthodox sense: it was rather to offer a series of 'amendments' and corrections to what he saw as a range of mistaken emphases in orthodox Marxist theory.

There can be no doubt that his rejection of the base and superstructure argument was intended as a direct challenge to the related strains of economism and functionalism which he was not alone in finding at work in a great deal of Marxist theory, including Marx's own.[32] Williams argued consistently against those who would construe the mechanisms of social reproduction in any way which reduced people to the status of mere 'bearers' of social relations, the dupes of ideology. He argued consistently for a better understanding of the situational complexity of human agency, and came to figure his case, in the end, on the idea of the constitutive force of language in a way which was the product of some forty years of thinking on, through and against the orthodox ideas of literature and Marxism.

In the end, this oppositional thinking came through as a theory of cultural materialism which Williams was willing to set against what he saw as the dogmas of historical materialism. In the next chapter, we shall examine cultural materialism in relation to the other great *doxa* that Williams set himself against: the formation he came to call the 'bourgeois idea of literature'.

6   Towards a cultural materialism 1977–81

The previous chapter traced some of the main contours of Williams's complex relations to Marxist cultural theory. We saw how his central emphasis on the constitutive force of culture in social and political reproduction culminated in the advocacy of a cultural materialism. Cultural materialism challenged the Second International's commitment to the singular, absolute and unicausal priority of the economy, and refused its equally firm relegation of cultural activity to a secondary role in the reproduction of the social order. The means and relations of communication belong alongside the means and forces of production as one of the constituents of any explanation of the functioning of the social totality.[1] Williams's cultural materialism argued instead for the centrality of a line of thought occluded in the usual accounts – Marx and Engels's stress on the importance of 'practical consciousness' – and suggested that culture be recognised as a primary force in the reproduction of, and therefore all challenges to, any existing social order.

But the theory of cultural materialism looks two ways. As *cultural* material- ism, it is the name Williams gave to his distinctive version of Marxist theory, but, as cultural *materialism*, it refers to his response to the theory and practice of literary analysis at work in the existing institutions of English studies. This theory and practice, the discipline of English literature, is distinctively bourgeois in nature and effect. Bourgeois literary analysis is marked by an overemphasis on the individual at the expense of the social; and a tendency to ahistorical and apolitical analysis. To borrow and adapt Edward Said's useful terms, bourgeois literary theory produces an idea of literature as a pure textuality cut off from the entanglements of all worldly circumstance.[2]

Cultural materialism versus Cambridge English

In Williams's view, both Leavisism and literary structuralism share a series of family resemblances, the common features of the bourgeois response to the pressures of modernity and mass culture. In *Culture and Society*, he had argued that this structure of response, first articulated in the 1920s, was repeated with renewed vigour and stridency in the post-1945 period and *Marxism and Literature* found a further continuity between the modernist dilemma and the advent of structuralist and post-structuralist theory in their restrictive definitions of textuality. The theory of cultural materialism was intended as a challenge and check to these subterranean continuities. This chapter examines how the case for a cultural materialism, first argued in *Marxism and Literature*, was deployed in the debates around 'structuralism' provoked by the 'MacCabe Affair', and subsequently extended and developed in Williams's later study, *Culture* (1981).

Few reviewers of *Marxism and Literature* attempted the daunting task of trying to chart or to assess the book's argument as a whole; and few of the broader discussions of his work have done so either. Reviews focused largely on the first item in the title – Marxism – and much less attention was paid to the second, Literature. This has had the unfortunate consequence – which I discuss further in the conclusion – that while the term 'cultural materialism' has been adopted by a number of progressive academics, that adoption has always involved a certain translation of Williams's own concept, and consequently, as with most translations, a certain loss or simplification of the original. This chapter seeks to revive the force and complexity of Williams's own arguments.

Marxist stalwart Arnold Kettle reviewed the study unsympathetically, rejecting it because of its foundation in Cambridge English and New Left attitudes. For Kettle, any Marxism in which 'concepts are given so central a place…and in which the particular concept of "reflection" is placed on a sort of Stalinist dunce's or whipping stool, is almost bound to err on the side of theoreticism and academicism' (Kettle 1977: 72). From a different perspective, George Woodcock belittled the book as a 'confessional document – the autobiography…of a true believer [in Marxism]' (Woodcock 1978: 593), while Bernard Sharrat saw little in it save 'a summary and summation of most of Williams's already published work' (Sharrat 1982: 37). The most detailed account appeared in the American journal *Telos*, where Michael Scrivener wrote (against Anthony Barnett's view that Williams 'pleads too much for the continuity of his position') of the 'real continuity' between his arguments in 1958 and 1977, but notes how the chapter on language demonstrates just 'how innovative Williams actually is' (Barnett 1977: 145; Scrivener 1979–80: 193). Many commented on the daunting abstraction of the language and the arguments as the book sought to compress the competing idioms of a century's thinking on Marxism and culture into one volume and one argument.[3] Generally missed was the attempt in *Marxism and Literature* to forge the theory of a new discipline through the critique of the existing discipline of English studies.

The principles of the cultural materialism which Williams developed as the theoretical and disciplinary critique of Cambridge English are given most fully in the third part of *Marxism and Literature*, but the main lines of attack are anticipated in the chapter on Literature in Part I of the study, where he deconstructs or defamiliarises the orthodox idea of literature by tracing its emergence from the eighteenth century to the present day.

'It is relatively difficult', Williams writes, 'to see "literature" as a concept' (Williams 1977a: 45). In the terms offered by Cambridge English:

it is common to see 'literature' defined as 'full, central immediate human experience', usually with an associated reference to 'minute particulars'. By contrast, 'society' is often seen as essentially general and abstract: the summaries and averages, rather than the direct substance, of human living.

(1977a: 45)

The references are, of course, to the work of F.R. Leavis, undoubtedly the most influential critic of the Cambridge English school, though shamefully neglected by the university for most of his career.[4] Leavis argued over some fifty years for the value and specificity of literary criticism through an extremely strong negative contrast of it with both traditional conceptions of literary history, and against any criticism based in theory, be it psychoanalytic, Marxist or philosophical.[5]

This stance came through strongly in Leavis's responses to the two most explicit challenges to his and *Scrutiny*'s procedures.[6] As Leavis put it in his essay, 'Literary Criticism and Philosophy', 'the reading demanded by poetry is of a different kind from that demanded by philosophy....Philosophy, we say, is "abstract", and poetry "concrete" ' (Leavis 1952: 212). René Wellek's challenge, in a review of Leavis's *Revaluation* (Wellek 1937), was met – or avoided – with a stinging response in which Leavis refused Wellek's request to make his theoretical assumptions explicit on the grounds that he was a literary critic and not a philosopher. If he, Leavis, 'avoided such generalities, it was not out of timidity. It was because they seemed too clumsy to be of any use'. 'I thought I had provided something better', he offered. 'My whole effort was to work in terms of concrete judgement and particular analyses' (Leavis 1952: 215) – to work through the particularity of textual analysis and literary evaluation.

And again, some sixteen years later, faced with the challenge of F.W. Bateson's new Oxford journal *Essays in Criticism*, and its promotion of a new 'contextual reading', one which demanded a consistently historical dimension to literary analysis, Leavis could only reply by refusing to meet the grounds of the accusation, and launching a counter-accusation at Bateson and other contextual critics. Such critics were guilty of 'the academic over-emphasis on scholarly knowledge', one which 'accompanies a clear lack of acquaintance with intelligent critical reading' (Leavis 1953: 281). In the end, as far as Leavis is concerned Bateson's proposed discipline of contextual reading 'is not merely irrelevant; it isn't, and can't be, a discipline at all: it has no determinate field or aim' (1953: 292). All that 'Bateson's posited relation between poem and "social context" can amount to 'is a matter of vain and muddled verbiage' (1953: 296–7). Or, as Williams summed it up, with a rather different emphasis:

Arguments from theory or from history are simply evidence of the incurable abstraction and generality of those who are putting them forward. They can then be contemptuously rejected, often without specific reply, which would be only to fall to their level.

(Williams 1977a: 45)

Leavis's project – the project of Cambridge English in its most powerful form – represents an 'extraordinary ideological feat', one in which the specific literary process of 'formal composition within the social and formal properties of language' is effectively elided, 'or has been displaced to an internal and self-proving procedure in which writing of this kind is genuinely believed to be (however many questions are then begged) "immediate living experience" itself' (1977a: 46). To fully understand this ideological and theoretical achievement – one which 'can hardly be examined or questioned at all from outside' – we need, he urges, to grasp the history of the concept of literature itself. For it is only in terms of this history that we can find a point of entry into an otherwise self-supporting structure of arguments, and prise open an otherwise closed system of assumptions.

From literacy to literature

The history of the term literature is one of the increasing specialisation and reification of its component senses. This is summed up in the striking shift in the meaning of literature away from its original sense as literacy, to the now dominant sense of literature as 'a category of use and condition rather than of production' (Williams 1977a: 47). He locates the beginnings of this shift in the eighteenth century, where, in a new extended meaning, literature goes 'beyond the bare sense of "literacy" ' to become the 'apparently objective category of printed works of a certain quality'. Once this has happened, the term loses the basic reference to 'reading ability and reading experience' (1977a: 48) which it initially held and could express. Since the eighteenth century, 'three complicating tendencies' have emerged, tendencies which have by now become 'received assumptions'. First, there was a move from 'learning' to 'taste' as the criterion for literary quality; second, the meaning of literature was increasingly restricted to imaginative works only (in the early part of the century, literature covered history, philosophy and virtually all forms of bound and printed communication); and third, the period saw the development of the concept of a national literary tradition.

All of these came together in the idea of a canon of national literature, a selective tradition which is apparently – but only apparently – based in objective judgements of literary value and worth. Long before it became a regular professional move to 'question the canon', Williams was sharp and to the point in his assessment of its foundational rhetoric, the grounding of the canon in apparent norms of aesthetic judgement. Properly considered, the apparent 'norms' of 'taste' and 'sensibility' are no more than 'characteristically bourgeois categories' which only 'acquire their apparent objectivity from an actively consensual class sense' (1977a: 48–9). Indeed, the very history of literary criticism as a practice and discipline is similarly constituted by forms and pressures of class-control. Williams is harsh on its emergence as an academic discipline in the twentieth century: the so-called (in Basil Willey's phrase) 'Golden Age of Cambridge English' – the moment of its entry as a 'new conscious discipline into the universities' in the 1920s – was no more than 'forms of class specialization and control of a general social practice, and of a class limitation of the questions which it might raise' (1977a: 49).[7] In fact, by the time of this development:

> the category which had appeared objective as 'all printed books', and which had been given a social-class foundation as 'polite learning' and the domain of 'taste' and 'sensibility', now became a necessarily selective and self-defining area: not all 'fiction' was 'imaginative'; not all 'literature' was 'Literature'. 'Criticism' acquired a quite new and effectively primary importance, since it was now the only way of validating this specialized and selective category.... What had been claimed for 'art' and the 'creative imagination' in the central Romantic arguments was now claimed for 'criticism', as the central 'humane' activity and 'discipline'.
>
> (1977a: 51)

This was precisely Leavis's idea of the discipline.[8] With the idea of the canon, the practice of literary criticism was justified by literature, and the idea of literature was confirmed by literary criticism, in the mutually supportive dynamic which Williams had identified as the dynamic of a 'selective tradition' in which:

> the 'national literature' soon ceased to be a history and became a tradition. It was not, even theoretically, all that had been written or all kinds of writing. It was a selection which culminated in, and in a circular way defined, the 'literary values' which 'criticism' was asserting.... To oppose the terms of this ratification was to be 'against literature'.
>
> (1977a: 51–2)

This was exactly the structure of argument and assumption so powerfully welded together in Leavis's seminal series of canonical studies, his famous 'revaluations'.[9]

Williams rightly regarded this transformation, within the discipline of literary studies, of a full history into a selective tradition as an 'extraordinary ideological feat'. The first step in combating it was to grasp the idea of 'literature' as 'a specialising social and historical category' (1977a: 53), and next, to seek to recover some of the basic senses of literature as literacy which have been repressed in and through the developing history of the word. Literacy in this sense goes beyond the basic mastery of reading and writing to become a secondary or critical literacy; and it also extends the usual boundaries of textuality to include the relatively new practices of composition and communication available in film, television and video.

The argument moves on, from this point in *Marxism and Literature*, to a similarly challenging discussion of the Marxist idea of ideology, and from there to his analysis of the Marxist debates on cultural theory which we have examined in Chapter 5. In Part III, 'Literary Theory', he returns to the discussion and dissection of bourgeois literary theory and its particular idea of literature. He begins by questioning the restricted sense of literariness underlying traditional conceptions of the literary.

The multiplicity of writing

In the orthodox terms of the discipline, 'literature' has been restricted to aesthetic writing, and its study has taken the form of a largely evaluative criticism. Against this, Williams urges what he calls the 'multiplicity of writing'. In *The Long Revolution*, he had argued for the recognition of creativity as an everyday activity, rooted in perception itself, rather than as a special instrumental feature of the artistic temperament alone.[10] The concept of literature, he reprises in *Marxism and Literature*, has operated a 'specialization and containment' of this ordinary creativity, though never with complete success. The main obstacle to the full recognition of the ordinariness of creativity, and the consequent acceptance of the multiplicity of writing, is the orthodox division established, in theory and across time, between literary and non-literary writing. Against this falsely specialising opposition between 'fictional' and 'factual' writing, he insists that the:

> range of actual writing similarly surpasses any reduction of 'creative imagination' to the 'subjective', with its dependent propositions: 'literature' as 'internal' or 'inner' truth; other forms of writing as 'external' truth. These depend, ultimately, on the characteristic bourgeois separation of 'individual' and 'society' and on the older idealist separation of 'mind' and 'world'. The range of writing, in most forms, crosses these artificial categories again and again, and the extremes can even be stated in an opposite way: autobiography ('what I experienced', 'what happened to me') is 'subjective' but (ideally) 'factual' writing; realist fiction or naturalist drama ('people as they are', 'the world as it is') is 'objective' (the narrator or even the fact of narrative occluded in the form) but (ideally) 'creative' writing.
>
> (1977a: 148)

In other words, the artificial categories deny the most significant feature of all forms of writing, namely 'the very fact of address...stance' (1977a: 149). Stance, the mutual positioning of reader and writer through the process of composition and address, was constitutive in all writing.[11] And this fact of address includes, and is perhaps even especially relevant to, writing in which the stance is consciously and conventionally 'impersonal', as in the composition of scientific papers and their 'necessary creation of the "impersonal observer" ' (1977a: 149). There is a rhetoric of objectivity, one which can range from the activation of the conventions of scientific writing and research, to their rather more suspicious troping and deployment in other forms, where, by sleight of phrase, the rhetoric of impersonality cloaks the figure of an interested observer, as occurs in exemplary fashion in the case of Orwell.[12]

In the end, the bourgeois dichotomies of fact and fiction, and the orthodox positing of objective versus subjective, work to contain and occlude nothing less than the social and ideological bearings of all composition and language-use, and alongside this, the real sociality of the human subject. Against the banal assertions of the independence, separation and 'freedom' of the individual subject of bourgeois and liberal theory, but also against the arguments of Althusserian theory and its many variants, and against the carceral subject of Foucauldian analysis, endlessly repeating its initial conditions of socialisation as the content of its subjectivity, Williams argues for a conception of the human subject in which the agency of human subjectivity is given a measure of recognition equal to that accorded to the idea of its determinations. Acceptance of the 'actual multiplicity of writing' makes of every person – as at the starting-point of Gramsci's theory – an intellectual in the basic sense of an active and responsive language-user, rather than merely the subject of an always determining language-structure, the product and 'bearer' of always external determinations.[13]

The social and the aesthetic

A part of the problem with the orthodox category of literature is the ways in which it embodies the constitutive tensions of the larger concept of the aesthetic. The aesthetic shares some of the negative aspects of literature in its careful selection and specialization of human creative energy to forms of class culture; but it also has positive aspects, as Williams had argued – though in a very different theoretical language – in *Culture and Society.* For the history of the concept of the aesthetic is 'in large part a protest against the forcing of all experience into instrumentality' and represents a resistance to those same alienating and reifying forces of bourgeois culture which make literature such a restrictive and specialised category.

Following the work of his former research student, John Fekete, Williams praises Lukács's attempt to place the aesthetic as a category of action and agency, one which is neither 'practical' nor 'magical', but which represents 'a real mediation between (isolated) subjectivity and (abstract) universality' (1977a: 151).[14] Nonetheless, he argues that Lukács's placing of the aesthetic as a distinguishable category of material production is open in the end to the same difficulties which plagued the Russian Formalists' earlier attempt to distinguish and separate out a specific 'poetic language' from within the ordinary social processes of language.[15] It is better, he argues, in the end to 'face the facts of the range of [aesthetic] intentions and effects, and to face it as a range':

All writing carries references, meanings and values. To suppress or distort them is in the end impossible. But to say all 'all writing carries' is only a way of saying that language and form are constitutive processes of reference, meaning and value, and that these are not necessarily identical with, or exhausted by, the kinds of reference, meaning, and value that are also evident, in other senses and in summary, elsewhere.

(1977a: 155)

The aesthetic, whatever else it is, is always a particular response to a specific situation, in a given signifying medium. At this point, Williams once again deploys his new sense of the constitutive force of language to great effect: 'language and form are constitutive processes of reference, meaning and value'. To argue otherwise is to see language merely as the medium for expression, understood as an essentially private act, one made possible by the individual possession of language as an instrument under the control of the sovereign ego of the bourgeois subject. That is, to see the aesthetic as Williams had himself seen it, particularly in his early work, where an ideology of artistic expression and instrumentality – elements of which, as we saw in Chapter 2, were derived from Eliot and fetishised in the theory of cinema as 'Total Expression' – held sway. In order to stress the importance of this new sense of the constitutivity of language, he examines some of the dynamics of that misleading term, medium, and the role it plays in the orthodox view in which language is simply the transparent medium for an always instrumental expression, the property of an always centred and always knowing subject.

Language as medium

The constitutive properties of language are all too easily abstracted and objectified in the orthodox idea that 'thoughts exist before language and are then expressed through its "medium" ' (1977a: 158).[16] Against this, he argues that if language is to be understood as a medium, then it needs to be grasped as a medium which – far from being neutral or value-free – is in itself the concrete embodiment of social, political and ideological conflicts. Language is never merely a system; it is always a social practice. And it is in this notion of language as a social practice that the radical aesthetics of modernism – which so stressed the potential defamiliarising effects of language use – joins the revolutionary theory and practice of Marxism. In the end, the 'full sense of practice' in Marxism or modernism 'has always to be defined as work on a material for a specific purpose within certain necessary social conditions' (1977a: 160). As Williams had argued in Part 1, Chapter 3 of *Marxism and Literature*, language 'is not a medium; it is a constitutive element of material social practice', even, indeed, 'a special kind of material practice; that of human sociality' (1977a: 165).

Full recognition of the real constitutive force of language in human sociality has been evaded by the two alternative views of language available to orthodox literary theory. Here language is either seen as instrumental or systematic, 'expressive' or 'formalist'. 'Each of these general theories' writes Williams, 'grasp real elements of the practice of writing, but commonly in ways which deny other real elements and even make them inconceivable' (1977a: 165). Following Vološinov, whose work he had discovered by a happy accident on the open-stack shelves of Cambridge's University Library, Williams insists that 'meaning is always produced; it is never simply expressed'.[17] 'No expression', he emphasises:

> no account, description, depiction, portrayal – is 'natural' or 'straight forward'. These are at most socially relative terms. Language is not a pure medium through which the reality of a life or the reality of an event or an experience or the reality of a society can 'flow'. It is a socially shared and reciprocal activity, already embedded in active relationships, within which every move is an activation of what is already shared and reciprocal or may become so.
>
> (1977a: 166)

And with a theoretical insight refreshed by his encounter with Vološinov, Williams reiterates the core of the theory of communication present in *Culture and Society* and *The Long Revolution*: 'to address an account to another is, explicitly or potentially, as in any act of expression, to evoke or propose a relationship' (1977a: 166).[18]

The Russian Formalists had grasped one aspect of this, drawing attention to the devices through which expression could be strengthened; but in the end they lost their way. Reacting against notions of language and expression as 'natural', they reduced language to what they saw as its basic elements, to 'signs' within a totalised 'system of signs', anticipating in this regard the inner dynamic of the new 'critical structuralism'. In the end, the Formalists were responsible for the creation of 'a new myth': the idea:

> that the 'system of signs' is determined by its formal internal relations; that 'expression' is not only not 'natural' but is a form of 'codification'; and that the appropriate response to 'codification' is 'decipherment', 'deconstruction'.[19]
>
> (1977a: 167–8)

Williams sees this form of analysis – which, once again following the arguments first put forward by John Fekete, he associates with both French structuralism and American New Criticism – as dangerously compatible with the very forms of alienation it seeks to analyse. For, he argues, what really follows from this position 'is the universality of alienation, the position of a closely associated bourgeois idealist formation, drawing its assumptions from a universalist (mainly Freudian) psychology' (1977a: 168). In this sense, the Russian Formalists anticipate the arguments of the structuralist movement, and all those caught up in what he calls elsewhere, again borrowing from Fekete, the 'language paradigm'.[20]

What is in the end necessary to combat this paradigm is, he argues, a 'fully social theory of literature' in which the overemphases of both expressionism and formalism are refused, rejected and redefined. The notations beloved of the 'language paradigm' are in fact 'relationships, expressed, offered, tested and amended in a whole social process, in which device, expression and the substance of expression are in the end inseparable' (1977a: 171–2). Such is the founding argument of cultural materialism, and Williams argues that evidence for this could be established through any fully social history and analysis of existing literary concepts such as convention, genre, form and author.

These indeed are the key terms whose analysis constitutes the remainder of the study, demonstrating in each case the ways in which the force of these concepts is lessened by their failure to fully comprehend the force of language in the constitutivity of the social process in the way that cultural materialism recommends. Thus Williams argues – drawing on the arguments and evidence gathered in *The Country and the City* – that 'the presentation of place depends on variable conventions':

> Descriptions of great houses, of rural landscapes, of cities, or of factories are evidence examples of these variable conventions, where the 'point of view' may be experienced as an 'aesthetic' choice but where any point of view, including that which excludes persons or converts them into landscape, is social.
>
> (1977a: 177)

Similarly, genre is described as 'neither an ideal type nor a traditional order nor a set of technical rules' but a 'social relationship' (1977a: 185); while the discussion of an orthodox literary theory in which 'the figure of the individual author' – 'a characteristic form of bourgeois thought' (1977a: 193) – needs to be challenged by the 'reciprocal discovery of the truly social in the individual, and the truly individual in the social' (1977a: 197). In all of these assertions, language needs to be seen as in a strong and indeed constitutive sense the social practice, 'the practice of human sociality itself'.

At the centre of cultural materialism is the call for a critical attitude towards all forms and practices of representation, and not only those associated with literature. A key characteristic of cultural materialism is its bringing together of three dimensions of intellectual analysis and enquiry which are far too often kept apart, to the detriment of each: the textual, the theoretical or conceptual, and the historical. Cambridge English, at least in the evaluative mode bequeathed by Leavis and his followers, had tended to privilege the textual at the expense of the theoretical and the historical, as Leavis's non-debates with Wellek and Bateson had shown. Contemporary structuralism, as Williams understood it, tended to focus on the theoretical over the historical and, in a curious sense, over the textual, often allotting texts only the role of example in the demonstration of the 'truths' of theory, just as in some historical analysis – both liberal and Marxist – texts were regarded merely as 'illustrations' of a historical process which was already comprehended in full.

In all of these partial approaches, bourgeois and Marxist alike, what might be called the productivity of the text was ignored – that productivity which meant that texts could contest as well as articulate or embody given ideologies. This, in turn, exemplified the ways in which the constitutive role of culture in the production and reproduction of society was badly understood and in consequence marginalised in most liberal and Marxist accounts. The task of a cultural materialism was to attend to that constitutive role of signification within cultural process, and so to seek to integrate the three usually separated dimensions of textual, theoretical and historical analysis. Only through this kind of integration could the fundamentally social role of language and communication be fully understood and asserted against the separated and reified analyses of both bourgeois and also (in so far as it had insufficiently freed itself from bourgeois categories) Marxist literary and cultural theory.

Against the orthodox emphases of the 'bourgeois theory of literature', which limits and reifies the workings of expression through the category of the aesthetic, cultural materialism emphasises the depth, richness and complexity of the fully theorised sense of language as constitutive. Cultural materialism is the analysis of the constitutive grounds and force of all forms of signification at work in human society.

Crisis in English studies

Published in 1977, *Marxism and Literature* presented equal challenges to the orthodoxies of both Marxist cultural analysis and traditional literary criticism through its arguments for a cultural materialism. In many ways, these arguments anticipated or participated in the emergence of a new body of work whose theoretical force and impetus led to a widespread sense of a 'crisis in English studies', one which continues some twenty years later as the self-contained discipline which English literature was for the first fifty years of its professional existence struggles to respond to the infusion of ideas, concepts and practices from the diverse constituents of 'theory'.

It is beyond the scope of this chapter to examine, in the necessary detail, the relations between Williams's work and what Anthony Easthope has usefully dubbed 'British post-structuralism' (Easthope 1988). A full-scale comparative exercise, placing Williams's work in direct comparison with the work of European thinkers, would require a different framing than this narrowly focused study of its relations to English studies. It would entail the establishment of a discursive common ground that would accommodate Williams's theoretical vocabulary, and the conceptual vocabulary of post-structuralism, as well as a detailed reading and analysis of the major works of Foucault, Derrida, Lacan *et cie*, and at the same time a detailed appraisal of the selective deployment of the work of the French school in British work.

Yet it is worth saying, before examining the detail of some of Williams's arguments, that Easthope's study, which does much to establish that larger frame, is interestingly blind to and silent on the ways in which cultural materialism was an attempt to come to terms with the problems of that whole formation.[21] Easthope, like many of Williams's other obituarists, locates the main force and value of his work with the arguments of the *Culture and Society* period, rather than with the later and more sophisticated arguments of *Marxism and Literature* and *Culture*. Against this placing of it, which has the effect of limiting its force and relevance to the 1950s ('left-liberal, culturalist and empiricist' in Easthope's description (Easthope 1988: 2)), let us examine some of the ways in which the arguments were intended to carry some force in and against the emerging theories of 'British post-structuralism'.

The MacCabe Affair

In Cambridge, 'British post-structuralism' came into focus in the arguments and debates surrounding the notorious MacCabe affair of 1980–1, 'Cambridge's biggest academic row since the bitter days of Dr. F.R. Leavis'.[22] A few remarks about the tenure system at the University of Cambridge are necessary to set the scene.

Generally speaking, to become a tenured lecturer in the English Faculty at Cambridge University, it is necessary first of all to go through a five-year probationary appointment as an Assistant Lecturer. This is then followed – or not – by what is known as 'upgrading' to the tenured position of University Lecturer. Assistant Lectureships are themselves hard fought for, and promotion or upgrading is usually dependent upon maintaining a good record of academic publication, the translation of the completed Ph.D. into a publishable book, and demonstrated competence and expertise in the field of the appointment. There is, in other words, general agreement and consensus about the workings of promotion. The MacCabe Affair attracted unusual national attention in the press as that consensus visibly broke down, and brought into focus emergent shifts and trends in the study of literature and moves beyond the given paradigm of literary study, as British academic work in literary studies began to move away from its intensely enclosed and nationalist focus and to examine work from Europe and the USA.

Colin MacCabe was hired by the Faculty as an Assistant Lecturer in 1976, and was refused tenure in the second of a number of meetings of the Faculty Board in 1980 (the first meeting was apparently inconclusive). This seemed a highly unusual decision, as MacCabe had already made a name for himself in British intellectual and political life through the publication of a number of seminal essays on film, literature and theory, and the publication of his thesis as a provocative book on James Joyce.[23]

This already significant body of work represented some of the first stirrings of Easthope's 'British post-structuralism', that heady mixture of Lacanian psychoanalysis, Althusserian Marxism and the textual analysis of film and literature.[24] As David Simpson wryly remarks, MacCabe's publications alone made him 'by any publicly recognized standard spectacularly overqualified for tenure' (Simpson 1990: 251); but he was none the less refused upgrading. The decision was bitterly fought and the occasion of much debate both within and without the university.[25] One moment in this debate was a lecture given by Williams to the English Faculty in March 1981, later revised and published as 'Crisis in English Studies'.[26] Criticised by many at the time for too distanced and magisterial a view of the conflict, the lecture can best be read in terms of Williams's prediliction for the longer historical view of crises and debates.

The lecture opens with an oblique and ironic reference to the MacCabe affair ('Recent events in Cambridge, of which some of you may have heard') as the occasion for the lecture. Williams describes his main purpose as one of 'identifying and briefly explaining some currently controversial positions beyond the labels which are being so loosely attached', of clarifying, in effect, the ideas of Marxism and 'structuralism' which were being used to identify, and vilify, MacCabe's work and positions in the dispute over his promotion.[27] In the first instance, argued Williams, it was necessary to stress the simple diversity of available positions in both Marxism and structuralism. While several of these positions are in fact in sharp opposition to each other (Williams is far from endorsing MacCabe's own position, as we shall examine in the next chapter), what is at stake in the present dispute is the general compatibility of these tendencies with the existing paradigm of work in literary studies in Cambridge, that is, with the current 'working definition of a perceived field of knowledge', one which 'as object of knowledge, based on certain fundamental hypotheses...carries with it definitions of appropriate methods of discovering and establishing such knowledge' (Williams 1981b: 192).[28] For Williams, the MacCabe affair was a symptom, 'although at a relatively early stage', of crisis in the explanatory power of the Literature paradigm, and consequently a moment for the elaboration of his alternative, cultural materialism.

In an impressive piece of synthesis and condensation, Williams outlines many of the main themes of *Marxism and Literature*, focusing on the question of the compatibility of Marxist and structuralist arguments with the dominant literary paradigm. Structuralist literary criticism, he argues, is in the end no more than 'an indirect inheritance from the kind of thinking which Richards had been doing about the isolated internal organization of a poem' (1981b: 206). The apparently new literary structuralism of the 1960s and 1970s 'is not only congruent with the paradigm.... It is the paradigm itself in its most influential modern form' (1981b: 206). Indeed, argues Williams, Althusserianism – a key influence on MacCabe's own work – can itself be understood as a particular variant of this literary structuralism. Here society is understood as a rule-governed system, determined in the last instance by the economy, in which there are a number of sub-systems or practices which enjoy a relative autonomy from that determination. The binding force of this is ideology in general, understood as 'the condition of all conscious life'. In Althusserian theory, human experience itself is seen as 'the most common form of ideology. It is where the deep structures of the society actually reproduce themselves as conscious life' (1981b: 207), and Williams's tone is mocking as he writes that ideology is in this account 'so pervasive and so impenetrable...that you wonder who is ever going to be able to analyse it' (1981b: 207). For Althusser, theory made this possible; but literature itself also enjoyed a 'relatively privileged situation':

> Literature is not just a carrier of ideology, as in most forms of reflection theory. It is inescapably ideological, but its specific relative autonomy is that it is a form of writing, a form of practice, in which ideology both exists and is or can be internally distanced and questioned. Thus the value of literature is precisely that it is one of the areas where the grip of ideology is or can be loosened, because although it cannot escape ideological construction, the point about its literariness is that it is a continual questioning of it internally.
>
> (1981b: 208)

While Williams admits that this method has been used in some 'very detailed and interesting analysis', it still participates in the logic of the dominant paradigm.[29]

Finally, he turns to semiotics, understood as bringing an important new emphasis to structuralism. This new emphasis comes through the readmission of the category of agency into the idea of structure. Instead of seeing literary works 'as produced by the system of signs...this later semiotics has emphasised that productive systems have themselves always to be constituted and reconstituted'. Because of this, he adds:

> there is a perpetual battle about the fixed character of the sign and about the systems which we ordinarily bring to production and interpretation. One effect of this shift is a new sense of 'deconstruction': not the technical analysis of an internal organization to show where all the parts, the components, have come from, but a much more open and active process which is continually taking examples apart, as a way of taking their systems apart.
>
> (1981b: 208–9)

Here Williams moves a little away from the rather slight definition of 'deconstruction' he had adopted and criticised in *Marxism and Literature*, and finds some common ground with the emerging 'post-structuralism' of his Cambridge colleagues like MacCabe and Heath, suggesting that this new 'more open and active process' of analysis might be better termed a 'radical semiotics'. This radical semiotics, despite its connections to the 'structuralist version of production and reproduction which has been much more widely influential – and more welcome and at home – in literary studies' (1981b: 209), differs significantly from it and could contribute to the challenging of the dominant paradigm of literary studies. In this challenge, there is common ground between a radical semiotics and cultural materialism.

While ready to admit that much of his own work – as we saw in Chapter 4 – is located well within the dominant literary paradigm, though 'with an exceptionally strong consciousness of the social determinants upon it' he argues, and most critics seem to agree, *The Country and the City* signalled a break with the dominant paradigm:

> because it sets out to identify certain characteristic forms of writing about the country and the city, and then insists on placing them not only in their historical background – which is within the paradigm – but within an active, conflicting historical process in which the very forms are created by social relations which are sometimes evident and sometimes occluded.
>
> (1981b: 209)

The key word is 'active'. Cultural materialism and radical semiotics come together in their recognition of subjective agency, the ways in which systems of language and conventions of representation not only coerce but also enable expression. And it is this recognition which places them 'outside the paradigm altogether' (1981b: 210). Nonetheless, this does not mean the abandonment of the study of literature as such. Cultural materialism has 'moved much wider than literature in its paradigmatic sense':

> but it still centrally includes these major forms of writing, which are now being read, along with other writing, in a different perspective. Cultural materialism is the analysis of all forms of signification, including quite centrally writing, within the actual means and conditions of their production.
>
> (1981b: 210)

It is this emphasis on the analysis of the means and conditions of production of all forms of signification that cultural materialism and radical semiotics may connect. There are still major differences, writes Williams, especially with reference to the ways in which radical semiotics draws on structural linguistics and psychoanalysis, 'but I remember saying that a fully historical semiotics would be very much like the same thing as cultural materialism' (1981b: 210).

'Very much like the same thing as cultural materialism' – this is how Williams refers, in a characteristically oblique fashion, to MacCabe's own work, and to what Christopher Ricks, a brilliant liberal professor of English at Cambridge and a major player in the MacCabe Affair, described as the work of 'a particular radical, Marxist, semiological clique' (cited in Simpson 1990: 264). In retrospect, it seems clear that though the local battle against this new work was lost in MacCabe's own case, the war was not. In reality, there were many diverse strands to this work, ranging from the emphasis on psychoanalysis to be found in the theory and practice of film analysis of what became known as 'Screen Theory' of MacCabe himself and his mentor Stephen Heath, as well as feminist critics such as Laura Mulvey and Jacqueline Rose; the exciting extension of this to the analysis of painting to be found in the work of Norman Bryson; and the more historically-based work of critics such as John Barrell and David Simpson, to name but few.[30] Indeed, if anything has come to dominate contemporary literary studies, it has been the combination of theoretical and textual analysis characteristic of structuralist writing; but what is less evident is whether the third dimension of analysis, the historical, so crucial to Williams's own project of a cultural materialism, has been so widely adopted.

Some indication of the importance which Williams gave to the historical dimension comes through in his discussion of the procedures of cultural materialism in *Politics and Letters* in his opening remarks concerning the aims of *The Country and the City*. First of all, he notes how in his project he wanted to get away from the theoretical project associated with Macherey and Eagleton in which 'since all literature is a mode of production employing certain conventions, what we must now do is systematise our perceptions of this fact into an overall literary theory' (Williams 1979: 304).[31] Instead, his project was 'quite different'. The emphasis of cultural materialism lay in the ways in which in 'the very process of restoring produced literature to its conditions of production reveals that conventions have social roots, that they are not simply formal devices of writing' (1979: 306). The lecture closes with some serious questions concerning the future viability of English literature as a unitary discipline, asking whether 'radically different work' can

> still be carried on under a single heading or department when there is not just diversity of approach but more serious and fundamental differences about the object of knowledge (despite overlapping of the actual material of study)? Or must there be some wider reorganisation of the received divisions of the humanities, the human sciences, into newly defined and newly collaborative arrangements?
>
> (Williams 1981b: 211)

This emphasis on the possibilities offered by such 'newly defined and newly collaborative arrangements' is taken up in Williams's next major study, *Culture*, published as the first volume in Gavin Mackenzie's *New Sociology* series in 1981.[32]

Culture

Culture is a relatively neglected work in Williams's *oeuvre*. Mainly, I think, this is due to the ways in which his usually very clear sense of an opponent is too internalised in this work.[33] Bruce Robbins, an American scholar with a long and consistent record of intelligent interest in Williams's work, provided a defensive Foreword to the second American edition, retitled *The Sociology of Culture*, where he notes its 'strange, austerely formal, somewhat unprepossessing appearance' (Williams 1992: xi). He attributes this, in part at least, to the book's desire to 'see the big picture...to rise above the usual signposts, landmarks, and boundaries by which the cultural landscape has been known' (1995: xi). What is lacking in the account (and in Robbins's too) is the small picture: any foregrounding of the fact that the book is best understood as the attempt to sketch out the contours of a new discipline, one which could replace actually existing literary studies, and based in the theory of a cultural materialism.

As such, it calls for the analysis of all forms of signification, including quite centrally the diverse forms and occasions of writing, but an analysis which is conducted at all times in terms of the means and conditions of production. As Anthony Giddens, a Cambridge sociologist who shared many of Williams's reservations about structuralism, put it in a respectful review which also made the key link to the Cambridge English debate around 'structuralism', cultural materialism:

> regards culture as a 'signifying system', but not in the abstract way charac-
> teristic of structuralist thought; for Williams emphasises strongly the need
> to analyse the ways in which signifying practices are constituted institution-
> ally, and reproduced over time.[34]
>
> (Giddens 1981b: 216)

Williams writes, in the familiar accents of the New Left arguments he had helped to develop in the 1950s, of the need for a sociology of culture which would challenge the 'general social and sociological ideas within which it has been possible to see communication, language and art as marginal and peripheral, or as at best secondary and derived social processes' (Williams 1981a: 10). Instead, and here he puts to work the more precise theoretical vocabulary he had acquired through the writing of *Marxism and Literature*, it would take as its starting point the 'constitutive' features of cultural practices, and emphasise the ways in which culture is better understood as 'the signifying system through which necessarily a social order is communicated, reproduced, experienced and explored' (1981a: 13). The new sociology of culture emphasises 'the social as well as the notational basis of sign-systems', adding 'a deliberately extended social dimension' to what would otherwise remain a textual analysis confined within the barrenness of purely formal attention (1981a: 31).

Throughout the book, Williams is wary of what we might call the tendency for premature theorisation at work in much of the available sociological inquiry. 'Theoretical constructs derived from empirical studies', he warns, 'and their extension or generalisation are always likely to presume too much, in the transition from local and specific to general concepts' (1981a: 33), and in Chapter 2, 'Institutions', he examines the relations between cultural producers and institutions and the ways these have always been historically mediated by cultural formations – 'the variable relations in which "cultural producers" have been organised or have organised themselves' (1981a: 35). In this way, he is able to present a far more nuanced view of the relations between artistic production and patronage than the usual formulae – of the artist and his public, or of economic base and cultural superstructure – allow. Chapter 3, 'Formations', similarly focuses on another problem which is usually ignored in the orthodox sociology of culture: that posed by artistic movements, cultural formations in which 'artists come together in the common pursuit of some artistic aim' (1981a: 62). While 'orthodox sociology' has found it easy to 'analyse cultural effects, where large numbers and control groups are available' as in the press, the publishing combine or the broadcasting company, the small and temporally specific groups which occur so often in the actual history of cultural production tend to slip through the wide mesh of orthodox investigation. Williams writes suggestively – but rather too schematically – of just how important such analysis can be in brief accounts of the Godwin Circle and the Bloomsbury Group (1981a: 74–7; 79–83).

The study constantly urges the need for a more narrowly focused analysis, one which attends to the specificities of textual analysis, and yet with an equal eye to the means and conditions of that textual production. The advice is good; but it is not followed through in *Culture* itself, which remains, in the true sense of the term, a theoretical study: the urging through abstract argument of the need for a historically precise and theoretically specific form of cultural analysis which accepts the full force of the idea of the primacy of cultural production. The difficulty is that *Culture* argues abstractly for a cultural materialism whose explanatory force is less embodied in abstract theory and assertion, and more in the practice of a precise contextual analysis which draws a great deal on textual evidence for its strength.

Indeed, *Culture* is best read alongside the essays in *Problems in Materialism and Culture* and *Writing in Society*, which more fully embody the theoretical insights at work in it. Far too many of the interesting and central assertions made in *Culture* remain too abstract in the primary sense of the word – too summary, too withdrawn from particular examples, and the particularity of examples – in a (negative sense of the) word, too theoretical. The interesting claim that the establishment of soliloquy as a convention in English Renaissance drama was at one and the same time a development of social practice and the discovery 'in dramatic form, of new and altered social relationships' (1981a: 142) is better made as a case in the essay 'On Dramatic Dialogue and Monologue' (1983i: 31–64); similarly, the idea that in 'French mid seventeenth-century neo-classical tragedy...the social content of the formal changes is especially clear' (1981a: 153) reads only as a bare assertion in *Culture*, while in the essay 'Form and Meaning: Hippolytus and Phèdre' (1977c: 22–30), this general point is given specific substance. So it is that while an essay such as 'The Bloomsbury Fraction' represents Williams's work at its best – theoretically sophisticated, historically nuanced, textually acute – the four or five pages in *Culture* are simply too compressed to do justice to the depth and sophistication of the arguments, and Williams's fine insight – that 'the extreme subjectivism of...the novels of Virginia Woolf belongs within the same formation as the economic interventionism of Keynes' (1981a: 81) – can only come through as an unsubstantiated claim in a somewhat tedious blur of abstract argument.[35]

All in all, the book as a whole calls in a thin theoretical way for the necessity of a thick analysis. Cultural materialism, if it were to become a professional academic discipline, would be the analysis of all forms of signification within their means and conditions of existence, with these conditions understood in terms of both their formal and socio-political context. In this way, cultural materialism promises to supersede the usual opposition between 'formalist' and 'sociological' approaches which has been so damaging to progressive analysis, the cause of such 'damaging and widespread' confusion (1981a: 138). It is only when we pause to articulate that what Williams means by that damaging and widespread confusion is virtually the whole of existing literary studies, whether orthodox literary, orthodox Marxist or orthodox theoretical, that we realise the real scope of his ambitions for cultural materialism. *Culture* is Williams's sketch for a sociology of culture which is not, but could become, 'a new major discipline' (1981a: 233).

A constitutive feature of this new discipline would be its supersession of orthodox literary studies. Williams had begun his professional career as an academic student of literature and culture with great uneasiness, torn, as we saw in Chapter One, between a Communist party orthodoxy he could not sustain in the face of the greater explanatory power of the discipline of English, and yet equally unable to accept its deliberately liberal or conservative apoliticism. Cambridge English – the local version of English studies which nourished his oppositional thinking – saw itself as an attempt at solving or at least responding critically to the pressures of modernity and the new mass society. What the ever-deepening critique of Cambridge English led him to was, as we have seen, the formation of the theory of cultural materialism.

'We begin to think where we live' was one of Williams's most striking – and most characteristic – formulations, the formulation of the very typicality he often seemed to claim for his own experience of the social and political divisions of Great Britain.[36] Certainly, with regard to the study of literature and culture, there can be no doubt that Williams lived and thought and argued in Cambridge.[37] We saw in Chapter 1 just how decisive a starting point Cambridge English was for him – it represented the 'tight place' from which he had to escape – and in the chapters which followed, just how much of his subsequent work and thinking was the product of a more or less continuous oppositional dialogue with Cambridge English, whether focused on drama, tragedy, the novel or the country house poem. As he later noted, he was involved with Cambridge English for a full two-thirds of its history.[38] Similarly, in his autobiographical essay 'My Cambridge', he notes just how important it was for him 'to work out [his] particular argument in Cambridge' (Williams 1977d: 12), and this despite – or rather precisely because of – the fact that he detested so many things about it:

after fifteen years I am intellectually more isolated from it, and from anything at all likely to happen in it, than I was when I came. The key moment, perhaps, was my rejection of literary criticism: not only as an
academic subject but as an intellectual discipline.

(1977d: 13)

'My rejection of literary criticism…But nobody quite believes I mean it', he
went on. 'I no longer believe in specialized literary studies. In fact', as he put it
in a 1977 interview, 'I don't believe, in any simple way, in the specialization of
literature' (Williams 1977b: 14). Strong and paradoxical words from someone
whose professional life had been devoted to literary criticism! And yet the
paradox was absolutely defining, determinately constitutive. *Marxism and
Literature* is the summary, in the necessarily abstract terms of theoretical
exposition, of that continued narrative of opposition. Or, as Williams put it with
his usual dry humour, the book spells out 'theoretically a position that has been
developing over a long time' (1977b: 16): over, in fact, a working lifetime. As
we shall see in the chapter which follows, it was from within the theory of
cultural materialism that Williams was able to articulate, in the last phase of his
thinking, the deep irony that Cambridge English was in the end a part of the
problem of the modernity it sought to transcend.

7   Against the new conformism 1981–7

This chapter examines the last phase of Williams's work, the writing completed after the publication of *Culture* in 1981, and before his untimely death in 1988. It left his final projects incomplete, though we are fortunate to have some of their major components. Tony Pinkney assembled most of the essays intended for the projected study, *The Politics of Modernism*, and these were published in 1989; and two of the projected three volumes of novels dealing with the history of Wales, *People of the Black Mountains*, have appeared. 1983 saw the publication of his most directly political book since the collaborative *May Day Manifesto* of 1967, the study *Towards 2000*, as well as the monograph *Cobbett*. Throughout, Williams's impressive industry produced the usual range of cultural, political and literary essays, lectures and reviews, as well as a further novel, *Loyalties*, in 1985. *Writing in Society*, a collection of literary essays appeared in 1984, and in 1989 Alan O'Connor edited the collection *Raymond Williams on Television*, largely made up of the television reviews written for *The Listener* between 1968 and 1972. Two further posthumous selections also appeared in 1989: *Resources of Hope*, edited by Robin Gable, drawing mainly on Williams's political writings; and *What I Came to Say*, selected by Francis Mulhern, and focusing primarily on literature and culture. These brought Williams's critical writings up to a total of some twenty-four volumes, the most substantial body of work in cultural politics produced by any socialist academic of his generation.[1]

What were Williams's main preoccupations in this final period? Virtually all his work in this period, though on different levels and in different ways, sought to provide a socialist response to the agenda of political and ideological issues which were largely set by the emergence and ascendancy of the New Right.[2] The phenomenon of Thatcherism provided the dominating cultural and political context. In this chapter, we shall examine the terms of the active opposition to, and critique of, what he came to call the 'New Conformism': a political mood of the moment whose cultural roots, he argued, lay in the long history of twentieth-century modernism and its appropriations. Something of this history, and its particular relation to the formation of Cambridge English, formed the focus of his retirement lectures in 1983.

Revisionary retirement

Williams took up the option of early retirement from his post as Professor of Drama at Cambridge University in the summer of 1983. He wanted to devote himself full-time to writing, though he did in fact continue to teach a few classes on practical criticism, and to give a number of seminars on modernism for the Modern Languages Faculty, and these formed the basis for *The Politics of Modernism*.[3] On 25 and 26 April he delivered two formal retirement lectures, and took the opportunity both to look back on the troubled history of Cambridge English as an intellectual and academic project, and forward to the new focus of interest for his own continuing work: the ideas and differential practices of modernism.

In the first of these, 'Cambridge English, Past and Present', Williams reviewed the history and future prospects of English studies at Cambridge in the light – or rather the pall – cast by the MacCabe Affair. 'Was there ever in fact a "Cambridge English"?' he asks. For certainly the situation of literary studies in Cambridge was just 'as tangled, as problematic and as unresolved' as it had been in 1961, on his return to Cambridge as a Lecturer in the English Faculty, though no more and no less so than it had been in his undergraduate years in the late 1930s and early 1940s. Why this tangle, why this confusion?

In Williams's view, Cambridge English was flawed from the start by the very condition of existence it so prided itself upon: its deliberate separation, as an academic discipline, from the formal study of language.[4] 'Theoretically' he urged, 'it is clear that it is in language that the decisive practices and relations which are projected as "literature", "life" and "thought" ' – the triple focus of attention in Cambridge English – 'are real and discoverable' (Williams 1983g: 188). But in its founding gesture, Cambridge English had turned away from the history of language – 'Language in history: that full field' (1983g: 189), as he put it – and the consequent possibility of treating it as something more than 'a background to be produced for annotation', in some private transaction of reading pleasure. Despite the self-regarding myths of a Tillyard or a Willey, it was because of its abandonment of the study of language as a social practice that Cambridge never did develop a fully coherent course of study around the discipline of English Literature.[5] In reality, there was never a 'Cambridge English', if by that one were to understand 'a distinctive and coherent course and method of study. The Golden Age was golden only in its beginnings, its searchings, its open and freespeaking and for some years tolerant experimentation and enquiry' (1983g: 190). 'For some years' indeed, since, as we saw in the previous chapter, the MacCabe Affair had precisely demonstrated at least the present absence of any such intellectual and academic virtues.

In the second lecture, 'Beyond Cambridge English', Williams reframes the substance of his own career as an attempt to challenge and question the assumed relations between the methods, practices and techniques which had come together as Cambridge English, and the larger cultural formation of literary modernism. He repeats and amplifies his central concern – the strange fact that 'many people still think that "language" is self-evidently a separate "subject" from "literature" ' (Williams 1983h: 213) – and reiterates his view that it would be in the matter of how the complex general problems of language 'are dealt with, in the coming years, that the success or failure of English studies, will…be decided' (1983h: 213). In line with the core arguments of *Marxism and Literature*, the social reality and effectivity of language is emphasised, a reality in which language is to be understood neither as absolutely determining system, nor as absolutely spontaneous expression, but rather as constitutive in the active and dialogical sense which Williams had learned from Vološinov. This emphasis provides the core for what was to be his challenge to the complacent self-understanding of Cambridge English, and the focus of the final phase of his writing and research: what North American critic Jonathan Arac has called his 'remarkable retrospect on modernism' (Arac 1986b: xxxviii).

Cambridge English had always assumed a defensive stance in relation to the perceived pressures of modernity, acting as the champion of figures such as Eliot and Lawrence against the dark forces of mass society and mass civilization. From the beginning of his career, Williams had argued against the anti-democratic bias which was all too evident in many of the founding arguments of the Cambridge English school and its allies.[6] In the retirement lectures, he is firmer than ever in placing the discipline of English within modernism, rather than, as it wished to be seen, outside it as a bulwark against the sinister forces of mass civilization, shoring its cultural fragments against the threatened ruin of civilization. Cambridge English was not the ground of some possible solution to the pressures of modernity: it was itself a part of the larger problem posed by the conservative response to modernity. With an insight sharpened by some thirty years of argument and analysis, he suggested there were significant connections between contemporary theory and argument and the wider structures of early twentieth-century modernism.

In a review written around the same time as the retirement lectures, Williams suggested that the 'central problem' was 'the understanding of "modernism" itself. 'Is it a general name for a group of diverse innovations and experiments in the arts?' he asked, or, 'are these innovations and experiments the specific elements of a much more general shift in social relationships, which has led to theoretical changes in a much wider field, including the theoretical positions from which "modernist art" is favourably or unfavourably interpreted?' (Williams 1983d: 439). The cultural materialist perspective – which emphasises the role of the arts in any shifts in social relationships – favoured the second option. Hence his assertion, in the second lecture, that a great deal of contemporary analytical orthodoxy is in fact derived from an unexamined structure of modernist thinking:

Formalism in literary analysis; the epistemological break that is said to distinguish Marxism; the break and innovation of psychoanalysis; the break and innovation of theoretical linguistics, from Saussure; structuralism in anthropology and sociology: these, as forms of thinking and in the cultural practice that accompanies them, compose 'modernism'.

(Williams 1983h: 220)

This should be recognised as an unusually broad definition of a much contested term, and one which moves decisively beyond its ordinary deployment in literary history.[7] Indeed, it is striking that in many ways the definition is best read as referring to the literary theory emerging in Britain through the mid to late 1970s. The definition thus encompasses and seeks to connect the work of figures in very different discursive fields across some sixty years of intellectual history, assembling a montage of the ideas of a Victor Shklovsky in 1916 with those of the school of Althusser in the 1960s, as well as placing Freud with his great interpreter Lacan, and suggesting connections between all of these and developments in and from the work of Saussure, Lévi-Strauss, Goldmann and others.[8]

For Williams, all of these – the staple constituents of Theory – compose the 'specific cultural formation' generally known as modernism. As the single most decisive aspect of this formation, Williams singles out how it 'has been at once a response to and governed by an underlying and decisive unevenness of literacy and of learning: the unevenness, specifically, of a class society, at a definite and critical stage' (1983h: 221).[9] This 'unevenness' comes through in the symptomatic emphasis on alienation and estrangement in this whole cultural formation. 'The common factor', he argues,

in the different theories and practices that are grouped together as modernism is an estrangement – a sense of both distance and novelty – which is related in its own terms to some large characterisation of the 'modern world' but is in reality the response of a disturbed and exposed formation – writers, artists and intellectuals – to conditions which were blocking their own most significant kinds of work.

(1983h: 221–2)

This estrangement, celebrated as the *ostranenie* of Russian Formalism, was never only a question of form or technique.[10] According to the theoretical and historical emphases of cultural materialism, literary explanation does not come to an end with formal observation. The fact of technique needs itself to be interpreted socially. This is the key emphasis of cultural materialism, whose methodological commitment is to examine cultural expression in terms of its means and conditions of existence. In this perspective, the 'aesthetic universality' claimed by the modernists was forged from an 'initial strangeness', the product of 'experiences of both estrangement and exposure', and, as product, marketed from a newly metropolitan civilization: 'What began in isolation and exposure ended, at many levels, in an establishment: as the decisive culture of an international capitalist world, which could trade both the original and the adapted forms' (1983h: 223). At the same time, a significant constituent of this whole cultural formation was constituted, expressed and disseminated in the activities and practices of educationalists and intellectuals, mainly based in the universities, where, as Williams argues it, a:

> new sense of the objectivity of systems, and of this objectivity as something that needed to be penetrated by new forms of analysis, taking nothing as it appeared but looking for deep forms, deep structures, with the eyes of a stranger, came through in field after field: in linguistics, in anthropology, in economics, in sociology, in aesthetics, in psychoanalysis....The whole text was to be read without date and author: this was the new and necessary discipline.
>
> (1983h: 223)

The implicit logic of Williams's whole argument is easy to follow. This discipline, this mindset, had been anticipated as an academic discipline in the 1920s and 1930s as the 'new and necessary' discipline of Richards's *Practical Criticism* (1929). It re-emerged in the 1950s and 1960s as the structuralism of Saussure, and became influential in the work of figures such as Lévi-Strauss, Goldmann, Todorov and Lacan.[11] In the post-1968 period this mutated into the new and necessary discipline of the postmodern in the work of writers such as Lyotard and Baudrillard. For Williams, there is a significant continuity of position running through all of these, and it is that stance he is concerned to identify.

With an unusual rhetorical colouring, he turns to look back on this whole development 'in turn, with the eyes of a stranger':

> What I then see is not only what they have achieved but their own deep forms. I can feel the bracing cold of their inherent distances and impersonalities and yet have to go on saying that they are indeed ice-cold. I see, practically and theoretically, the estranging consequences of the general assumption – as active in modernist literature as in theoretical linguistics and structuralist Marxism – that the systems of human signs are generated within the systems themselves and that to think otherwise is a humanist error.
>
> (1983h: 223)

Just the humanist error which had been the target of so many critical positions since the 1960s, ranging in idiom from Lacan's insistence that 'a signifier represents the subject for another signifier', across Althusser's stirring call, in the sharp tones of a structuralist Marxism, for a revival of 'Marx's theoretical anti-humanism' (Althusser 1965: 229), to Foucault's enigmatic wager 'that man would be erased, like a face drawn in sand at the edge of the sea' (Foucault

1966: 387), as well as many other claims of the 'death of the subject' by Barthes, Deleuze, Derrida and others.[12] What most concerned Williams was – as we shall see below – the terms of its local manifestation in the debates around the 'classic realist text' in both film and fiction. He found these arguments, based as they were in a broadly Althusserian theory of ideology, to be theoretically compromised and historically incorrect. Ironically, the arguments of the *avant garde* theorists of the cultural left shared too many basic assumptions with the New Conformism. We shall first examine how Williams saw these basic assumptions in *Towards 2000*, and then examine how these came through, though in different guise, in the arguments around ideas of modernism and the 'classic realist text' in the work of some of Williams's Cambridge colleagues and broad political allies.[13]

Towards 2000

The 'estranging consequences' of the bourgeois modernist worldview are taken up as the central thrust of Williams's arguments in his most specifically political essay since the collaborative *May Day Manifesto*, the book-length study, *Towards 2000*, published in 1983. Thatcherism, and the debates on the left which it provoked, provide the essential context for understanding the book's central arguments and address.

Thatcherism and, more importantly, Thatcherism apparently triumphant. Margaret Thatcher had rather surprisingly defeated Edward Heath in the leadership contest of 1975, two years after his administration had been brought down in the 1973 general election. Heath's failure was generally attributed to his inability to deal forcefully enough with the miners' strike of 1972. The indomitable Maggie – the 'Iron Lady' – went on to win three successive election victories in 1979, 1983 and 1987. As had been promised, the period saw a significant redistribution of wealth, largely through selective income tax cuts and the increase in VAT, from the poor to the rich; a massive and unparalleled increase in unemployment and in bankruptcies in the manufacturing sector; a partial dismantling of the welfare state; increased political centralisation; a significant erosion of trade union rights; and – to contain the protests, riots and disruptions provoked by these aggressive policies – an equally significant strengthening and militarisation of the police force.[14] 'To those who had, much was given': Hugo Young's summary encapsulates much of the agenda and achievements of Thatcher's administrations (Young 1989: 502).

Thatcherism was the object of some major analysis and rethinking on the left, and the occasion for not a little immediate despair. The jingoism and jubilation following Britain's victory in Falklands War of June–July 1982 marked perhaps the nadir of leftwing feeling, summed up in Tom Nairn's desperate cry that the lesson of the Falklands War was to show that the 'real England is irredeemably Tory' (Nairn 1983: 288). Similarly, in a series of provocative articles, Stuart Hall brought the arguments and insights of the Birmingham Studies Cultural Centre into play, emphasising the strength and force of Thatcherism as an ideology and, above all, as an ideology that had found something the left was missing: 'a powerful means of translating economic doctrine into the language of experience, moral imperative and common sense' (Hall 1983: 28).[15] Thatcherism enjoyed hegemony because it had created an almost unassailable 'authoritarian populism'. While many were swayed by Hall's arguments, others were more cautious and refused to lend Thatcherism the kind of internal coherence apparently granted to it in Hall's analysis. Bob Jessop and others preferred to stress the internal contradictions of Thatcherism, and urged that it 'must be seen less as a monolithic monstrosity and more as an alliance of disparate forces around a self-contradictory programme' (Jessop *et al.* 1984: 34).[16]

Throughout this entire period, Williams maintained a sturdy sense of his own political identity, holding to the continued force and relevance of socialist ideas. In 1983, just four weeks before the general election, Williams had argued against the easy conclusion that if Thatcher were to win, this would show 'that the majority of the British people can be defined as Thatcherite in conscious-ness' (Williams 1983e: 163), and warned of a danger on the left of acquiescing to 'an interpretation which, as it were, would blame the majority of the British people for not accepting a socialist analysis' (1983e: 164).[17] Later, in 1986, he lamented what he saw as too defeatist a tendency on the left, asking with some anger and disdain whether it was 'only an accident that one form of the theory of ideology produced that block diagnosis of Thatcherism which taught despair and political disarmament in a social situation which was always more diverse, more volatile and more temporary? Is there never to be an end to petit-bourgeois theorists making long-term adjustments to short-term situations?' (Williams 1986c: 175). In July 1987, in one of his final interviews, when asked whether he felt 'disillusioned' by the rise of the Right and Thatcher's recent election victory (her third), his reply was characteristic: 'Disillusionment, not at all; disappointment, of course': it was clearer than ever 'that the socialist analysis is the correct one' (Williams 1987c: 315). Williams's political writing – but not only his political writing – set out to combat and challenge that block diagnosis and the sense of despair which fed it.

Against Stuart Hall's idea of an 'authoritarian populism', Williams set the idea of Thatcher's 'constitutional authoritarianism', preferring to focus attention on the actual mechanisms and contradictions of state democracy than on ideological explanation. In a striking essay on the TV coverage of the Falklands War, he stressed the ways in which the reporting raised questions crucial to the 'culture of contemporary democracy', and what was happening to it in Thatcher's administration. What was evident was 'the unique modern combination of a Cabinet with absolute sovereign power, acting within a complex of parliamentary parties, opinion polls and television'. This combina-tion represented 'a new political form, latent for many years but now at least temporarily made actual' (Williams 1982: 42). Its name was constitutional authoritarianism, and it needed to be thought as an expression of that larger 'culture of distance' which Williams associated with Thatcherism, but also more broadly with the New Conformism which underlay Thatcherism, that 'latent culture of alienation, within which men and women are reduced to models, figures and the quick cry in the throat' (1982: 43).

Similarly, in an essay 'Mining the Meaning', written for the *London Review of Books* during the bitter, prolonged and ultimately failed miners' strike of 1984–5, he put out a challenge to the key words of Thatcherite economic 'common sense'. The destructive catchwords of management, economic and law and order, he argued, work to conceal 'the real operations of a new and reckless stage of capitalism' (Williams 1985c: 127). Against the new 'common ground' proposed by Thatcher and her ideologues, Williams argued that the miners' struggles 'outlined a new form of the general interest' (1985c: 127), one which could challenge 'the logic of a new nomad capitalism' (1985c: 124), and its confident belief that 'all the redundant people and discarded communities can continue to be politically marginalized or, if they act on their own behalf to be controlled by centralized communications (the political argument, as in this strike, taking place not in Parliament but on radio and television) and [accepting here some of Hall's arguments] by new forms of policing' (1985c: 127).[18]

In other essays and speeches – many delivered for the Socialist Society, at whose inaugural meeting Williams spoke in 1981, or written for its fortnightly political magazine, *New Socialist* – he addressed the issues of nuclear disarmament, ecology, and the need for labour party reform and called for a thorough reassessment and redefinition of socialist goals and strategies. All of this came together with the publication in 1983 of Williams's most extended piece of socialist analysis and advocacy, *Towards 2000*. Never was Williams more active as a socialist thinker than in this last decade of his life.

What is striking, argues Williams, in the book's central insight, is the ways in which the 'innovative forms' of modernist representation – which were originally composed to challenge 'the fixed forms of an earlier period of bourgeois society' – have themselves become 'stabilised as the most reductive versions of human existence in the whole of human history':

> The originally precarious and often desperate images – typically of fragmentation, loss of identity, loss of the very grounds of human communication – have been transferred from the dynamic compositions of artists who had been, in majority, literally exiles, having little or no common ground with the societies in which they were stranded, to become, at an effective surface, a 'modernist' and 'post-modernist' establishment.
>
> (Williams 1983a: 141)

These new forms have now become 'a widely distributed "popular" culture that is meant to confirm both its own and the world's destructive inevitablities' (1983a: 142) as if every active citizen was no more than a Vladimir or an Estragon, a Hamm or a Klov.[19]

Although *Towards 2000* is concerned with the local struggle against Thatcherism in Britain, it also seeks to address that struggle in the global context of late capitalism. In a controversial move, Williams takes as his starting point the final section of *The Long Revolution* (1961), the prescient analysis 'Britain in the 1960s', which is reprinted in full as the first chapter of the new book.[20] In a 1965 note, Williams had already admitted, under the pressure of criticisms from historian Asa Briggs, that the original framework of the essay suffered from too nationalistic a focus.[21] In *Towards 2000*, the terms of the nationalist focus are themselves examined alongside the orthodox forms of international analysis.

The book as a whole is concerned with the fixed terms of 'normal' political analysis of late modernity. He contrasts public with private projections of the future, and questions the supposedly 'objective' projections which are used as the basis for current party-based political thinking. In fact, argues Williams, the political manifesto, based as it is on the rhythms of the electoral process, is too short-term in focus to deal with social and political phenomena which are only susceptible to proper analysis and adjustment in a much larger time-scale. Such a time-scale has more in common with our private thinking where, for example, the:

> relatively ungraspable date of 2050...is within the normal lifespan of my grandchildren, and all the more traditional ways of thinking about the future would certainly include this kind of natural human foresight and concern. The apparently more practical urgencies which foreshorten calculation, for temporary advantage, are in this respect as in others more damaging to the most basic human order.
>
> (1983a: 16)

Williams notes how modernism has favoured the 'systematic dystopia' (*1984, Animal Farm, Brave New World*) as a form, and how these works commonly suggest that 'the very attempt to achieve a systematic utopia leads straight to a systematic dystopia'. They imply 'a complacent projection of actual and historically instituted social orders as permanently necessary and exclusive', and it is this implication which 'most deeply discourages those who see very clearly that their own social order is in crisis'. Against this, Williams calls for a renewal of positive utopian thinking, one which offers 'an imaginative reminder of the nature of historical change: that major social orders do rise and fall, and that new social orders do succeed them'. Such a reminder is a necessary part of the formation of any socialist discourse which wishes to offer a projection of the future contrary to the prevailing negative and modernist versions.

Indeed, a large part of the book is devoted to a critique of just these prevailing versions, which Williams associates with modernism. Deploying the particular kinds of linguistic, historical and ideological analysis of language which are essential components of his cultural materialism, it is argued that there is an ideological unity to the basic prevailing attitude towards the world, a distinctively modernist frame of thinking and analysis: 'The dominant version' he writes:

> has been a basic orientation to the world as raw material. What has been steadily learned and imposed is a way of seeing the world not as life forms and land forms, in an intricate interdependance, but as a range of opportunites for their profitable exploitation.
>
> (1983a: 261)

Against this, we need to assert the 'principle of a society sustained by its economy has to replace the practice of a society determined by a market' (1983a: 97). The argument, in other words, turns partly on the force of representation as a systematic 'way of seeing' which provides or enforces 'a basic orientation to the world as raw material'.[22] As such, this same way of seeing is active both in modernism and in our contemporary understandings of modernism, though with one significant difference. As Williams was to argue in his final essays, the orthodox interpretations of modernist practice itself tended to select just one strand of the ideology of modernism and so repeat and enforce it, the strand of 'bourgeois dissidence' which he had first criticised in relation to Orwell, and which he renamed, in his final essays, the New Conformism.[23]

New Conformisms

Tony Pinkney has collected most of the essays which Williams had intended for publication, adding some cognate supplementary material, together with a lengthy editorial introduction, and this was published in 1989 as *The Politics of Modernism: Against the New Conformists*.[24] Many readers found the collection somewhat unsatisfactory. Prendergast wrote of 'an uncomfortably strained quality in much of the writing' (1995b: 196), while Loren Kruger described it as 'thought-provoking but sometimes sketchy' (1991: 144). Chris Baldick, in a review for the *Times Literary Supplement*, found Williams's division of interest between 'the original modernist formation itself and an academically processed version of it' highly problematic, and suggested that the first 'is not carried through to substantial detail, while the second suffers from a characteristic reluctance to name or even adequately describe the position polemically assailed' (Baldick 1989: 1205). In the account which follows, I seek to describe a little more fully the positions under attack and to show why, for Williams, there was no division of interest between the original modernist formation and the later academic histories of it. First, though, it is necessary to examine some of Pinkney's framing of this final phase of work.

In a substantial introduction to the selection – 'Modernism and Cultural Theory' – Pinkney sets up a fascinating intellectual, political and historical context through which to frame and read the final essays. These same arguments are taken up, extended and amplified in a related essay, also published in 1989, 'Raymond Williams and the "Two Faces of Modernism" ', and together these form the basis for a later monograph on the novels.[25] In his introduction, Pinkney distinguishes between the '"official" line' which Williams takes in his final essays, and what he claims as an equally important but implicit 'sub-text' to the book. This sub-text 'runs the case rather differently', and consequently there are 'two almost incompatible views of Modernism and the avant-garde' at work in *The Politics of Modernism*. The second, concedes Pinkney, only comes through only 'as trope rather than argument' (Pinkney 1989a: 26). As trope indeed: for there are several moments at which he has to twist the evidence to fit his case that 'it was Expressionism that aesthetically formed Williams' (1989a: 25).

Thus, in support of his assertion that Williams must have known about Brecht in the late 1930s, he quotes him as saying that 'there were ways of knowing about [Brecht's] work, if distant and specialized ones' (Williams 1979: 215–16, cited in Pinkney 1989a: 26), but neglects to mention Williams's own admission of his own 'lack of awareness' of Brecht's work in this period, or his defensive remark that such ignorance concerning Brecht was 'very common at the time'. 'It was only in the mid and late fifties that most of us got to know Brecht', he states (Williams 1979: 215–16), in direct contradiction with Pinkney's view. Similarly, Pinkney writes that Williams 'adds the name of German Expressionism' (1983b: 19) to the modernist litany, and quotes Williams as saying that 'in the late thirties admiration for *Dr Caligari* or *Metropolis* was virtually a condition of entry to the Socialist Club at Cambridge' (Williams 1979: 232). The only problem is, that read in context, this is a wry remark, the phrase 'condition of entry', heavily ironic. For far from demonstrating an admiration for German Expressionism, Williams is actually engaged in distancing himself from it. His own stated admiration – in complete accord with the arguments of *The Politics of Modernism* – is for the 'early Soviet cinema', which had always seemed to him to be 'the major work that took up the original naturalist project' (1979: 232). He praises Eisenstein's work against that of the German Expressionists, and German Expressionist cinema is identified as the forerunner of the mistakes and excesses of avant-garde cinema. 'In the sixties', he says:

> there was a development of incredibly complex seeing, but of nothing very much. The complexity became a fetishized concentration on the point of view at the expense of what was viewed. This cinema could genuinely be described as formalist in the sense that it was preoccupied with problems of the medium without any adequate relation between its methods and the kind of content these were supposed to interpret.
>
> (Williams 1979: 232)

Nothing could be clearer: the quotation which Pinkney picks as evidence for Williams's interest in and support for German Expressionism comes in reality from a context of argument which is critical of expressionism as an avatar of the arid formalism of the 1960s. *Pace* Pinkney, Williams is criticising – not endorsing – the German Expressionist experiment.

In arguing for the 'sub-text' of *The Politics of Modernism*, Pinkney over-states his case, and can only support it by bending the available evidence to fit his preconceptions. Indeed, the larger case compounds the problems discussed in Chapter 2, apropos of Pinkney's discussion of Williams on drama. There is a repeated overestimation of the impact and appeal of Expressionism, and a tendency to substitute his reading of the dynamics of modernism for Williams's own which leads to a certain blurring or misalignment in explana-tory focus, as well as a substantial neglect of the political context which Williams was always addressing, however indirectly. Pinkney is much more correct – though in contradiction with some of his own assumptions – when he writes that Williams had, from the beginning, 'major reservations' about Brecht's work, and particularly what Williams called its 'enthronement of the critical spectator' (cited in Pinkney 1983b: 20): this issue will be discussed further below.

The reason for the overestimation doubtless lies in Pinkney's desire to overturn the usual idea of Williams as an 'English Lukács'. He chooses Lukács's expressionist opponent Ernst Bloch as an alternative figure of comparison (Pinkney 1989b: 28–31).[26] In both cases, Williams/Lukács, Williams/Bloch, it would be a mistake to try and turn what works as a partially illuminating comparison into any theoretically substantial case. Williams's own formation was very different from either that of Lukács or Bloch, notwithstanding Pinkney's attempt at making common ground in expressionist modernism. The simple fact was that Williams's main formative influence was Cambridge English, which can be understood, and as Williams grew to understand it, as itself a modernist cultural formation rather than an objective analytic response to the pressures of a perceived mass modernism.[27]

Rather than seeking the 'sub-text' of *The Politics of Modernism*, let us examine the ways in which the book continues the argument against the 'new critical structuralism' which had begun in *Marxism and Literature*, and which was now continued, under the new pressures of Thatcherism, as an argument against the 'New Conformism'. This dimension of address – Williams *contra* Thatcher – lies outside the scope of Pinkney's fascinating but in the end academicist and anachronistic analysis. Writing against the New Conformism meant writing against the new right-wing forces represented in the Thatcher regime of 1979–90, and anticipated in the period in opposition which the Conservative Party spent from Edward Heath's defeat as Prime Minister in 1974 until the election of Margaret Thatcher in 1979. This also meant arguing against those modes of analysis in literary theory which leant unwitting support to the conceptions of the self, individual or subject which Thatcherism drew upon for its representation of an acquisitive and asocial world. That these modes of analysis could be found in theoretical work intended for the left only made these criticisms the more urgent.

The sovereign individual

The 'New Conservatism' which became known as 'Thatcherism' set out by defining itself against the 'social-conscience Conservatism' which had dominated the British Conservative Party since Labour's victory in 1945 (Riddell 1985: 2). Sir Keith Joseph was the first to articulate its main directions as something of a conversion experience. In April 1974 he realised that though he had believed himself a true Conservative for some twenty years, he had been mistaken: only now could he see what true Conservatism really was (Young 1989: 79). In a series of speeches and articles, Joseph argued that the Conservative Party had betrayed itself by granting too much to the imaginary 'middle-ground' of the postwar consensus on the centrality of welfare state policies. This 'middle-ground' was unstable, with a built-in drift leftwards 'dictated by extremists of the left' claimed Joseph (Joseph 1976: 21). The party needed to identify and occupy a new and distinctively conservative 'common ground' if they wished to re-establish the real principles of conservatism. As a part of this, think-tank ideologues Norman Strauss and John Hoskyns prepared a strategic plan for Joseph in the autumn of 1977, one whose main component was a direct challenge to trade union power. Though the report was never published, and had no immediate effect on policy, it did articulate for the first time the 'subterranean impulses of hard-right Conservatism' which slowly made their way into the Thatcherite agenda (Young: 115).

A new common ground: new, or perhaps at least distinctive, in the fervour and forthrightness with which socialism was excluded from any rightful part or participation in the social whole. 'The choice facing the nation is between two totally different ways of life' urged Thatcher on the eve of the 1983 election. 'And what a prize we have to fight for: no less than the chance to banish from our land the dark, divisive clouds of Marxist socialism.' On another occasion: 'I have always regarded part of my job as – and please do not think of it in an arrogant way – killing socialism in Britain'; and again: 'Britain and socialism are not the same thing, and as long as I have health and strength they never will be' (cited in Hayes 1994: 98). Another way of putting this, which came through in a notorious moment in an interview with *Woman's Own* magazine in October 1987, was more brutal and much more contentious: 'there is no such thing as society. There are individual men and women, and there are families' (cited in Hayes 1994: 89).

This remark was the cause of much immediate controversy, and provided a useful way in to the full implications of Thatcher's free-market ideal of the non-society. 'To say there is no society but only individuals is fundamentally an amoral position', thundered Ralf Dahrendorf. 'It's the philosophy of social darwinism' (Dahrendorf 1988: 197).[28] As Mark Hayes has emphasised, what this meant in practice:

> was that certain groups were deprived of full citizenship by material depri-
> vation: social security claimants, the unemployed, the sick, the disabled, the

homeless and many pensioners began to constitute a new alienated under-
class....Under Thatcher citizenship status very much depended upon one's
position in the market – a citizen had no tangible value independent of the
market order.

(Hayes 1994: 91–2)

The linchpin of this asocial social philosophy was a conception of the individual which placed a particular emphasis on the subject's moral capacity, or
rather, on an unusual definition of just what moral capacity was. As Thatcher
herself put it, 'a moral being is one who exercises his own judgement in choice.
In so far as a citizen's right and duty to choose is taken away by the state, the
party, or the union, his moral faculties atrophy and he becomes a moral cripple'
(Thatcher 1977: 108). Seen in a positive light, Thatcher's moral code simply
insisted 'on treating people as rational and responsible rather than as candidates
for special favours' (Minogue 1988: 141). But as Minogue also emphasises, this
soon shades into 'the repudiation of collective guilt' around the issue of
pursuing profit above all else (Minogue 1988: 125). From there, it was easy to
see Thatcherites as 'supremely selfish to the exclusion of all other concerns'
(Letwin 1992: 18–19). Kenneth Baker summed up this aspect of Thatcher's
moral vision nicely in April 1988: 'Tories did not need to apologise for the
increased scope to what might be called acquisitive individualism' (cited in
Young 1989: 526).

'Acquisitive individualism': the phrase could be Williams's, though uttered in
an angry rather than complacent tone. This definition of the human subject as
essentially an acquisitive individual, with this acquisitiveness somehow the
necessary property of a moral subject, was central to the 'new conformism' of
Thatcher's 'counter-revolution' (Williams 1986c: 172). As one defender of
Thatcherism put it, the 'Thatcherite conception of the individual is the most
important and at the same time the least understood element of Thatcherism'
(Letwin 1992: 32). For Williams at least, it was best understood as one line of
descent from a particular branch of bourgeois dissidence. Many of the
arguments of these post-modernists of the New Right rested on a certain
conception of the subject as the 'sovereign individual':

The politics of the New Right, with its version of libertarianism in a dissolution or deregulation of all bonds and all national and cultural formations
in the interests of what is represented as the ideal open market and the truly
open society, look very familiar in retrospect. For the sovereign individual is
offered as the dominant political and cultural form, even in a world more
evidently controlled by concentrated economics and military power.

(Williams 1988a: 62)

What was curious was that the conservative promotion of the 'sovereign
individual' should share some common ground with the idea of the 'critical
spectator' deployed in some leftist literary and cultural criticism. The 'sovereign

individual' was essentially asocial, its definition of freedom an illusion. The 'critical spectator' occupied – or would like to occupy – a place impossibly outside social determination – as Williams had argued *vis-à-vis* Eagleton's critical commentary: the 'basic fault' was to assume that 'by an act of intellectual abstraction you could place yourself above the lived contradictions both of the society and of any individual you choose to analyse, and that you yourself are not in question' (Williams 1977b: 12). Common to both was the denial of the precisely constituted social materiality of the human subject, an aspect which the rationalist (or irrationalist) critique of the knowing subject failed to grasp.[29]

Some of the main components of Williams's arguments against this New Conformism came together in the Guardian Film Lecture he gave on 21 July 1985. Here he took up one of the main themes of *Towards 2000*, arguing that the 'celebration of possibility is the most profound need' (Williams 1985a: 129). In the lecture, Williams dwells on the overdeterminations of the idea of cinema as a 'popular' medium of entertainment. At best, he says, this classification is 'double-edged': it celebrates the possibilities for working-class culture that some early theorists and practitioners saw in cinema as a popular medium, but this celebration all too often ignores the ways in which cinematic narration presents a swerve away from any genuinely radical solutions to common problems. For a key element in film melodrama:

> is that after many twists and turns, and seemingly hopeless situations, the poor victim is saved and the poor hero or heroine lives happily ever after. There is no problem in understanding why these resolutions were popular. But there is a problem, in trying to relate these often magical or coincidental lucky escapes of individuals to anything that could be called, in the easy slide from 'popular', a genuinely radical or socialist consciousness.
>
> (1985a: 111)

Similarly, Williams argues that the common claim that film 'was inherently open, as against the relatively closed forms of other media' (1985a: 111) needs careful examination, especially when this assertion settles into 'the now conventional rejections of what are called "naturalism" and "classical realism" ' (1985a: 111). These are 'muddled and muddling concepts' he warns, and goes on to reiterate some of the objections to the 'contemporary radical rejections of Naturalism' that he had first made, pointedly enough, at a *Screen* summer school in 1976. 'Naturalism' he reminds us:

> has close historical associations with socialism. As a movement and as a method it was concerned to show that people are inseparable from their real social and physical environments. As against idealist versions of human experience, in which people act under providence...naturalism insisted that actions are always specifically contextual and material.
>
> (1985a: 113)

It is therefore a 'a bitter irony' that in the terms of contemporary debate on film, 'Naturalism came to be understood as the very thing it had challenged: mere reproduction' (1985a: 114). 'In our kind of time', he warns, 'the dissident bourgeois is not necessarily a radical, though that is often the self-presentation' (1985a: 114).[30] In discussion after the lecture, he had harsher words still for those who falsely claimed the terrain of the popular:

> All I would say is that those whom with some deliberateness I called enemy artists – I don't just seem them as different, I see them as enemy – endlessly harp on the failure of relationships, the dislocation of communities, the defeat of noble efforts, the end of idealism. This really is the only thing with which they can defend this social order: not that it's good, but that it's inevitable...And because of that there is what I called a bourgeois dissident form of art which shows all this with great power.[31]

It was this 'deliberateness', and the anger which Williams's use of the word contained, which powered these final essays on modernism, and their repeated attacks on the broad formation which he named and understood as the New Conformism.

The critical spectator

A central component of the orthodox version of modernism which Williams wished to challenge came through as an academic argument about modernism, one which had focused particularly on the idea of language. A part of the reticence to name his opponents, commented on many times by critics, and mentioned in particular relation to *The Politics of Modernism*, might be read as the necessary delicacy – or unworthy indirection – of political solidarity: Williams was at times criticising his allies here. More generously, and I think more correctly in this case, it can be seen as the refusal to entirely associate intellectual positions with the fullness and complexity of individual identity. Williams had an unusually equal respect for both the specificity of theoretical argument, with its sometimes too easy talk of 'positions', and the specific agency and historicity of any embodied human subject. The case of Orwell – so critical and yet so respectful – need only be recalled.[32] The work of at least two of Williams's Cambridge colleagues and allies – Stephen Heath and Colin MacCabe – was at issue with regard to the arguments of *The Politics of Modernism*.[33] I shall focus in particular on the arguments put forward by Colin MacCabe, as these exemplifed some of the trends criticised by Williams, and particularly what he came to call the 'enthronement of the critical spectator' (Williams 1977a: 216).

As we saw in the previous chapter, Williams had supported and defended MacCabe through the violent Cambridge dispute over the question of his tenure in the English Faculty. But, within that general support, there were a few critical and theoretical reservations. In particular, as he had put it in his 1981 lecture on the affair, there were still 'radical differences' between his own position and the 'reliance on structural linguistics and psychoanalysis' which characterised the work of his Cambridge fellows, though he had put it to them 'that a fully historical semiotics would be very much the same thing as cultural materialism' (Williams 1981b: 210). We can take MacCabe's arguments in the 1970s – culminating in his controversial study *James Joyce and the Revolution of the Word* (1979) – as points where these 'radical differences' come through in the elaboration of what has come to be known as 'British poststructuralism'.[34]

MacCabe's arguments – in common with what has become generally known as the 'Screen-theory' – assumed a broadly Brechtian stance on the politics of culture, arguing the critique of realism as an urgent necessity.[35] His seminal essay, 'Realism and the Cinema: Notes on Some Brechtian Theses', takes its focus from Brecht's remark that realism 'is an issue not only for literature: it is a major political, philosophical and practical issue and must be handled and explained as such – as a matter of general human interest' (cited in MacCabe 1974: 34). Brecht's original arguments on this matter were sharpened by the application of a powerful new theoretical vocabulary, drawn from Althusser's work on ideology, and the theories and arguments concerning the subject's relation to language to be found in Freud and Lacan. These came together in a focus on the idea of the 'classic realist text', and the political necessity of mounting a formal challenge to it. In some sense, the 'classic realist text' threatened to freeze its reader into a stance of ideological complicity as unchallengeable as that ascribed to the subject in Althusser's theory of ideology. Challenging it therefore offered a way out of the functionalism inherent to Althusser's theory and the political impotence associated with it. In cinema, this meant adopting a critical stance towards apparently progressive films such as *Klute* or *Days of Hope* on the grounds that 'the classic realist text cannot deal with the real as contradictory' (1974: 39), and endorsing the more avant-garde work of film-makers like the Straub-Huillet team and Jean-Luc Godard which seemed to offer 'the possibility of articulating contradiction' (1974: 50).[36] To 'change the position of the subject within ideology' (1974: 53) was the task of cultural practice and therefore of any progressive film-making and film criticism. In literature, the critique of classic realism and the liberating potential of contradiction could be found at work in the classic modernism of James Joyce.

For MacCabe, Joyce's work gave an unparalleled 'primacy to the material of language' and in so doing offered 'a different experience and...different political consequences, from the classic realist text' (MacCabe 1979: 133). In a powerful and persuasive argument, he charted Joyce's increasing challenge to realism across *Dubliners, Stephen Hero* and *A Portrait of the Artist as a Young Man,* and through to its culminating point in *Finnegans Wake.* In this text, he concludes, the 'acceptance of movement and process, coupled with the awareness of identity as a constant effect of the passage of language, has profound political implications for a society based on the notion of the individual as an independent and self-sufficient entity. It is only by the acceptance of the most reductive account of the relation between politics and literature that Joyce's texts can be dismissed as non-political' (1979: 152). These 'political implications' are primarily the result of Joyce's deconstruction of the ideological implications of a classic realism. 'Instead of a traditional organisation of discourses which confer an imaginary unity on the reader' he argues:

> there is a disruption of any such position of unity. The reader is trans-
> formed into a set of contradictory discourses, engaged in the investigation
> of his or her own symbolic construction. What is subverted in the writing is
> the full Cartesian subject and this subversion is a political event of central
> importance.
>
> (1979: 152–3)

This position – and the work with which it was associated – was powerful, stimulating and controversial and helped to launch a whole wave of similar studies which, predictably enough, found something of the same challenge to classic realism and its liberal humanist subject in an increasing variety of writers, forms and periods.[37] In an interesting autobiographical sketch, MacCabe later noted how he and others of the 'radical semioticians' had been strongly influenced by the French interpretation of modernism as a form of 'writing which disrupted the stability of meaning and identity' (MacCabe 1985: 8). At the very least, the work of theorists such as Derrida, Barthes and the *Tel Quel* group on writers such as Mallarmé, Bataille and Artaud 'broke with the sterility of Leavis's restriction of modernism to Lawrence and Eliot' (1985: 8). Yet MacCabe also acknowledged, with the benefit of hindsight, the ways in which the 'political weight' he and others gave to their arguments 'was deeply problematic' (1985: 8).

MacCabe's own retrospective judgement in 1985, if not prompted by Williams's arguments, would certainly have been shared by him. In *The Politics of Modernism* Williams repeatedly criticises any literary-historical interpretation which would reduce the complex historicity of actual modernist works and the question of their address to the status of mere evidence for the truth of the theories of a self-proclaimed contemporary avant-garde in literary theory. It was surely no accident that Williams chose the Strathclyde conference of 1986, 'The Linguistics of Writing', organised by Colin MacCabe, Derek Attridge, Alan Durant and Nigel Fabb, and with guests including Jacques Derrida and Gayatri Spivak, as the moment to argue this point very fully.[38]

Williams begins the lecture combatively with two quotations from August Strindberg's Naturalist manifesto, the Preface to *Lady Julie*. Strindberg writes of his characters in terms reminiscent, for Williams, of current post-structuralist dogma: they are 'conglomerations from past and present stages of civilization; they are excerpts from books and newspapers, scraps of humanity, pieces torn from festive garments which have become rags – just as the soul itself is a piece of patchwork' (cited in Williams 1986a: 65). His point in doing so, and the polemical focus of his essay as a whole, is to act as 'a challenge to certain tendencies in applied linguistics, and to forms of literary analysis seemingly derived from them, which have appropriated a selective version of Modernism, and within this an internal and self-proving definition of the avant-garde, as a way of ratifying their own much narrower positions and procedures' (1986a: 65). The first consequence of this appropriation is a fundamental distortion of the actual history of modernist and avant-garde movements: 'We can still not say,' he argues, 'of either supposed movement, that what we find in them is some specific and identifiable position about language, or about writing, of the kind offered by subsequent theoretical or pseudo-historical propositions' (1986a: 66). He finds no evidence to support the idea that there is in modernism 'a common rejection of the representational character of language and hence of writing' and insists that 'we shall misunderstand and betray a century of remarkable experiments if we go on trying to flatten them to contemporary theoretical and quasi-theoretical points' (1986a: 66).

All of Williams's suspicions regarding the idea of the 'classic realist text', the critique of representation, the explanatory value of psychoanalysis and the utility of any attempt to conjoin it with Marxism come through in the harsh tones of this reference to 'contemporary theoretical and quasi-theoretical points'.[39] Against any such appropriation, he returns to the 1920s debates around Russian Formalism which had become increasingly central to his own arguments.[40]

Shklovsky's slogan, the 'resurrection of the word', has often, argues Williams, been taken by contemporary theorists as the core definition of literary Modernism. In this appropriation, it is read in relation to Saussure's deconstruction of the sign, and used as the basis for an argument in favour of the non-referentiality of language. Against this, Williams points to Eichenbaum's account of his participation in the movement (Eichenbaum 1926). For him, 'the basic slogan uniting the initial group was the emancipation of the word from the shackles of the philosophical and religious tendencies with which the Symbolists were possessed' (cited in Williams 1986a: 67). In its historical context, Shklovsky's emphasis is best understood as a rejection of the religious and idealist elements of the Russian Symbolist movement, that is, as 'a secularisation, a demystification, of the "poetic word" of the Symbolists' (1986a: 68).

In fact, there were two broad attitudes towards language to be found in the diversity of modernist writing. The first is that which 'treats language as material in a social process' and the second, that which 'sees it as blocking or making difficulties for authentic consciousness' (1986a: 77). For Williams, Breton's surrealism is a major manifestation of the second tendency, as can be seen by its preoccupation with and promotion of 'automatic writing'. Here, language is:

simultaneously identified with the blocking of 'true consciousness' and, to the extent that it could emancipate itself from its imprisoning everyday forms and, beyond that, from the received forms of 'literature', as itself the medium of the idealized 'pure consciousness'.

(1986a: 73)

But what is absent from this kind of account is any recognition of the real sociality of language. This absence comes through particularly strongly in the case of Artaud, where 'the purpose of writing (as we have since often heard) is not communication but illumination'; a contrast, which Williams wryly notes 'seems necessarily to modify the second term to self-illumination' (1986a: 71).[41] What this can then lead to, and what in practice it did lead to, is 'an emphasis – which indeed became a culture – on the experience itself, rather than on any of the forms of embodying or communicating it' (1986a: 71).

Against Surrealism, Williams poses the forces of social rather than subjective Expressionism, and its emphasis on the cry.[42] While surrealism sought to transcend contradictions, he argues, social expressionism confronted them, even to the point of 'raising them to a principle of form' (1986a: 74). In this form, the individual cry may carry a social charge, and even become, as in the dramas of a Toller or a Brecht, 'a slogan, a fixed form, to shout as a means of collective action' (1986a: 75).

He then returns to the crucial case of Russian Formalism, which, 'as it came through into an influential tendency in literary theory, was a disastrous narrowing of the very facts to which it pointed' (1986a: 75). The formalist arguments were taken to imply the rejection of any notions of 'content', 'representation' and 'intention'; but this interpretation misses out entirely the great contribution of Vološinov, whose argument regarding the 'multiaccentual' nature of the sign. What the theorists all too often forgot was their own conditions of practice, the existence of their own intentions in what Williams calls 'a characteristic error':

> Under the spell of their own selected examples, of valued but highly specific uses, they forgot that every act of composition in writing, indeed every utterance, at once moves into specific processes which are no longer in that way open: which indeed, as acts, even in the most seemingly bizarre cases, necessarily have 'content' and 'intention' and which may, in any many thousands of ways, even in these terms 'represent'.

(1986a: 76)

And this was the case even in such an extreme example as that of Hugo Ball's famous reading of Gadji Beri Bimba, where, as Williams illuminatingly remarks, the 'relapse to the rhythms of the mass in the middle of an outraging Dadaist spectacle is not only funny; it is, like the sudden locating appearance of Zanzibar, a reminder of how deeply constituted, socially, language always is, even when the decision has been made to abandon its identifiable semantic freight' (1986a: 68–9).[43]

Though each of the two positions is historically located in the period we know as modernism, the first, with its emphasis on language as material in a social process is, for Williams, 'modernist in both theory and practice', while the second, though modernist in practice, needs to be understood 'in its underlying theory' as 'intransigent idealism' (1986a: 77). In conclusion, he summarises:

> what we have really to investigate is not some single position of language in the avant-garde or language in Modernism. On the contrary, we need to identify a range of distinct and in many cases actually opposed formations, as these have materialized in language...Formal analysis can contribute to this, but only if it is firmly grounded in formational analysis.
>
> (1986a: 79)

This is the formational analysis which brings history together with theory in cultural materialism.

Williams was deeply suspicious of a view of literary history in which texts from the past somehow confirm the theoretical paradigms of the present. In the first instance, he challenged the all too easy periodisation and unitary description of modernism, and from that, what he saw as a dangerous formulation of the present as the postmodern. So, while in the talk 'Metropolitan Perceptions and the Emergence of Modernism', he accepts the general idea that 'the metropolis of the second half of the nineteenth century and of the first half of the twentieth century moved into a quite new cultural dimension' (Williams 1985b: 44), and that this did indeed result in some common themes and forms, he nonetheless closes his argument by challenging the consequent 'metropolitan interpretation of its own processes as universals' (1985b: 47). This was the burden of his lecture on 17 March 1987 at Bristol University, 'When was Modernism?', when he warned against 'a highly selected version of the modern which then offers to appropriate the whole of modernity' (Williams 1987a: 33), and again, with some warmth, repeated in the W.D. Thomas Memorial lecture, 'Country and City in the Modern Novel', on 26 May 1987, where he urges 'we must not make the mistake of supposing that the contemporary is really the universal, but lately discovered' (Williams 1987b: 4). Modernism, he warns:

> not so much in practice but as a set of ideas, really does reduce all past experience in this way: the contemporary becomes the universal, even the eternal. A genuinely modern consciousness, on the other hand begins by recognising that its very modernity is historical, that is to say, that it is a product of specific and discoverable social and historical changes.
>
> (1987b: 4–5)

The case was pursued with renewed vigour in two essays published in 1988. In 'The Politics of the Avant-Garde' and 'Theatre as a Political Forum', both written for the collection *Visions and Blueprints* (Timms and Collier 1988), he further develops his case for the necessity of a more historically differentiated view of the avant-garde.

In the first essay, Williams argues that differentiations between modernist and avant-garde artists are best achieved through a formational rather than an individual analysis. He then distinguishes between modernists and the avant-garde in the following terms: 'Modernism had proposed a new kind of art for a new kind of social and perceptual world. The avant-garde, aggressive from the beginning, saw itself as a breakthrough to the future' (1988a: 51), that is, these belong to the third phase of the modernist movement as a whole. In the first phase, innovative groups of artists 'sought to protect their practices within the growing dominance of the art market and against the indifference of the formal academies' (1988a: 50) and in a second moment, these groups shifted to 'the defence of a particular kind of art became first the self-management of a new kind of art and then, crucially, an attack in the name of this art on a whole social and cultural order' (1988a: 51). It is only in this third phase that the term avant-garde can properly be used.

Though both groups might call for revolution, the substance of that call could be very different. For sure, the 'Futurist call to destroy "tradition" overlaps with socialist calls to destroy the whole existing social order', but Williams finds a 'decisive difference' between 'appeals to the tradition of reason and the new celebration of creativity which finds many of its sources in the irrational, in the newly valued unconscious, and in the fragments of dreams' (1988a: 52). Hostility to the bourgeois order could similarly develop in two directions: the conservative, with its claim that the artist was the only true aristocrat, and the consequent rejection of both the unwashed masses and the bourgeoisie; and the radical, in which the artist affiliated himself or herself directly with the people or the workers against the bourgeoisie and the aristocrats (1988a: 55). In the end, he suggests, many modernists are best seen and understood as 'bourgeois dissidents' only, and one way of recognising them as such lies in the emphasis they give to the idea of the 'sovereign individual'. The real inheritors of this 'bourgeois dissidence' are the postmodernists of Thatcherism and the New Right.

In 'Theatre as a Political Forum', Williams further substantiates his case, and in the process offers a significant correction to his own early views on twentieth-century drama.[44] Where Yeats and particularly Eliot had figured large, with the promise that their poetic drama apparently held for a work of Total Expression, they are confined, with Paul Claudel, to a telling parenthesis at the end of this essay as examples 'of an avant-garde as an arrière-garde' (Williams 1988b: 94). He insists above all, in this telling piece of cultural materialist analysis, on the necessity for understanding the theoretical claims of any avant-garde in relation to their historical circumstances. This is particularly important in the case of something like the avant-garde, a movement whose rhetoric characteristically insists 'even the immediate past', and is especially so when

> the rhetoric of the avant-garde, characteristically rejecting even the immediate past, has survived into what appears to be scholarly and critical discussion, with deeply negative effects not only on the work of the earlier period but, more to the present point, on the understanding of the complex character of avant-garde theatre itself and especially its relation to politics.
>
> (1988b: 83)

As a first and necessary move, the work of the avant-garde in theatre must be located in relation to what it so stridently rejected in its origins, and whose rejection has become almost meaningless in repetition: the broad movement known as Naturalism. It was from within this movement (which he traces back to the emergence of bourgeois drama in eighteenth-century England) that the first phase of the modernist revolt began, in the work of figures such as Ibsen and Strindberg. In their work, a division between the deep conventions of naturalism and the surface of what by then had become the mere naturalist habit is effected. The 'furious denunciation' which this deep naturalism produced represents, argues Williams, 'a direct continuity from Modernist Naturalism to the work and the reception of the avant-garde' (1988c: 85).

And yet, he continues, the common rejection of naturalism has worked to conceal 'the only important question: that of the alternative directions in which a continuing bourgeois dissidence might go' (1988c: 86). The example of German Expressionism shows some of the main differences between 'social' and 'subjective' Expressionism. Here the case of Brecht is central, passing as he does from the subjective Expressionism of the early plays, through to the social Expressionism of the *Lehrstücke*, the teaching plays, in which there was a 'direct interaction of avant-garde theatre with a militant working-class movement which has found the appropriate cultural institutions' (1988c: 90). This moment was cut short by the brutality of the Nazi regime; and Brecht moved ahead to what he became most known by – the theatre of estrangement, and its emphasis on 'complex seeing'. Against the apolitical Brecht of mainstream commentary, Williams argues for the insights yielded by the cultural materialist method:

> To abstract the specific methods, or the theoretical phrases attached to them, as determining forms without reference to their very specific and limiting social situations, is to confirm the actual development of the avant-garde, culturally and politically, towards a new aestheticism.
>
> (1988c: 91)

In this cultural politics, which he associated both with the critique of the classic realist text and the arguments underlying Thatcherism, the 'fragmented ego in a fragmented world has survived as a dominant structure of feeling' (1988b: 93).

The main consequence of this 'is to render all activity and speech as illusory and to value theatre, in its frankly illusory character, as the privileged bearer of this universal truth' (1988b: 93). Taken in this direction, as Williams feared was the direction of contemporary theory as well as some contemporary theatre and writing, the avant-garde becomes an arrière-garde, and the provocative images of the avant-garde settle into the conventional representations of a powerful new conformism.

Conclusion

Williams did not to live to write the concluding essay of the book, 'Against the New Conformists', or to fully decide on the contents of the book as a whole. But it is clear enough that the new conformism only repeated the main tenets of the old conformism that Williams had spent his life refuting. Both expressed a counsel of despair and subjugation that needed to be challenged and rejected whether it was expressed in the claims of monetarist economic theory or structuralist Marxism. As we have seen, a substantial amount of Williams's writing in these final years was devoted to the critique of the New Right and the need to develop strategies on the left to meet the challenge of Thatcherism and its key conception of the 'sovereign individual'. At least an equal amount of energy and force was spent in developing a critique of its strange mirror image: the critical spectator.

For Williams, contemporary theory had internalised the most passive images of human subjectivity available in the modernist repertoire: trapped and frozen in place like characters in *Endgame*, ideologically defined as the mere bearer of economically determined social relations, contemporary theory, as Williams understood, threatened to produce a subject whose idea of liberation was reduced to the politics of textuality. While these New Conformists might claim to wield the cutting edge of structuralist or post-structuralist theory, and to give authentic voice to the rigours of postmodernity, their claims needed to be read against the longer history in which they participate but would prefer to forget; their theoretical assumptions to be checked against the findings of a broader intellectual analysis.[45]

Conclusion

Ten years after his death, memories of Raymond Williams fade and the particular tone and force of his voice – positive yet sceptical, querying yet assertive – grows ever more difficult to recall. What becomes of the body of work and writing that remains behind, now no longer animated by that voice and presence? As a conclusion to this study, I take issue with some of the more negative representations of Williams and his work as these have appeared in the past decade. My contention is that some of the ways we have been choosing to remember Williams threaten to have the paradoxical effect of forgetting the substance, value and explanatory power of his intellectual and academic project.

In the decade since his death, some of the real limitations of his work have begun to come into focus, and the cases where he was wrong – specifically wrong – are, by now, reasonably well known. His overestimation of Eliot's poetic drama proved spectacularly incorrect, while the concept of Total Expression which it mobilised was undoubtedly the strongest manifestation of literary critical idealism to be found in his work (see Chapter 2). His sketch of the nineteenth-century culture and society tradition, and, more importantly, the notion of tradition on which it was based, have long been questioned and criticised (Kermode 1959; Kiernan 1959; Thompson 1961; Hall 1980). And despite the desire to unite literary with historical scholarship – epitomised in *The Country and the City* – his particular readings often failed to achieve the accuracy necessary to fully historical explanation (Barrell and Bull 1973; Barrell 1980; Simpson 1987; Samuel 1989; de Bolla 1995). Meanwhile, his identification and restriction of literary studies and literary theory to what was known and practiced as Cambridge English seems parochial in the extreme, and damaging to the pretensions of his critical project (Gorak 1988; Williams 1979: 337). These and other such observations appear to put in question the continued relevance of his work for students of literature.

Similarly, with regard to specific questions of theory, it is easy now to see various faults, failings, errors and misunderstandings. The central notion of a 'structure of feeling' amounts to little more than an ingenious instance of theoretical impressionism, in which a rhetorical figure tries to assume the explanatory force of a distinctly articulated theoretical concept (see Chapters 2 and 5 of the present study). Williams's take on Marxism fails to pay enough attention to the basic concepts of class or state, and fundamentally ignores the economic dimension, and the determining position given to it in Marx's mature theory (Kiernan 1959; Kettle 1961; Eagleton 1976b, 1989b; Williams 1979). His interest in so-called 'historical semantics' is amateurish, and seems to be ignorant of the basic professional protocols of this area of study, while his reading of Saussure's fundamental work appears merely tendentious (Burchfield 1976; Skinner 1988; Moriarty 1995). His idea of psychoanalytic theory – which casually conflates the very different paradigms of Freud and Jung – are too rooted in the 1940s to meet the challenge of the Lacanian rereading of Freud and its subsequent deployment in the fields of literary and cultural studies in the 1970s (Higgins 1990, 1995). Despite the claims of his later work, Williams signally fails to engage directly enough with the work of his structuralist and post-structuralist antagonists, while his positive notions of identity, social rootedness and community owe too much to, and are ultimately compromised by, their own roots in conservative thought (Johnson 1979; Mulhern 1984). Throughout, he appears to be constitutively blind to the politics of race and gender, and the dynamics of imperialism.[1]

Such critical points are undoubtedly a necessary corrective to what one reviewer referred to as the host of 'essentially fan club books' which appeared immediately after Williams's death (Johnson 1990: 6).[2] But we must be careful not to press the scales too far down on the other side. Just as with any scholar, Williams is open to correction, and a part of the internal dynamism of academic scholarship lies in the necessary correction and elaboration of given views and assertions. What ultimately counts in this process may be less the initial correctness of someone's views, than the directions their work gives to future research. In this sense, there is no doubt that, despite any particular errors of fact or interpretation, Williams's work opened up new dimensions and directions for research. To take only work on the late eighteenth century, contemporary scholars such as John Barrell, David Simpson, Peter de Bolla and Alan Liu all record debts of substance to Williams, even as they criticise particular errors in his work.[3] In this sense, Williams's work in literary studies clearly remains a resource for contemporary scholarship.

With regard to questions of theory, the matter is more complex, and it is often difficult to distinguish stance from substance. Before judging Williams's theoretical contribution, perhaps we need first to acknowledge that the field of theoretical debate is an essentially antagonistic one, one in which unresolved questions clash, and that the most strident calls for consensus on some point often betray the inner anxieties of dogma. In this regard, we should certainly be sceptical of any criticisms of Williams that take the form of unargued assertions, or simply take differences in vocabulary for failings in a presumed theoretical correctness. This was a danger already evident in some of the first valedictory accounts, and in representations and assessments of Williams's work which followed.

At least by implication, Cornel West's characterisation of Williams as 'the last of the great European male revolutionary socialist intellectuals' (1989: ix) suggests that the moment of the relevance of his work has ended; and this is put much more forthrightly in the memorial editorial of the British journal *New Formations*, which argued that though Williams's work 'constituted a sustained critique of the content of the Arnold–Mill–Leavis tradition', it 'retained from it a paradigm of the form of culture which made him reluctant to question the integrity of identity as such'. Against Williams, the editors set Stuart Hall's 'vision of a radical pluralism', and suggested that Homi Bhaba's 'account of an agonistic political fluidity' is 'certainly more fragmented and, if you like, more "post-modern" than Raymond Williams's Enlightenment ideal of a common culture' (New Formations 1988: 2–3). And this representation of Williams's work as outdated, outmoded and superseded by more recent theory was taken up and extended in a number of subsequent accounts. For Dennis Dworkin, 'though [Williams] has been dead for only five [sic] years, he is already part of a different political age' (1993: 54); while he and his co-editor Roman remark, in the introduction to their fine collection of essays on Williams, *Views Beyond the Border Country*, how many of their contributors 'remain critical of his failure to employ psychoanalysis, deconstruction, and other avant-garde approaches to theorise the relationship between colonial and post-colonial formations' (Dworkin and Roman 1993b: 13).[4]

It is not surprising, given the negative emphasis of these representations of Williams's work, that even those who wished to lay claim to at least a portion of his intellectual legacy have felt inclined to do so only in a particularly guarded and defensive manner. For the whole dynamic is one in which Williams is remembered in such a way that his work seems better off forgotten. This comes through most strongly and most critically in and around the various ideas and definitions of cultural materialism in current circulation.

Cultural materialism is surely the key to the understanding and assessment of Williams's intellectual legacy, so that it is a serious matter when those who wish to lay claim to cultural materialism also feel it necessary to assert their theoretical distance from it. Scott Wilson, for instance, in his study *Cultural Materialism: Theory and Practice*, goes so far as to distinguish between his conception of cultural materialism and a 'mainstream' form associated with Williams's work. Williams is credited with devising 'the *term* "cultural materialism" ' (my emphasis), but Wilson wishes to revise its conceptual content by drawing on 'the general economic theories of George Bataille' and 'the work of Lacan and Derrida' (Wilson 1995: xi). Similarly, Jonathan Dollimore describes 'cultural materialism' as a '*term*...borrowed from its use by Raymond Williams' (my emphasis again), and goes on to mark his own reworking of it to refer to a more 'eclectic body of work', one which includes 'the convergence of history, sociology and English in cultural studies, some of the major developments in feminism, as well as continental Marxist-structural and post-structuralist theory, especially that of Althusser, Macherey, Gramsci and Foucault' (Dollimore 1985: 2–3).

What such revisions – for this is what they are – clearly demonstrate is a sense that Williams's work, and its terms of argument and analysis, are increasingly distant and unfashionable. There is a consequent need to translate its unfamiliar vocabulary into something more closely resembling our own: the aim is to familiarise an increasingly different mode of thinking and analysis. These familiarising pressures are apparent in the very language used to characterise and represent some of Williams's arguments and opinions. To remark on his 'reluctance' to 'question the integrity of identity as such', or to speak of his 'failure to employ psychoanalysis, deconstruction, and other avant-garde approaches' threatens to blind the reader to the fact that Williams had arguments on and around these issues, arguments against the 'eclectic body of work' associated with Lacan, Derrida, Althusser and Macherey. Representing cultural materialism in this way threatens to distort the force of it in Williams's thinking, and reiterates the lesson: if we take the trouble to remember Williams, it should only be to remind us just how safely we can forget him.

The dangers in such procedures are evident. By reading and reducing Williams's cultural materialism to a term, a signifier without a consistent signified content, its force as a concept is displaced and ultimately lost. I believe it is now necessary to get beyond this stage of assessment and the representations it embodies, and in which it appears to be enough – at least in some cases – to register differences of theoretical jargon, or field of focus, as the grounds for the dismissal of Williams's work. For the claims made – or at least implicitly present – in many of these accounts run the risk of refusing the basic rule of historical interpretation: that an author's thought needs to be understood within its means and conditions of production, if commentary on it is not to fall into mere anachronism. Any claims that our own theoretical vocabulary is indeed superior to Williams's clearly needs to be tested in practice, rather than simply assumed as a starting point.

Any real assessment of the force of Williams's work needs to be historical as well as theoretical. It needs to attend to the terms of the conceptual vocabularies available to him, a sense of their limits, as well as a sense of what use and difference he made of and to them, before seeking to describe the limitations of Williams's thinking. The analysis of his work can best be made in terms of its cultural, conceptual and political means and conditions of production, in line with the theory (or at least Williams's theory) of cultural materialism. At least as far as Williams was concerned, the 'term' cultural materialism was intended to have a clearly defined conceptual content, and, indeed, one which would put it at odds with the 'Marxist-structural and post-structuralist theory' of the accounts of Dollimore and Wilson.[5] This content can in fact best be described in terms of the two dimensions of oppositional address which it sought to articulate: the opposition to both 'official English culture', and to 'orthodox Marxism'.

As we have seen in the course of this study, cultural materialism is the deliberate product of Williams's opposition to 'official English culture' as it came through to him as the discipline and discourse of English studies. Cambridge English, as he knew and understood it, served primarily an aesthetic and evaluative function: its principal aim, through that lingeringly close textual analysis known as 'practical criticism', was to judge and discriminate the quality and sincerity of an author's thought with the ultimate aim of promoting discrimination, maturity and sincerity among the reading public as a whole, as well as encouraging these virtues in writers themselves, as the necessary constituents of the good society.

Williams's break from this – the founding discourse of Cambridge English – took the form of two equally decisive moves. First, there was the rejection of the opposition between 'high' and 'low' culture, an opposition which founded the cultural authority of literary criticism in its precisely calibrated distance from mass culture. This was the achievement embodied in the great works of the late 1950s, *Culture and Society* and *The Long Revolution*, and summed up in the seminal essay 'Culture is Ordinary' (Williams 1958b). With these, Williams helped to make the shift from 'literary' to 'cultural' studies, that is, away from the study of a high cultural literary canon and towards the investigation and analysis of signifying practices in general, and including forms such as film, television and advertising, as well as questions of social, political and cultural identification.

Secondly, and within literary studies themselves, Willams helped to shift the discipline away from the aesthetic and evaluative function which had been its raison-d'être since the 1920s, and to map out a new set of tasks and coordinates for the critic. This meant the bringing together of the three dimensions of textual, historical and theoretical analysis into the distinctive practice of cultural materialist investigation. In this new paradigm of study, a text is read formally, in terms of the play of its generic and internal construction; it is located historically, both in terms of its means and conditions of original production, and also in relation to the history of its readings; and it is read theoretically, in terms of whatever questions can be productively put to it. Such were the lessons evident in the great revisionary studies *Modern Tragedy* and *The Country and the City*, in the shorter works *Orwell* and *Cobbett*, as well as in essays such as 'The Bloomsbury Fraction'.

At the same time, the concept (and not the term) cultural materialism is equally the product of Williams's deliberate opposition to orthodox Marxist thinking, both on cultural and ideological theory in general, and on literature in particular. From his critical take on the Zoschenko affair through to his final formulations of Marx and culture, Williams consistently rejected dogmatic formulations of Marxist theory and argued the need for far more flexible and historical accounts, attuned to the specific limits and potentials of human agency. Cultural materialism challenged both the reductive content of the dominant accounts of literary and cultural history in writers such as Caudwell and Fox, Plekhanov and Engels, as well as the structures of economistic and functionalist thinking which informed them. To suggest, as one critic has recently done, that the whole base and superstructure argument amounts to no more than 'a spectacular red herring' (Simpson 1995b: 35) is perhaps best read as a tribute to the almost complete success Williams's arguments have enjoyed in this regard.

And at the very least, cultural materialism has reanimated discussion concerning the central question of agency, both with regard to Marxism, as well as to other competing accounts of social reproduction. Williams argued throughout his work against any interpretation of Marxism in which the human agent is represented only as a passive and servile subject, whether the argument was presented in the form of the 'mechanical materialism' which he knew from the 1930s debates, and in which 'the arts are passively dependent on social reality' (Williams 1958a: 274), or whether it appeared in its 1970s guise, as that 'fashionable form of Marxism' – the more sophisticated Althusserian argument – 'which makes the whole people, including the whole working class, mere carriers of the structures of a corrupt ideology' (Williams 1976b: 241).

Similarly, Williams differs significantly from one strand of thinking in structuralist and post-structuralist theory. In this profoundly textualist emphasis, the language-system appears to be seen as entirely constitutive of human subjectivity, a nightmarish view apparent – at least at times – in the writings of a wide range of thinkers from Adorno and Althusser, through to Foucault and Derrida. Against this, Williams was scrupulous in assigning a fully dialectical function to language, as a system which at one and the same time enables even as it tends to determine the possibility for the production of human thought and subjectivity. For Williams, the self or subject is never simply an effect of language, as it sometimes appears to be in the more extravagant versions of structuralist and post-structuralist positions.[6] Language does not simply determine self-consciousness; it also enables it.

To recognize these – the actual arguments of cultural materialism – as the central arguments in Williams's work is to represent it in a way that its real achievements become visible. But to read him in this way – to read him historically – is to read against the grain of some of the current representations of his work. The implication of this is that to read historically may work to challenge rather than confirm our own positions and opinions: perhaps the hardest lesson that can be drawn from Williams's work as a whole. For this is the sceptical and deconstructive lesson that our conceptual vocabularies are never quite as stable as we would like them to be, and that to imagine otherwise is to blind ourselves to the sheer historical density of language, and the social and political conflicts figured within it.[7]

One way of figuring the overall nature of Williams's achievements is to consider it the particular force which he lends to the idea of literacy. The enduring force of Williams's writing surely comes from that articulation of the personal and the political, the academic and the activist, which characterised its particular address and integrity, apparent in works such as *The Country and the City*. Here the study of literature is put to work, yet without ever becoming purely instrumental, in a personal and political interpretation. This active interpretation presents us with a powerful refocusing of literacy as above all a critical literacy. While primary literacy develops the basic skills of reading and writing, critical literacy is a secondary literacy, which brings into play particular forms of analysis and interpretation which treat all texts as representations, and not presentations, of the world.[8]

Literacy is a term which comes into focus in the final phase of Williams's work. Looking back over the essays collected in *Writing in Society*, he describes them as examining 'the changing relationships...between writers and assumed or intended readers, in conditions that developed from uneven or partial literacy to a more general literacy in which there were persistent inequalities in access to writing and reading' (Williams 1984a: 5); and again, in one of his retirement lectures, he noted that while it is often said that 'there are more than six centuries of English literature', it is less often remarked that 'there are less than two centuries of English literacy' (1984a: 212); while in 1987 he emphasises that 'the struggle for literacy was as real a social struggle as any struggle for subsistence or food or shelter' (Williams 1987d: 154). His final recorded interview was focused on the 'politics of literacy' (Williams 1987e).

Yet a concern with literacy, in the particularly powerful sense with which Williams invested it, had been there from the start. In *Reading and Criticism*, he had urged the need for a 'mature reading' which would be the 'extension of literacy in the fullest sense' (1950: 21). What was this 'fullest sense'? One thing it wasn't was the literacy offered by orthodox literary criticism. In *Culture and Society*, Williams criticised the ways in which even the valuable work of an I.A. Richards embodied 'a kind of servility to the literary establishment' (Williams 1958a: 251). Despite the fact that Richards, with the publication of *Practical Criticism*, 'did more than anyone else to penetrate the complacency of literary academicism', he remained in thrall to the idol of 'Aesthetic Man', 'alone in a hostile environment, receiving and organizing his experience' (1958a: 251–2). His central idea of 'literature as a training ground for life' was 'servile' (1958a: 252). 'Servile' is the key word of the rejection of orthodox literary criticism, and points to the development of the sense of a critical literacy. It sums up that sense of subjection to class norms of aesthetic judgement which was a disabling component of traditional conceptions of literature, and worked as a major impediment to the proper understanding of the dynamics of cultural process.

The point was forcefully made in *Politics and Letters*, where Williams summed up one of the main arguments of *Marxism and Literature* as the realization that the 'categories of literature and of criticism were so deeply compromised that they had to be challenged *in toto*' (Williams 1979: 326). Criticism, and the highly trained skills of literacy which went with it, had come to be understood as a 'detached process' so that the process of judgement was 'something which occurs above any specific instances or situations' (1979: 335). 'I had this training very hard', he acknowledges:

and what you were told to do was to forget yourself, to forget your situation, to be in a naked relation – but with your training, of course – to the text; while the text itself was similarly taken out of all its conditions and circumstances. My whole encounter with literary criticism really revolved around this pseudo-impersonal attempt to judge works without any sense of the presence of the individual making judgement.

(1979: 335)

Williams's resistance to this 'servile' textualism provides the strongest thread of continuity across his work as a whole, linking early works such as *Reading and Criticism* and *Culture and Society* with the 'Cambridge English' studies such as *Modern Tragedy* and *The Country and the City*, and connecting these in turn with the theoretical expositions of cultural materialism, *Marxism and Literature* and *Culture*. Literacy, in cultural materialist terms, was a means to cultural empowerment and political emancipation, uniting the connections between education and politics. This active literacy was at the very centre of his vision of the role of education in the 'long revolution', that third (after the industrial and democratic revolutions), and 'most difficult' to interpret (Williams 1961a: 11). All education participates in the reproduction of social consciousness; but, potentially at least, it can give some of the intellectual tools for challenging existing social consciousness. This was, I think, the main lesson Williams drew from his formative experience in adult education, and comes through in the suggestive comments he made, looking back over the history of adult education in 1983. 'The true position', he writes, was:

> that the impulse to Adult Education was not only a matter of remedying deficit, making up for inadequate educational resources in the wider society, nor only a case of meeting the new needs of the society, though those things contributed. The deepest impulse was the desire to make learning a part of the process of social change itself.
>
> (Williams 1983f: 158)

And, as he concluded, the 'building of social consciousness is of real consciousness, of real understanding of the world' (1983f: 166). There is no better description of the force of Williams's work as a whole than this active and critical literacy.

Again, some recognition of the importance of this to Williams comes through in the very different context of a lecture given to the Classical Association in 1984, where he emphasised the social and political importance of a 'high literacy':

> It is high literacy...which calls the bluff of authority, since it is a condition of all its practical work that it questions sources, closely examines offered authenticities, reads contextually and comparatively, identifies conventions to determine meanings.
>
> (Williams 1984d: 55)

Training in all of these related skills of critical literacy help to form 'habits of mind which are all against, or should be all against, any and every pronunciation of a singular or assembled authority' (1984d: 55). To be sceptical of, and questioning towards, 'any and every pronunciation of a singular or assembled authority': a difficult task indeed, but one certainly embodied by the fiercely oppositional and independent turn of Williams's own critical intelligence.

One certainty is that Williams's own work, and the reading and representation of it, now belongs to an ongoing conflictual history in which we all still participate. 'He could be wrong, as anyone can be wrong, in specific cases, but it is [the] nature and foundation of his thinking which remains relevant' (Williams 1983b: 76). This was Williams's judgement on the work of William Cobbett. Ten years after his death, I believe it can serve as the starting point for future assessments of Williams's own work, as well as the conclusion to this one.

Notes

Introduction

1 See, for example, *The Independent*, 28 January (Terry Eagleton and Frank Kermode); *The Guardian*, 29 January (Frances Mulhern); *The Morning Star*, 4 February (Tony Benn); *The Listener*, 4 February (Anthony Barnett); *Times Higher Educational Supplement*, 5 February (Fred Inglis); *The New Statesman*, 5 February (Stuart Hall); *The Nation*, 5 March (Edward W. Said and Edward P. Thompson). Channel Four television broadcast a special tribute to Williams on 28 February. Warwick University also organised a memorial conference on 30 April: for a brief account, see Lovell (1989). The British journal *News from Nowhere* devoted a special issue to Williams: *Raymond Williams: Third Generation* in February 1989, as did the US journal *Social Text* in 1992. See also Blackburn (1988) and Eagleton (1988). Patrick Parrinder's remark is drawn from his 'Diary' (Parrinder 1988), and Juliet Mitchell's from the report on the National Film Theatre forum 'Raymond Williams – Towards 2000' (30 June 1989) in Higgins (1989). I borrow and adapt a few paragraphs from that essay in this introduction.

2 The interviews with the *New Left Review*, conducted in 1977 and 1978, and published as *Politics and Letters* in 1979, remain an extraordinarily useful, detailed and stimulating account of Williams's life. They can now be supplemented, and at times corrected, by Inglis (1995), though this study is marred by a marked degree of ambivalence, and even hostility, towards Williams and his work (see Raphael Samuel's important review (Samuel 1996) for some warnings in this regard). Alan O'Connor's thin study (1989) provides an outstanding bibliography of Williams's writing, and of criticism on Williams, though one in need by now of some extension.

3 For a scrupulously detailed account of this period of Williams's life, as well as an outstanding selection of work from this period, see McIlroy and Westwood (1993).

4 See E.P. Thompson (1961): 'His work is very important indeed, and...so far as we can speak of a New Left – he is our best man' (p. 24). See also Perry Anderson's repeated praise of Williams: *Culture and Society* and *The Long Revolution* are said to 'undoubtedly represent the major contribution to socialist thought in England since the war' (1965: 11); and, above all, in his seminal essay, 'Components of the National Culture' (Anderson 1969).

5 Or so Williams tells the story (Williams 1977d). Inglis (1995: 176) contests this view, but gives no sources for his disagreement.

6 See my report on Said's memorial speech in Higgins (1989: 83–4); Said (1990); and, more generally, Said (1994).

7 This initial phase of public mourning was followed by a surge of critical interest in Williams, as the first attempts were made to get his work as a whole into focus. See Gorak (1988); O'Connor (1989); Tredell (1990); and, the best of these mono-

graphs, Milner (1993). These were followed by Eldridge and Eldridge (1994) and Inglis (1995). Various aspects of Williams's work were examined separately in volumes of essays edited by Eagleton (1989c), Dworkin and Roman (1993), and Prendergast (1995a).

8 For Williams as a novelist, see Davey (1989); Robbins (1990); Pinkney (1991); Di Michele (1993); discussions of Williams's own plays are to be found in Gorak (1988: 32–9), and Sharrat (1989: 136–49). Accounts of Williams's political identity are to be found in Eagleton (1976b); Barnett (1976); Hirschop (1989); Blackburn (1989) and Brenkman (1995). For Williams on the mass media, see Williams (1962a) and (1974a), and the lengthy interview in Williams (1986e). Accounts of this work can be found in Eldridge and Eldridge (1994: 98–110); Hitchcock (1995); and, for general discussion, see Lusted (1989).

9 See, for instance, the memorial editorial 'Identities' in *New Formations* 5 (Summer 1988), as well as Cornel West's statement, 'Raymond Williams was the last of the great European male revolutionary socialist intellectuals born before the end of the age of Europe (1492–1945)' (West 1989: ix). More explicitly, D.L. Dworkin's remark that 'though he has been dead for only the last five [sic] years, he is already part of a different political age' (Dworkin 1993: 54). I examine the implications of the *New Formations* editorial in Higgins (1995). Prendergast (1995b) makes a careful interrogation of the implications of West's statement. I examine Dworkin's comment – and the whole issue of Williams's relevance to us today – in the conclusion.

1 The tight place

1 Most commentators follow Eagleton's assessment of this early period as probationary, and pass over it without serious consideration. Ward (1981) makes no mention of these early works, beginning his analysis only with *Culture and Society*. For Gorak, the early work is 'programmatic…[it] reflects Cambridge training and Cambridge tastes' (1988: 19). O'Connor (1989) similarly focuses on the post-*Culture and Society* works. Recent exceptions to this blindness are Pinkney (1989a, 1989b) (these accounts are discussed in Chapters 2 and 4); McIlroy (1993a, 1993b); and Eldridge and Eldridge (1994), where there is brief discussion of the early works on drama (1994: 115–21).

2 See Eagleton (1976a, 1976b). My references are to (1976b). Eagleton's relations to Williams's work have a long and complex history, and really need attention as an item of discussion in their own right. Eagleton himself later writes of the 'brisk impatience of relative youth' (Eagleton 1989a: 4) which had characterised his 1976 assessment; but, at the same time, he reaffirms the central drift of his criticisms in Eagleton (1989b). See also Eagleton (1984: 108–15).

3 Notably Kiernan (1959) and Thompson (1961) in their respective review essays. I examine their views in some detail in Chapter 4.

4 The words are uttered by the hunter, Ulfheim, to the artist Professor Rubek in Act III of the play. A more recent translation renders them as 'No, nothing seems difficult at first; but then you come to a tight corner where you can't go forward or back. And there you stick – "tree'd", we sportsmen call it' (Ibsen 1974: 286).

5 See Annan (1955) for a description of the closely-knit society of 'Oxbridge'. For his particular response to Williams, see Annan (1991), where his work is described as 'rhetorical, evasive and vacuous' in tones heavily marked by class condescension (1991: 360).

6 Other 1950s 'scholarship boys' included Kingsley Amis, Donald Davie, John Wain and Richard Hoggart. It is interesting to distinguish Williams amongst these. The usual casual identification made between Williams's and Hoggart's respective projects, seen as the founding moments of British Cultural Studies, stands in need of

some serious questioning. See, for instance, the debate in adult education between Hoggart and Williams (Hoggart (1948) and Williams (1948), now easily available in McIlroy and Westwood (1993: 136–45)); Williams's review of *The Uses of Literacy* (Williams (1957b); also in McIlroy and Westwood (1993: 106–10)); and the later discussion between them (Willams and Hoggart 1960; McIlroy and Westwood 1993: 111–20). See also Williams (1957c) where he explicitly criticises Hoggart's separation of politics from family life: 'Hoggart is wrong, however, in supposing that these are to be set on one side of a line [family values, neighbourhood, etc.], while on the other is set the wider social product – the Labour movement – which he describes as the work of a minority. Of course only a minority is really active, politically but we must not be confused by bourgeois ideas of the nature of a minority. There, a minority is thought of as isolated, self-defensive, opposed to the majority's values' (1957c: 31).

7   See, in particular, Williams (1977d): 'There was little personal difficulty or dislike, but the formation was easy to hate – and I have to record that I responded aggressively. The myth of the working-class boy arriving in Cambridge...is that he is an awkward misfit and has to learn new manners. It may depend on where you come from. Out of rural Wales it didn't feel like that. The class which dominated Cambridge is given to describing itself as well-mannered, polite, sensitive. It continually contrasts itself favourably with the rougher and coarser others.... If I then say that what I found was an extraordinarily coarse, pushing, name-ridden group, I shall be told that I am showing class-feeling, class-envy, class-resentment. That I showed class-feeling is not in any doubt. All I would insist on is that nobody fortunate enough to grow up in a good home, in a genuinely well-mannered and sensitive community, could for a moment envy these loud, competitive and deprived people' (1977d: 5–6). Inglis gives an excellent and well-researched account of Williams's schooldays in his *Raymond Williams*, especially pp. 38–69.

8   Gorak bends the evidence a little in order to argue his case that Williams's entire intellectual identity was grounded in his own profound alienation. He writes, for instance, of how '[Williams's] working-class status in an emphatically middle-class university marginalised him still further' (Gorak 1988: 10). But, as O'Connor usefully points out, the Socialist Club 'claimed 1,000 members in 1939, or almost 20 per cent of the university membership' (O'Connor 1989: 7). Pinkney also stresses the 'intensely Modernist political sub-culture around the university Socialist Club' available to Williams (Pinkney 1989a: 8). For details of the very active social life of young communists in the 1950s, see Samuel (1986a, 1986b), and for Williams's own recollections of the period, see Williams (1979: 39–54, 1977d).

9   See *Cambridge University Socialist Club Bulletin* 6 March 1940 and Vol. 4 No. 4 Tuesday 5 November 1940, p. 2.

10 Lionel Elvin was a Fellow of Trinity Hall 1930–44. See McIlroy and Westwood (1993: 24) for useful biographical notes. E.M.W. Tillyard, along with Mansfield Forbes and I.A. Richards, was one of the trio of new appointments made to lead the new English school. Tillyard, a former Classicist, specialised in Shakespeare and Milton. His study, *The Elizabethan World Picture* (1952), can be taken as an exemplary instance of the 'background' approach to literary history that Williams detested.

11 Williams singles out Fox as the centre of leftist discussions of literature in Williams (1979: 44). For an excellent discussion of socialist realism in the Russian context, see Régie Robin, who concludes that it 'marked a historical period of Soviet society with, at heart, an aesthetic of transparency and clarity, a monologic dream of cultural and ideological homogeneity, and a very specific figuration, the positive hero' (Robin 1992: 299).

12 Cited in Hewison (1981: 23). The publication of *The Condemned Playground: Essays 1927–1944* in 1945 brought Connolly significant public attention. See Shelden (1989: 140): 'Given his ambition to influence the cultural policy of the new government, he could not have managed better the timing of the book's publication. The

argument of "Writers and Society" received prominent attention in many of the reviews of the book.'

13 For a useful account and history of the idea of 'participatory democracy', see Held (1987: 254–64).

14 See Leavis (1933: 63–7).

15 For *Politics and Letters*, as well as the Soviet Literary Controversy essay in vol. 1, no. 1, Williams wrote 'Lower Fourth at St Harry's', challenging Connolly to write about the American Congress Committee on Unamerican Activities as he had done about Zhdanovism in Russia; 'Radio Drama', a discussion of Macneice's *The Dark Tower* in relation to Williams's developing theory of naturalism; 'Dali, Corruption and his Critics', a review of Dali's autobiography in which Williams argues that 'biography and psycho-analysis have nothing to do with literary criticism' – all in vol. 1, nos 2 and 3. In the final Summer 1948 issue, a section from *Drama from Ibsen to Eliot*, 'The Exiles of James Joyce'; '...And Traitors Sneer', a review of Coward and West; and possibly, under the name Michael Pope, another review, 'The American Radio'. For *The Critic*, Williams wrote three reviews ('Saints, Revolutionaries and Carpetbaggers, Etc'; 'Ibsenites and Ibsenite-Antis'; and 'The Delicacy of P.H. Newby'); and one major article, 'A Dialogue on Drama'.

16 For an interesting account of the development of 'cold war culture' in Britain, see Sinfield (1989), and especially Chapter 6, 'Freedom and the Cold War' (1989: 86–115), though the Zoschenko Affair is not discussed.

17 Zhdanov echoes and elaborates the criticisms first made by the Central Committee of the Party and published in *Pravda*, 21 August 1946. See Zhdanov (1947). See also Lewis (1946–7a, 1946–7b). For a useful account of the whole affair, see Vickery (1963).

18 Connolly quoted extensively from *Culture and Life* (28 June 1946) and *Pravda* (21 August 1946) in his article 'The Fifth Form at St. Joe's', (first published in *Horizon*, September–October 1946). See Connolly (1953), especially p. 135: 'The artist who cares truly for individual freedom, aesthetic merit or intellectual truth must be prepared to go once more into the breach against the Soviet view with all the patience, fervour and lucidity with which, ten years ago, he went into action against the nascent totalitarianism of the Nazis.'

19 In fact the debates go back to the 1940s. See, for example, 'Writers and Society, 1940–43' in Connolly (1945: 260–87). These essays best represent the decadent aestheticism Williams so detested. An interesting comparative response from George Orwell can be found in his review of Connolly's *The Unquiet Grave* (1945), which he describes as 'a cry of despair from the rentier who feels that he has no right to exist, but also feels that he is a finer animal than the proletarian' (Orwell 1945: 365). For an excellent general discussion of the issues involved, see Sinfield (1989: 43–7).

20 For a fascinating study of Communist Party culture in the 1940s and 1950s, see Samuel (1986a, 1986b, especially 63–8). According to Inglis, Williams certainly had a very strong personal motive for leaving the Party. He quotes Annette Lees, a friend of Williams, and his wife-to-be, Joy Dalling, on the Party's check on their political suitability: 'They said we were "politically unconscious" – well, we were, to their way of thinking. Raymond was very angry at once, and that's why he left the Party. He said, "They're not telling me who I can marry" ' (Inglis 1995: 84). See also Williams (1979: 52–3).

21 As Mulhern noted, *Politics and Letters* was one of the journals which signalled a clear shift away from the *Scrutiny* paradigm. See Mulhern (1979: 226–7, 230–3) and Dworkin 1997: 86–7.

22 As Gorak pithily comments, 'Williams's greatest source of intellectual development was probably Williams' (Gorak 1988: 12). It was, he states, 'as if he must feel utterly isolated in order to work at all, so strident were his claims for independence from even the most elementary source' (1988: 12). Inglis's judgement – that Gorak

'hardly knows what to do with him across the Atlantic' (Inglis 1989: 19) – is far too harsh an assessment. While Gorak exaggerates considerably when he writes that Williams 'offers a case study in the psychology and methods of the alienated intellectual' (1988: 10), there are many valuable insights to be found in this monograph, whose virtue lies in part in its distance from its subject.

23 With hindsight, the chapter scandalously ignores any discussion of colonialism, as Williams ruefully admits (1979: 237).

24 Williams does use the term 'environment' to describe the contemporary cultural context and refers directly to Leavis and Thompson's book in footnote 7, p. 20.

2 Drama and the structure of feeling

1 See Williams (1991) for a fine bibliography compiled by Graham Holderness. See the 'Foreword' to the American edition of *Culture* (1981a), retitled *The Sociology of Culture* (1992) for Bruce Robbins's description of Chapter 6.

2 Anthony Barnett was the first to challenge Eagleton's view of the relevance of drama to Williams's work (Barnett 1976: 54). Pinkney picks up Barnett's point, and argues against the tendency to trivialise Williams's interest in drama as some kind of 'quaint, engaging, marginal hobby' with no real bearing on his 'general social concerns' (Pinkney 1989b: 19–20); but, as I shall discuss below, his essay misrepresents the nature of Williams's early interests. See also Graham Holderness's introduction to Williams (1991). More generally, see Sharratt (1989), Kruger (1993), and Eldridge and Eldridge (1994), especially Chapter 6, pp. 115–16.

3 O'Connor (1989) is symptomatic in this regard. No detailed examination of the early work is given. It is dismissed in the single sentence: 'The existentialist themes of his early work on Ibsen are revised and replaced by the idea of 'complex seeing' from Brecht' (O'Connor 1989: 80). See also Note 2 above.

4 In the *Politics and Letters* interviews, the *New Left Review* team do ask about Williams's 'high appreciation of Eliot's drama'; but his response avoids any direct mention of Eliot, or discussion of the question of his formative influence. The four pages of his response do not address the question of Eliot's influence directly: 'Let me say it was impossible for me to write adequately about dramatic forms until I fully understood the nature of the historical movement of naturalism and realism, which I did not at the time' (Williams 1979: 202). Gorak (1988: 21) is partially correct in stating that 'Williams remained locked within Eliot's guiding assumptions and values', as I shall discuss below.

5 Fred Inglis, for example, refers to *Drama from Ibsen to Eliot* simply as a 'critical guide to modern drama' (Inglis: 126).

6 See also his review of *Look Back in Anger* as 'the best young play of the decade' (Tynan 1964: 41–2).

7 Williams's impatience with the existing dramatic criticism can also be seen in his review of studies by Muriel Bradbrook and Brian Downs in *The Critic* where he argues 'there is no acceptable literary criticism of Ibsen's plays available in English' (1947e: 65). Inglis records that the publishers of *Drama from Ibsen to Eliot* sent on a letter from Kay Burton of Newnham College, objecting that Williams drew too much from Muriel Bradbrook's lectures of 1945–6 in his own study. Inglis quotes selectively from Williams's reply to the publishers, and notes that Ms. Burton was satisfied by Williams's account, but maintains his own scepticism (see Inglis 1995: 138–9). In point of fact, Bradbrook's study, *Ibsen the Norwegian*, is fully acknowledged in Williams's text, and is explicitly discussed at several points (1952: 42, 44, 56, 61, 65, 73). Even a casual comparison of the two suggests little in common save that they are writing about the same play. For Bradbrook, *Peer Gynt* 'is a far better play than *Brand*, which was written out of despair, but lacks the true clarity of tragedy. The story of Peer is the story of his struggle to get away from the trolls – in Christian

phrase, the search for salvation...he is also a comic character, a gaily caricatured typical Norwegian' (Bradbrook 1946: 54). Williams interprets the play around ideas of vocation and relationship foreign to Bradbrook's reading, and his reading owes more to Eliot than to any other single influence. See, for instance, his concluding remarks: '*Peer Gynt*'s success, and its difference from *Brand*, is that the mythological and legendary material which Ibsen uses provides a more completely objective formula for the central experience than any he found before or after.... In *Peer Gynt* words, once again, are the sovereign element of the drama' (Williams 1952: 60). Inglis misreads the book title as *Ibsen the Dramatist*, perhaps in a *Verlesen* which seeks to annul Bradbrook's central theme – to show how Ibsen's plays reveal typical aspects of the Norwegian character – and to seek to connect it more closely with Williams's interest in Ibsen's work as showing the possibilities of verbal drama.

8 See Williams (1947a, 1947e, 1947f).

9 See, for instance, Eliot's ' "Rhetoric" and Poetic Drama', 'A Dialogue on Dramatic Poetry', and 'Four Elizabethan Dramatists' in his *Selected Essays* (1966).

10 See Eliot (1924); Knights (1937); Wilson Knight (1930).

11 For a succinct overview of Eliot's career as a dramatist, see Innes (1992), especially p. 387: 'In the era immediately following the Second World War, too, when serious new drama was restricted to J.B. Priestley's restatements of his 1930s themes or Terence Rattigan's naturalistic problem plays, the religious vision of Eliot's poetic drama set the standard.... But their Establishment traditionalism relegated Eliot's plays to period pieces the moment the first post-war generation of playwrights stormed the theatre.'

12 Eliot's views on the social importance of such common systems of belief are most strongly expressed in 'The Idea of a Christian Society' (1939); and in *Notes Towards the Definition of Culture* (1948). Williams confronts Eliot's social philosophy head-on in Williams (1958a: 227–43).

13 These come through most strongly in Eliot (1934, 1939, 1948). For excellent recent assessments, see Asher (1995), Cooper (1995), and Julius (1995).

14 See Ellmann (1987) for some perceptive comments in this regard.

15 Inglis has described this well, suggesting that 'Williams made the mistake so many people make, that we know what we feel by introspection' (1995: 220), and there-fore believed that writing worked by 'producing in others a facsimile of his feelings' rather than through persuasion (1995: 221).

16 See Williams (1953c: 186). This essay was written prior to *Preface to Film*.

17 For more detail, see Williams (1979: 230–3).

18 The revised and extended version of *Drama in Performance* published in 1968 includes a new chapter on Bergman's film *Wild Strawberries* which repeats many of the same emphases. See, for example, Williams (1991: 150): 'What has happened in Bergman's case, though by no means in all films, is that the dramatic author has become his own director: the unity of text and performance is achieved, not conven-tionally, but in the phases of the work of one mind.'

19 See Pinkney (1989a, 1989b). I further discuss Pinkney's inflation of the evidence for Williams's interest in German Expressionism – necessary to make his 'anti-Lukácsian' case – in Chapter 6.

20 Thus he writes of Williams's 'overvaluing of [Eliot's] "break" with Naturalism in *Drama from Ibsen to Eliot* in 1952' (Pinkney 1989a: 9), but does not register just how central Eliot's ideas were to Williams in this early period.

21 Eagleton (1976b) focuses his discussion of the term on the book which came from the lectures he heard as an undergraduate student (Williams 1970, 1976b: 33–4). Simpson, in his acute essay 'Raymond Williams: Feeling for Structures, Voicing "History" ', begins his discussion of the term with *Culture and Society*, and only examines the term as it appears in the later versions of the books on drama (1995b: 29–50). Only Peter Middleton's essay, 'Why Structure Feeling?', examines its first use

in *Preface to Film*. Middleton asks the right question: 'To understand Williams's attachment to the concept we need to explore the nature of the problem he was trying to resolve by its introduction' (1989: 52); but his account is marred by its failure to recognise that Williams is less interested in attacking the 'post-Comtean philosophical tradition', and more concerned with criticising the Marxist tradition, or at least the scientist variant of it associated for us primarily with Althusser, and by Williams with the English Marxism of the 1930s and 1940s.

22　See Simpson (1995b), especially pp. 36–7, 42. Simpson shares many of Eagleton's doubts about the theoretical value of the term.

23　See especially Chapters 4–6, 'English Poets: (I) Primitive Accumulation', 'English Poets: (II) The Industrial Revolution', and 'English Poets: (III) Decline of Capitalism'. Here Caudwell argues, for instance, that in the 'period of primitive accumulation the conditions for the growth of the bourgeois class are created lawlessly....The absolute-individual will overriding all other wills is therefore the principle of life for the Elizabethan age' (Caudwell 1937: 73–4).

24　See J.R. Williams (1953), and the reply and counter-reply by Raymond Williams and J.R. Williams in McIlroy and Westwood (1993: 196–8).

25　Thus it is no surprise that in *Culture*, Williams's sketch of the form cultural materialism might take as a new discipline – the sociology of culture – the history of drama is the privileged example chosen to exemplify the central assertion that 'certain forms of social relationship are deeply embodied in certain forms of art' (Williams 1981a: 148).

3　Culture and communication

1　See Williams (1979: 7); Parrinder (1987a: 58); Anderson (1965: 15); Dworkin (1993: 41); Simpson (1995b: 36); Inglis (1995: 146); Gorak (1988: 40). John Beaver's review from *The Twentieth Century* is quoted on the back cover of *The Universities and Left Review*, vol. 1, no. 5 (1958): 'Among the young, not to know about – I won't say have read – *The Uses of Literacy* and *Culture and Society* is to brand oneself the literary equivalent of a square.' See also Dworkin 1997: 87–93.

2　See Eagleton (1976b: 25), and *New Formations* 5, Summer 1988, p. 4. The *New Formations* Editorial is further discussed in the Conclusion, and the issues it raises are discussed at length in Higgins (1995).

3　See John Mander's comment, in his 1960 review of Julian Symons's *The Thirties, A Dream Revolved*: 'In the thirties the working-class intellectual was a bit of a joke.... It is difficult nowadays to think of younger left-wing intellectuals who do not come from working-class or lower middle-class homes' (cited in Hewison 1981: 199).

4　See Morrison for an interesting portrait of the social, political and aesthetic tensions at work in the 1950s: 'Consciously identifying with socialist agents of change, Amis and other members of the Movement are nevertheless attracted to the "old" pre-1945 order....To be politically astute in the 1950s, the Movement implied, was to be politically inactive' (Morrison 1980: 77, 95). Unfortunately there is no space here for a thorough consideration of Williams's relations to contemporaries like Kingsley Amis and Donald Davie, although some of the strength of the antipathy is felt in Williams's only published poem 'On First Looking into New Lines' (Williams 1984a: 257–8). For Amis on Williams, see Amis (1962). See also Hewison: 'Amis and Wain prepared the stage for the Angry Young Man, Colin Wilson gave him an identity as the Outsider, John Osborne gave him a voice. John Braine proceeded to demonstrate that he had absorbed the materialistic morality of his times' (1981: 135), and Chapters 5 and 6 in general. Sinfield offers a useful distinction between 'middle-class dissidence' and a 'left-liberal class fraction' in his insightful study of the period (1989: 238).

5 See Inglis (1995: 109): 'His answers to the special paper on George Eliot...were clear in the memory of Muriel Bradbrook twenty years after she had marked them.'

6 As Williams later wrote, 'it should be stressed that it was a choice: it was distinctly as a vocation rather than a profession that people went into adult education – Edward Thompson, Hoggart, myself and many others whose names are not known' (Williams 1986b: 154). He also records that the extra money was welcome: 'Trinity offered me a senior scholarship at 200 a year for three years, but the adult education job I saw advertised at Oxford paid 300 a year. So a financial factor came into it' (Williams 1979: 64). But the main reason may well have been the extra time to write that this job gave him as he worked on the first drafts of his novel.

7 Richard Hoggart worked in the Department of Adult Education at Hull University from 1946 to 1959. *The Uses of Literacy*, usually associated with Williams's *Culture and Society*, appeared in 1957. Edward P. Thompson was Extra-Mural Lecturer at Leeds University from 1948 to 1965.

8 McIlroy sums up: 'We can, therefore, whilst granting the importance of his lonely professional regime, make too much of his intellectual isolation...he was in contact with and in dialogue with leading scholars, and in the first dozen post-war years was editor of three important journals' (1993a: 12). See also Inglis (1995), Chapter 6, 'Worker's Education in the Garden of England'.

9 Kermode (1959). Here, as in his later review of *Modern Tragedy*, Kermode prefers to turn a blind eye to the fundamentally political address of Williams's work, and to focus only on its literary critical aspect.

10 But see also reviews of *Culture and Society* by Dwight Macdonald: 'I don't think Mr Williams's ideas are effective. In fact I don't think they are ideas at all. They are, rather, prejudices – prejudices on the right side, generous and sincere and democratic prejudices, but still idées reçues, unexamined assumptions' (MacDonald 1961: 79); see also Briggs (1961) and especially Anthony Hartley's three essays, which for Williams, summed up 'that sector of right-wing liberal opinion...which saw it as a new attempt at a reassociation of culture [sic] and social thinking which it thought had been seen off after the thirties' (Williams 1979: 132) (Hartley 1958, 1959, 1962, especially p. 581: 'His [Williams's] own view of culture – which can roughly be called populist – seems to be based on a series of confusions as to the meanings covered by the word and to neglect the necessarily individual and aristocratic function of the creative artist.')

11 Cowling was later one of the founder members of the Salisbury Group, a gathering of Conservative academics, commentators and politicians, most of whom had present or past connections with Peterhouse College. This was established in 1977 to promote 'traditional conservatism'. Cowling expressed just what that meant in his keynote statement of the group's first publication, *Conservative Essays*: 'It is not freedom that Conservatives want: what they want is the sort of freedom that will maintain existing inequalities or restore lost ones' (cited in Edgar 1984: 44). The group also included Roger Scruton, author of an essay on Williams in his *Thinkers of the New Left* (1985) where he characterises Williams's interests in democracy and social justice as sentimental. See also Scruton (1984).

12 Williams took a characteristically longer view, and had drifted out of the Communist Party by 1941. In *Politics and Letters*, he describes the key event for him as the East German Rising and its suppression in 1953 (Williams 1979: 88–9).

13 See also Hall (1980). This essay remains one of the finest single essays on Williams's work as a whole. For useful discussion of some of the tensions around cultural studies between Hall and Williams, see Dworkin (1993), Milner (1993: 76–84, 87–90) and Dworkin 1997: 45–69.

14 Crossman is cited in Dwight Macdonald (1961: 83) from *The Guardian*, 9 March 1961; also cited in Inglis (1995: 170). Gorak's judgement betrays the overemphasis and tendentiousness which mars his study: 'In fact, without *Culture and Society* the

work of the British "new left" with its sustained critique of British social and political institutions, might never have occurred' (1988: 52).

15 Biographers Peter Ackroyd and Lyndall Gordon pass over Eliot's specific targets and prefer to see *Notes towards the Definition of Culture* merely as evidence for Eliot's increasingly pessimistic mood. See Ackroyd (1985: 291–2) and Gordon (1988: 221–3). Against this psychologisation and privatisation of public and political arguments, see Cooper (1995).

16 See Shaw (1959) for a survey of the 'Great Debate' concerning the attainment of 'university standards' in adult education, as well as a discussion of the related questions of 'voluntaryism' versus 'professionalism'. See also McIlroy and Westwood (1993).

17 The argument in adult education reflected broader ideological and political discussions: see, classically, Bell (1960). Lasch (1973) gives a useful account of the 'end of ideology' movement in the US context. For a useful survey of the British arguments, see Stedman Jones (1984b).

18 See Raybould (1948, 1949, 1951).

19 For Williams's own account, see Williams (1979: 78–83). See also McIlroy and Westwood (1993: 203–6).

20 Bell's identification of civilization with the values of a well-educated elite who would, if necessary, be supported by an ignorant working-class gives an excellent idea of the kind of arguments Williams was opposing. A particularly revealing passage reads: 'The rich men and women of the eighteenth century cultivated their taste. The poor, as I hope presently to show, so long as to be poor means to be unfree and uneducated, are concerned actively with civilization only in so far as by their labours they make it possible, and, passively, in so far as their manners, habits, opinions and sentiments are coloured by it....I have not yet noticed that the soon-to-be sovran [sic] proletariat, the working men of old England, manifest any burning desire to avail themselves of such means of civilization as they already dispose of. Rather it appears to me their ambitions tend elsewhither. Far from discovering amongst them any will to civilization I am led to suspect that the British working man likes his barbarism well enough' (Bell 1928: 49–50, 156). Perhaps Williams's definitive reply is to be found in the essay 'The Bloomsbury Fraction', where he sums up their general position as one in which the function of the 'social conscience, in the end, is to protect the private conscience' (Williams 1978: 167).

21 Some recognition of this is to be found in Lloyd and Thomas's description of *Culture and Society* as 'a counterhegemonic work of enormous significance' (Lloyd and Thomas 1995: 271). See also Robbins's interesting discussion, and especially his comments '*Culture and Society* is so powerful and moving a case for professional legitimation not despite but because of its fundamental commitment to political opposition' (Robbins 1993: 79). And see the whole discussion in Williams (1979: 97–107).

22 Cobbett began like Burke as an opponent of the French Revolution. See Williams's monograph *Cobbett* (1983b) for a fine analysis of the continuity across Cobbett's differing political allegiances.

23 See, for instance, Viswanathan who argues, that Williams 'consistently and exclusively studies the formation of metropolitan culture from within its own boundaries....Despite [his] life-long commitment to contesting purely abstract categories of analysis that draw on system rather than history, his critical practice paradoxically reproduces them in the context of imperialism' (Viswanathan 1993: 218, 224). Apropos *The Country and the City*, see also Said (1993: 98–100). For a spirited defence of Williams in this context of argument, see Prendergast (1995b).

24 See, for instance, Eliot's description of the 'Community of Christians': 'It will be their identity of belief and aspiration, their background of a common system of education and a common culture which will enable them to influence and be influ-

enced by each other, and collectively to form the conscious mind and the conscience of the nation' (1982: 68).

25 As Mulhern remarks, in *Fiction and the Reading Public*, the 'notion of an original unity of "culture" and "civilization", which in F.R. Leavis's argument had been an unobtrusive assumption, was now expounded as the first principle of a theory of cultural history' (Mulhern 1979: 38). It was Williams's implicit criticisms of the Leavises that drew the ire of critics such as Green (1968: 108–9) and Watson (1977a, 1977b).

26 Eliot may well have played a central role in this. See, for instance, his statement, in *The Idea of a Christian Society* that 'the tendency of unlimited industrialism is to create bodies of men and women – of all classes – detached from tradition, alienated from religion and susceptible to mass suggestion: in other words, a mob. And a mob will be no less a mob if it is well clothed, well housed and well disciplined' (Eliot 1982: 53).

27 See Cunningham (1988), especially Chapters 9 and 10, 'Movements of Masses' and 'Mass Observations'. See also Carey (1992). Carey appears ignorant of Williams's arguments in *Culture and Society* while presenting a mirror image to them, and writing in terms very close to Williams's central point regarding the use of the term masses: 'I would suggest, then, that the principle around which modernist literature and culture fashioned themselves was the exclusion of the masses. The defeat of their power, the removal of their literacy, the denial of their humanity. What this intellectual effort failed to acknowledge was the masses do not exist. The mass, that is to say, is a metaphor for the unknowable and invisible. We cannot see the mass. Crowds can be seen; but the mass is the crowd in its metaphysical aspect – the sum of all possible crowds – and that can take on conceptual form only as metaphor. The metaphor of the mass serves the purposes of individual self-assertion because it turns other people into a conglomerate. It denies them the individuality which we ascribe to ourselves and to people we know' (1992: 21). Carey appears to be guilty either of plagiarism or an extraordinary oversight in his scholarly preparation for the study. See also Eldridge and Eldridge (1994: 64): 'The challenge to the use of "mass" as a concept is, threfore [sic], not some quirky pedantry, but a way of drawing attention to its ideological and control implications.' For a contrary and critical view, see Parrinder (1987a). What is at stake in Williams's discussion is the site of observation, one which is always implicated in society, and never free from interest and implication.

28 Both a fine phrase and conceptually central to Althusser's view of intellectual and scientific innovation.

29 Though Thompson had negative comments too, as we shall discuss in Chapter 5.

4 Cambridge criticism

1 See Inglis (1995), especially chapters 8 and 9, for a general sketch of the period. The *May Day Manifesto* was largely drafted by Williams after lengthy discussions with other members of the group, including Stuart Hall and Edward Thompson. See Hall *et al.* (1968); and for an account of this, and related matters, see Williams (1979: 369–76). See Williams (1971a, 1971b) for an extract from Williams's speech apropos of the Dutschke affair. For an account of Williams's role and activities in the Arts Council, see the essays 'Politics and Policies: The Case of the Arts Council' in Williams (1989a: 141–50), 'The Arts Council' in Williams (1989b: 41–55) and 'Middlemen' in Williams (1989c: 98–107). See *Stand* 12 (1971e: 17–34) for *A Letter from the Country*, broadcast in April 1966; and *Stand* 9 (1967c: 15–53) for *Public Inquiry*, broadcast 15 March 1967. The best discussion of them is to be found in Sharrat (1989). Williams's columns for *The Listener* have been collected (Williams 1989d). See also Williams (1974a) and Lusted (1989).

2 *Drama in Performance* includes extra chapters 'Plays in Transition', 'Modern Experimental Drama', and '*Wild Strawberries*, by Ingmar Bergman', as well as silent elisions of passages in praise of Eliot; *Drama from Ibsen to Brecht* is restructured, and has additional chapters: '*The Exiles* of James Joyce', 'Federico Garcia Lorca', 'Dylan Thomas's *Play for Voices*', 'O'Neill: *Mourning becomes Electra*', 'Giraudoux: *Electre*', Sartre, *The Flies*', 'Georg Buchner: A Retrospect', 'D.H. Lawrence: *The Widowing of Mrs Holroyd*', 'Arthur Miller', 'Bertolt Brecht' and a whole section, 'Recent Drama', as well as a completely new conclusion. Once again, a central revision lies in the downplaying of Eliot's example and achievement. In *Orwell* (1971a) Williams is much harsher in his assessment than in his discussion in *Culture and Society*. In his 'Introduction' to *The Pelican Book of English Prose*, Williams formulates some of the themes of writing and observation crucial both to the study Orwell, and to *The Country and the City*. The introduction is reprinted, with minor changes, as 'Notes on English Prose 1780–1950' in Williams (1984a: 67–118).

3 As mentioned in the Introduction, Inglis (1995: 176) disputes this, suggesting that Williams had been contacted by a Faculty legate before the letter arrived, and had already agreed to accept a lectureship if one were offered; but he gives no source or evidence for this view. For Williams's own account, see (1977d: 4).

4 This chapter – and indeed this study as a whole – assumes the centrality which Williams leant to Cambridge English. It comes through most evidently in his 1974 remark: 'If I take my example from Cambridge English, it is not only because of local experience and concern, but mainly because, by common consent, the changes embodied in Cambridge English, especially between the mid-1920s and the 1940s, have been so widely influential in many parts of the English-speaking world. If an old definition of the subject was anywhere broken up, and a new curriculum and new definitions decisively propagated, it was, at least in the early stages, in Cambridge' (1974b: 1293).

5 Williams's two talks for the BBC *Third Programme*, 'Literature and Rural Society' and 'Literature and the City' establish a starting point of the project as a whole (1967a, 1967b).

6 See in particular Williams (1971a), especially Chapter 4 'Experience and Observation', and Williams (1989e).

7 The main thrust of Williams's arguments are anticipated in his 'Dialogue on Tragedy' (1962b). This examines a spectrum of opinion on tragedy, stretched between the opposing views of Ridyear and Clark. Clark is closest to Steiner's views, and Williams to Ridyear's.

8 Compare Lunacharsky (1933).

9 In a curious way, Steiner shows his own awareness of the ahistorical features of his own interpretation, but manages at the same time to make a virtue of them. See especially p. 192: 'In the imagination of the nineteenth century the Greek tragedians and Shakespeare stand side by side, their affinity transcending all the immense contrarieties of historical circumstance, religious belief, and poetic form. We no longer use the particular terms of Lessing and Victor Hugo. But we abide by their insight. The word 'tragedy' encloses for us in a single span both the Greek and the Elizabethan example. The sense of relationship overreaches the historical truth that Shakespeare may have known actually next to nothing of the actual works of Aeschylus, Sophocles and Euripides. It transcends the glaring fact that the Elizabethans mixed tragedy and comedy whereas the Greeks kept the two modes severely distinct. It overcomes our emphatic awareness of the vast difference in the shape and fabric of the two languages and styles of dramatic presentation. The intimations of a related spirit and ordering of human values are stronger than any sense of disparity.'

10 Williams may be recalling some of the detail of Ralph Fox's argument in *The Novel and the People*. Compare Fox (1937: 99).

11 The final chapter on Brecht – 'A Rejection of Tragedy' – is in many ways the weakest and most schematic. As the anonymous reviewer in the *Times Literary Supplement* (possibly George Steiner) noted, it was irritatingly brief and paid little attention to existing scholarly work. See *Times Literary Supplement* (1966: 717–18).

12 Though for Walter Stein, *Modern Tragedy* was unusually successful in bringing together political sensibility and literary analysis. 'Unlike so many who have sought to bring modern literary and political concerns into active relation, he [Williams] really has the interests and equipment of a serious literary critic. *Modern Tragedy* bears the fruits of this conjunction; though its special significance, both literary and political, seems to have been almost entirely missed on its appearance' (Stein 1969: 22). Nonetheless, Stein criticises Williams's work for its tendency to 'overstatement' (1969: 211) and its overidentification of the everyday tragedies of modern experience with 'remediable social disorders' (1969: 210). As John O. Thomson (1980) also noted: 'Fabianism and Stalinism are the twin positions on the left which Williams is writing against' (1980: 49).

13 This was Anthony Barnett's personal response, recorded in Inglis (1995: 250). See also Barnett (1976). For a recent overview of the book, which focuses on the German Romantic tradition of tragic thinking marginalised in Williams's study, see Surin (1995).

14 See George Steiner, *Real Presences* (1989) for a very different critical assessment of modernity.

15 Compare Eliot's essay, 'Tradition and the Individual Talent', and its key assertion that 'the historical sense involves a perception, not only of the pastness of the past, but of its presence; the historical sense compels a man to write not merely with his own generation in his bones, but with a feeling that the whole of the literature of Europe from Homer and within it the whole of the literature of his own country has a simultaneous existence and composes a simultaneous order' (Eliot 1919b: 14).

16 Ward notes how the book is 'in effect an answer to Leavis's influential book' (1981: 53). Jon Thompson, for example, sniffs at Williams's 'propensity, as in *The English Novel from Dickens to Lawrence* (1971) [sic: actually 1970] to merely offer an alternate version of Leavis's Great Tradition' (1993: 73). Inglis describes the book as the 'unacknowledged correction by Williams the class-warrior to Leavis's *The Great Tradition*' (1995: 213), while O'Connor mentions *The English Novel* as 'a record of his lectures on the English novel', but curiously makes no mention of its direct opposition to Leavis (1989: 25), though he does lay stress on the importance of its concept of 'knowable community' in Williams in Chapter 5. Only Eagleton (1976b: 34) and Hall (in Eagleton 1989c: 63) appear to appreciate the theoretical substance of the book as a whole, though Eldridge and Eldridge have a good assessment of Williams's arguments concerning the book's discussion of the 'knowable community' (Eldridge and Eldridge 1994: 132–3).

17 Mulhern has described the self-enclosure of Leavis's thinking well: 'Premissed upon a refusal of "abstraction", Leavis's "system" could not consistently be defended – except in the name of a process offered as the alternative to "abstraction" and "system" as such. For the system as a whole, reticence was the price of cohesion' (Mulhern 1979: 170–1). See also Baldick (1983), Bell (1988) and Belsey (1982) for interesting accounts.

18 See Peter Widdowson's excellent account of the reception of Hardy's novels in his indispensable *Hardy in History: A Study in Literary Sociology* (1989), especially Chapter 1, 'The Critical Constitution of "Thomas Hardy" ' (Widdowson 1989: 11–76).

19 See 'Modern Fiction' in Woolf (1968), especially pp. 189–92. And compare Williams's further remarks, in 'The Bloomsbury Fraction': 'In the very power of their demonstration of a private sensibility that must be protected and extended by forms of pubic concern, they fashioned the effective forms of the contemporary ideological

dissociation between "public" and "private" life. Awareness of their own formation as individuals within society, of that specific social formation which made them explicitly a group and implicitly a fraction of a class, was not only beyond their reach; it was directly ruled out, since the free and civilized individual was already their founding datum....The final nature of Bloomsbury as a group is that it was indeed, and differentially, a group of and for the notion of free individuals' (Williams 1978/80: 168–9).

20 See, for instance, Said (1983: 240); Jameson (1991: 6).

21 See, respectively, Said (1989: 152); Ferrara (1989: 102); Eagleton (1976b: 39); Ward (1981: 46). See also Eldridge and Eldridge (1994: 175–97) for a useful general commentary on Williams's study.

22 See Simpson (1995a: 72–91) for a fascinating discussion and critique of more recent examples of this mode. In some senses, Simpson (1995b) can be regarded as a continuation of the same discussion.

23 Perhaps Williams's most direct response, though still evasive in that it does not address Kiernan or Thompson's points directly, and in some ways trivialises them, is to be found in his remarks at the *Slant Symposium* in 1967. Here he tries to escape the problem by using a different phrase – a 'culture in common' rather than a common culture; but he insists that in 'speaking of a common culture...one was speaking critically of what could be summarised as a class society'; and he closes by asserting that 'the fantasy that some critics have had, that a common culture would be a uniform and conformist culture, or the fear that some friends have expressed, that a common culture would be notoriously difficult to attain because it is impossible to find any large number of people in general agreement, do not seem to hold' (Williams (1968b): 34, 36, 38). See also Williams (1968c: 297): 'I would therefore agree that in this [Thompson's] sense the problem of a common culture is the problem of revolutionary politics: the problem of intervening constantly in society to extend and transform the institutions which enable people to get that kind of access.'

24 Though Williams does not discuss Hibbard's essay directly, it is included – though mis-referenced – in the bibliographical notes to *The Country and the City*.

25 See, for example, Barrell (1972); Barrell and Bull (1973); Barrell (1980); and Simpson (1987).

26 It may be that this partial identification with Crabbe blinds Williams to the need to place his work with far greater historical precision. More likely, it is a question of the large focus of the study as a whole which inevitably means it is often mistaken on particular points. Compare some of the critical comments in Barrell and Bull (1974: 380–1), and, again, in Barrell (1980), where he argues that 'the "real" history that Raymond Williams has praised Crabbe for introducing into the tradition of rural poetry, as opposed to the nostalgic mythology of Goldsmith, is revealed instead as an attempt to abolish the sense of history altogether' (1980: 87–8). See also Inglis (1995: 237–8).

27 For a more recent account, focusing particularly on Joyce, see Moretti (1995). There is much common ground between Moretti and Williams, though Moretti appears not to know Williams's work. Compare also the account of tragedy in Moretti (1983: 42–82).

28 Williams's attention to imperialism, and to some third-world writing, though cursory, was unusual at the time, and makes it important to be very careful with claims that Williams was absolutely indifferent to what has become known as colonial discourse. While it is certainly true to say that it was not the focus of his attention, it was there in the margins at a time when most criticism was absolutely blind to it: this itself seems something of an achievement. See, for instance, the ways in which Said's observation that the 'few tantalizing pages in *The Country and the City* that touch on culture and imperialism are peripheral to the book's main idea' (Said 1993: 77), are

transformed into critical attack in Viswanathan (1993), Pyle (1993) and Radhakrishnan (1993).

29 This argument was anticipated as early as 1961; see Williams (1961b). Though
Williams was not to know it, the Chinese Revolution – which he mentions with
respect alongside the Cuban revolution – in fact represented a similar catastrophe.
For very contrasting accounts, see Hinton (1966), and the play David Hare made
from it, *Fanshen*, 'an optimistic document' (Hare 1976: 9); and Becker (1996) for
new research on the whole period.

30 Compare Williams (1958a: 274): 'It certainly seems relevant to ask English Marxists
who have interested themselves in the arts whether this is not Romanticism absorbing
Marx, rather than Marx transforming Romanticism.'

31 For a survey and exemplary collection of such new work, see, for instance, Nussbaum
and Brown who declare that the 'new' defined in their collection *The New Eighteenth
Century* 'has its roots in recent renewed attention to interdisciplinary work and in
particular the relationship of literature and history' (1987: 9).

32 See Simpson (1995a, 1995b).

33 Compare, for instance, Jonathan Arac's focus in *Postmodernism and Politics*, on 'one
of the most vexed areas in contemporary theory, that of representation' (1986b: xx),
and his further discussion (1986: xx–xxviii).

34 See Williams (1961a), Chapter 1, 'The Creative Mind', and Chapter 5 below for
further discussion of this important essay.

5 Marxisms: contra Caudwell, against Althusser

1 I distinguish in this chapter between Williams's relation to Marxism as a socialist,
engaged in a wide variety of practical political activities, and the question of the
relation of his academic work and writing to Marxism. This chapter deals with the
latter, though there is considerable overlap between them. For accounts and assessments of the former, see Eagleton (1976b); Barnett (1976); Mulhern (1984);
Hirschkop (1989); Brenkman (1995).

2 And therefore participating in the dilemma first mapped out by Perry Anderson in
1976, in which the dominating characteristic of Western Marxism was its shift in
attention away from the practice of politics to the contemplation of culture as the
prospect of European-wide revolutionary insurrection declined. As Anderson later
summed up the case: 'the major exponents of Western Marxism also typically pioneered studies of cultural processes – in the higher ranges of the superstructures – as
if in glittering compensation for their neglect of the structures and infrastructures of
politics and economics' (Anderson 1983: 17).

3 The first is cited as Anthony Sampson's description in Williams (1975: 65); the
second, the judgement of C.L.R. James (1961: 115). We have already examined, in
Chapters 1 and 4, some of the arguments of Eagleton, Kiernan and Thompson.
Arnold Kettle's reviews of Williams present a usefully consistent record of the orthodox Marxist criticisms of Williams. See his reviews of *Culture and Society* and *The
Long Revolution* (1961), *Marxism and Literature* (1977) and *Politics and Letters*
(1979), in which he writes 'all this is typical of bourgeois sociology...[Williams fails
to] really get to grips with the nature of class division' (1961: 305), and, in summation, 'A Marxism in which "concepts" are given so central a place as Williams gives
them and in which the particular concept of "reflection" is placed on a sort of
Stalinist dunce's or whipping-stool, is almost bound to err on the side of theoreticism
and academicism' (1977: 72). For a more positive assessment, see Merrill (1978/9).

4 Indeed, so strong was the influence of Williams's judgements on Caudwell in
Culture and Society that they have only recently begun to be challenged. Eagleton's
comments reproduce Williams's own dismissive tone: 'Who is the major English
Marxist critic? Christopher Caudwell, hélas...there is little, except negatively, to be

learnt from him' (1976b: 21). Mulhern launched the first defence of Caudwell in an essay for *New Left Review* (Mulhern 1974); but, strangely, though Mulhern mentions *Culture and Society*, he does not try and meet Williams's arguments on Caudwell head on. E.P. Thompson joined the debate with an essay published in *The Socialist Register*, seeking to rescue Caudwell as 'an anatomist of ideology' (Thompson 1977: 234). In the most recent study, following Thompson's line but translating it into a somewhat Althusserian vocabulary which Thompson would have rejected, R. Sullivan sees Caudwell as primarily concerned with 'the problem of the subject, the role of language in the structuration of consciousness, and the nature of "reality" in relation to humanity's imaginary or illusory understanding of it' (1987: 161). The editors of *Marxist Literary Theory: A Reader* note that although 'it is one of the landmarks of British Marxist literary criticism, Caudwell's work has been dismissed more than admired. Raymond Williams, for example, commented that Caudwell was often not specific enough to be wrong' (Eagleton and Milne 1996: 91).

5 Mulhern is here citing Leavis 'Under Which King Bezonian?' (Leavis 1933: 171). See also Leavis (1933: 5–9): 'Marx as a Marxist, one ventures, was not really concerned about literature and art; his concern was for a simplification involving, as an essential condition, the assumption that literature and art would look after themselves...it is certain that for most Marxists the attraction of Marxism is simplicity: it absolves from the duty of wrestling with complexities; above all, the complexities introduced if one agrees that the cultural values – human ends – need more attention than they get in the doctrine, strategy and tactics of the Class War....There is, then, a point of view above classes; there can be intellectual, aesthetic and moral activity that is not merely an expression of class origin and economic circumstances; there is a "human culture" to be aimed at that must be achieved by cultivating a certain autonomy of the human spirit.' And Leavis (1952: 182–203).

6 Though Pechey, in a fascinating discussion of the *Scrutiny* image of Marxism, also draws attention to the significant influence of Alick West, whose 'antithetical reading of Romantic discourse' is seen as the 'precondition of *Culture and Society*' (Pechey 1985: 71).

7 Milner (1993: 23–32) gives an excellent concise account of Caudwell and others.

8 As Mulhern notes, the 'frequency with which the word "express" occurs in his text is due to no lexical frugality on his part: it denotes precisely the relationship between poetry and economy in his system' (1974: 50–1).

9 Williams wonders with evident frustration why Thompson did not publish his views at the time of the original debate. See Williams (1979: 77).

10 For an interesting and informed discussion of the history of this 'fundamental tenet' in the context of debates within the Second International, see Colletti (1972), especially Chapter 2, 'Bernstein and the Marxism of the Second International'. There is considerable common ground between Colletti and Williams on many points of theory, though, as Ferrara (1989) notes, there is little knowledge of Williams's work in Italy.

11 The literature on this is, of course, immense, and the debates continue. For a slightly hostile survey of the first century of competing definitions, see Kolakowski (1981).

12 Sullivan's study is perhaps marred by its too insistent attempt to see Caudwell's work as the precursor of post-structuralist doctrines, as in his assertion that Caudwell's 'emphasis on the role of the subject to effect change, to reshape reality through an "inner design"...opened up a debate within Marxism that still has contemporary relevence' (1988: 109). As Amigoni rightly observes, 'what his study lacks is a sustained attempt to theorize the contestatory historical relationships between the various strands of critical discourse that Caudwell was negotiating and Sullivan is tracing' (1989: 289–90).

13 Amigoni repeats Sullivan's error in his review, asserting – wrongly – that while Williams suggested that 'the interrogatory approach to "orthodox" Marxist positions...enabled him to reread Caudwell's aesthetics with new eyes...he never specified the nature of the vision' (1989: 287). By 1977, he had already done so in *The Long Revolution* where Williams takes his position on psychoanalysis almost word for word from Caudwell. Compare, for instance, Williams (1961a: 93–7) with Caudwell (1949: 160–2, 175, 177).

14 I examine these points more thoroughly in Higgins (1990, 1991).

15 See Taylor (1985), Chapter 9, 'Language and Human Nature'. And, for a magisterial extension of the general argument across the whole range of Western philosophy, see Taylor (1989a). Taylor was, of course, one of the founding editors of the *New Left Review*, and participated in the Slant symposium alongside Williams in 1967. For a concise account of his later move away from Marxism and towards a socialist humanism – worth comparison with Williams's criticisms of the 'transition from Marx to Marxism' – see Taylor (1989b). A similar critique of these 'naturalist' assumptions is to be found in Giddens (1979a) and, as one of the components of a powerful critique of orthodox Marxist assumptions, in Giddens (1981a).

16 As Williams himself was the first to admit: 'I was talking about the people and ideas I first focussed as Marxism when I was a student.... It was a deficiency of my own generation that the amount of classical marxism it knew was relatively small' (1979: 316).

17 Williams's activity as a reviewer gives some indication of this. Before 1970, only four reviews deal with Marxist works: reviews of Lukács's *The Historical Novel* in 1962, of Sartre's philosophy and of *The Left Review*, in 1968, and in 1969, a review of Marcuse. After 1970, some eleven reviews are published. These are from a total of over two hundred published in *The Guardian* alone. Nonetheless, we don't have to go quite so far as Aronowitz, who states that 'Williams first seriously engaged Marxist theory only in the 1970s' (1995: 321), and further suggests that Williams's rejection of the base and superstructure argument was present only in 'the last fifteen years of his life' (1995: 333).

18 There is no discussion of Goldmann's monumental work on Pascal and Racine, *The Hidden God* (1956), in Williams's *Modern Tragedy*, though the book was published in English translation in 1964. Explicit references to Goldmann's work all postdate his Cambridge visit.

19 See, for instance, Gareth Stedman Jones's perspicuous critique of Lukác's distinction between 'actual' and 'positive' consciousness (which he better translates as 'actual' and 'ascribed' consciousness), and his concern that in Lukács's argument, 'the economic history of modes of production – the "base"...is etherialized virtually out of existence' (Stedman Jones 1977b: 39). This is similarly the burden of many Marxist critiques of Williams.

20 The lecture rates as one of Williams's strongest single performances, and only the considerable overlap with the central ideas of 'Base and Superstructure in Marxist Cultural Theory' inhibits me from dealing with it more fully here. In it, he makes his case for his own cultural materialist analysis against both Cambridge English and orthodox Marxism. 'Looking at our work', he writes of the Cambridge English school, 'it could be said that we lacked a centre, in any developed philosophy or sociology. Looking at his [Goldmann's] work...it could be said that he had a received centre, at the level of reasoning, before the full contact with substance began' (1971d: 22). For succinct expressions of the views of Goldmann's which Williams discusses, see, for 'scientism', the lecture 'Dialectical Thought and Transindividual Subject' (Goldmann 1970, especially 90–2); for the concept of 'structure', the essay 'La Méthode structuraliste génétique en histoire de la littérature' (Goldmann 1964, especially 338, 344–5); for something of the nature of the debt to Lukács, 'Introduction aux problèmes d'une sociologie du roman' (1963: 21–57). His

relatively static methodological principles are spelt out in Goldmann (1952): for their most fruitful realisation, see Goldmann's masterpiece, *The Hidden God* (1956). Jay (1994) has a useful survey of Goldmann's work as a whole. For a probing account of Williams's essay, see Said (1983), where he writes in favour of Williams as a 'reflective critic' (1984: 238), noting 'however far away in time and place Williams may be from the fiery rebelliousness of the early Lukács, there is an extraordinary virtue to his distance, even the coldness of his critical reflections on Lukács and Goldmann, to both of whom he is otherwise so intellectually cordial' (1984: 240).

21 See Said (1984: 240).

22 For an insightful commentary on this passage, see Prendergast (1995b). He reads it as the location of a significant knot in Williams's whole thinking about the primacy of culture, noting that 'there are two stories, complementary but not fully compatible' at work, and pointing out that 'if everything is there at the beginning, it would seem that some things are more at the beginning than others' (1995b: 12–13). Compare also Simpson (1995b); Eagleton (1976b, 1989b).

23 Therborn's comment also seems accurate: 'What [Williams] has made less clear…is the equally important point that "indissoluble real forces" may in their actual operation have diverse, analytically distinguishable dimensions' (Therborn 1980: 6). Eagleton offers a persuasive and developed critique, warning of a tendency in Williams's formulations to fail to recognize that 'determinations are not symmetrical…in the production of human society some activities are more fundamentally determining than others' (1989b: 169).

24 Useful accounts include Lefèbvre (1969), Larrain (1979), Eagleton (1991) and Rosen (1996).

25 Bruno Bauer's sincere belief that his own philosophical positions were revolutionary could only be held through a mystificatory and self-defeating overvaluation of their real social impact. Despite the sincerity of his own convictions, his removal from his university position was never going to be the tinder which sparked off a full-scale social revolution. The example is David McLellan's, not Marx's (McLellan 1969: 61).

26 Derrida makes something of the same point, though in a very different vocabulary. See Derrida (1994: 389).

27 See, for instance, Hirst 1979, Larrain 1979, Abercrombie *et al.* 1983 and Higgins 1986.

28 I argue (Higgins 1996a) that Ahmad's criticisms of Said are open to just such objections, strangely, since in so many ways Ahmad shows himself to be a generous supporter of Williams's work and positions.

29 See also Clark and Holquist's valuable discussion of the whole question of Marxism and language in Chapter 10 of their study, *Mikhail Bakhtin* (1984: 212–37); and, more generally, Holquist (1990).

30 See, for example, Sharrat (1982). I discuss the reviews of *Marxism and Literature* more fully in Chapter 6.

31 See, for instance, Kiernan (1959) and Thompson (1961), and the discussion of these in Chapter 4. The interviews with the *New Left Review* team present a fascinating dialogue around all these questions. See especially Williams (1979: 164–72). For a more recent critique of Williams in this regard, see Robbins (1993: 144–7).

32 It is interesting to compare Williams's positions with those independently argued in and through the different disciplinary discourse of sociology. Giddens, for instance, suggests that 'Only if historical materialism is regarded as embodying the more abstract elements of a theory of human Praxis, does it remain an indispensable contribution to social theory today' (1981a: 2), and his subsequent discussions suggest much common ground with Williams. Not surprisingly, the *New Left Review* response to Giddens shares many of the same features as their criticisms of Williams. See Wright (1983), especially p. 32: 'Particularly once the simple functionalist version of the base-superstructure model is abandoned, it is difficult to argue systematically

for the structural unity of economic and political relations within the theory of social development and the concept of class.'

6 Towards a cultural materialism

1 For a usefully condensed account, not discussed in the previous chapter, see Williams (1978a). Anderson notes that the work of the Cambridge anthropologist Jack Goody shares something of this same emphasis with Williams (Anderson 1990a: 76–8). See especially Goody (1977, 1986); and his essay 'Alphabets and Writing' in Williams (1981c).

2 See Said (1983).

3 Gorak goes so far as to suggest that the 'work itself viewed independently remains too drastically abbreviated to be comprehensible' (1988: 75).

4 The history of Leavis's relations to the Cambridge English Faculty was itself a fraught and combative one. As Williams put it in a memorial essay, Leavis 'had worked a lifetime in a Faculty he opposed and despaired of' (1984c: 20).

5 For a sympathetic assessment, see Bell (1988). Bell's defence of Leavis can be summarised in his statement 'The critical impact of Leavis lies not in the complexity of his ideas about literature so much as in the quality of attention to it' (1988: 12). For a philosophically sophisticated defence, see Casey (1966). See also Inglis (1982). For more sceptical assessments, see Mulhern (1979) and Baldick (1983).

6 In Mulhern's words: 'The most notable feature of Leavis's humanism was its obdurate anti-scientism. The improper aggrandisement of the established sciences of nature and society, and misconceived attempts to transpose their models into the domain of culture, were in his view among the greatest threats posed by contemporary "civilization" to human integrity' (1979: 170).

7 For the rather self-congratulatory accounts of the 'Golden Age' of Cambridge English, see Willey (1964); Tillyard (1958); Bennet (1973); Bradbrook (1973). For more sceptical approaches, see Mulhern (1979); Doyle (1982); Baldick (1983).

8 As, classically, in Leavis (1943). I argued in Chapter 1 that Leavis's direct influence on Williams had been overexaggerated, and the extent of Eliot's influence relatively unregistered; but there is no doubt that Leavis's work formed a reference point for English studies *per se*. For more detail on Williams's actual and complex relations to Leavis and his work, see Williams (1959b, 1978c, 1984c).

9 See especially, Leavis (1932, 1936, 1948).

10 See Williams (1961a), especially Chapter 1, 'The Creative Artist'.

11 For a rich formulation and exemplification of this topic, see Williams (1969b).

12 For more on this, see Williams (1989e), and Williams's crisp monograph *Orwell* (1971a).

13 See Gramsci (1971: 5–23), especially p. 9: 'All men are intellectuals, one could therefore say: but not all men have in society the function of intellectuals.' For an interesting development of this, see Said (1994) and Williams's brief discussion in (1981b: 214–6). Here as elsewhere, there are strong similarities between Williams and Said: see Higgins (1996a) for some basic points of comparison.

14 See Fekete (1977) where he observes how the tradition of literary criticism 'becomes locked into an ideological subject/object dualism that separates experience and expression, instead of seeking significance precisely in their relationship' (1977: 21). The accompanying footnote, to be found on pp. 224–5, traces the idea back to Lukács's late work, *The Specificity of the Aesthetic*. See Lichtheim (1970: 116–29) for a brief but useful commentary.

15 For a succinct account of the Russian Formalist movement, see Bennet (1979); for a more sophisticated survey, see Jameson (1972). The standard scholarly account remains Ehrlich (1955). See also Trotsky (1923). Williams was particularly influenced by Bakhtin and Medvedev (1928).

16 This, of course, was the starting point for Ludwig Wittgenstein's revolutionary arguments concerning the role and status of language in thought and philosophy. Despite Wittgenstein's centrality to Cambridge philosophy, and to Cambridge thinking more generally, his work seemed to have no impact on Williams. See Eagleton (1982) for a provocative account. Similarly, many of Williams's arguments are put with great force in the particular context of structural linguistics by Emile Benveniste (1966), especially chaps 18–21.

17 See, for instance, Vološinov (1929), and especially its supercession of the 'two basic trends' in the understanding of language – 'individualistic subjectivism' and 'abstract objectivism' – in favour of a theory of language as 'verbal interaction' or 'utterance' in pt II, chaps 1–3, pp. 65–98.

18 Williams owed a large debt to Vološinov, many of whose works are now thought to be principally inspired or even written by Mikhail Bakhtin. In this regard, Clark and Holquist conclude 'a conclusive answer to the question of Bakhtin's authorship cannot be found' (1984: 148). I simply follow Williams's references here and make no attempt to adjudicate the issue. His accidental discovery of their work, in the early 1970s, was due to the open-stack system prevailing at the Cambridge University Library (personal communication, June 1987).

19 See Moriarty (1995) for a convincing critique of some of these claims.

20 See Williams's 'Foreword' to Fekete (1977): 'Since the middle sixties, and with gathering pace, there has been a form of apparent rejection of this critical tradition which is in fact only a new, more powerful but also more alienated version of its fundamental problematic of objectivist organization. Critical structuralism, often in confusing association with an objectivist form of Marxism, has indeed to be seen, as Dr Fekete argues, as a phase of this destructive tradition, rather than as any kind of alternative to it' (1977: xiii).

21 The best Easthope can say is that 'two pages' of Williams's essay, 'Base and Superstructure in Marxist Cultural Theory', 'inaugurate what will be referred to as "left-deconstruction" ' (Easthope 1988: 14), and later, that the essay opened the road 'for an analysis of literature not as texts but as a practice of reading in which they are institutionally constructed' (1988: 153) – a familiar deformation of Williams's cultural materialism in its restriction to and containment within literary studies, as I argue in the conclusion to this book.

22 See *The Guardian*, 17 January 1981 (cited in Simpson 1990: 256). The best accounts of the whole affair are to be found in Simpson (1990) and Inglis (1995: 278–85). See also Colin MacCabe's own discussion and analysis of events in 'Class of '68: elements of an intellectual autobiography 1967–81', in MacCabe (1985: 1–32).

23 See MacCabe (1985, 1979, 1981).

24 See Easthope (1988) for a good general overview, and especially pp. 40–1 and 135–41 on MacCabe.

25 See *Cambridge University Reporter*, 10 February 1981, pp. 1–35 for the discourses of Stephen Heath, John Barrell, Michael Long, Howard Erskine-Hill, Geoffrey Kirk and Williams himself.

26 The essay was first published in *New Left Review* 129: 51–66 as 'Marxism, Structuralism and Literary Analysis'. I quote from the retitled version, Williams (1981b).

27 As Simpson notes, the term 'structuralist' was the one that the ' "business as usual" faculty majority chose as their *omnium gatherum* definition of the enemy' (Simpson 1990: 246). Compare MacCabe's own account, in 'Class of '68': 'By calling me a "structuralist" my opponents revealed their ignorance about both structuralism and my own work' (MacCabe 1985: 30).

28 See especially the three essays, 'The Fiction of Reform', ' Forms of English Fiction in 1848', and 'The Reader in Hard Times' in Williams (1984a: 142–74), and my review of *Writing in Society* for a discussion of Williams's 'ambivalence' with regard to the

1970s 'critique of realism' (Higgins 1985: 169). MacCabe's influential essay, 'Realism and the Cinema: Notes on Some Brechtian Theses' was first published in *Screen*, vol. 15, no. 2, Summer 1974 (MacCabe 1974). See Docker (1989) for a useful survey of the whole debate between Williams and the *Screen* position.

29 See Althusser's own 'A Letter on Art' (1966) in Althusser (1984); and, under the influence of Althusser, Macherey (1966).

30 See, for instance, Bryson and Kappeler (1983), produced as a response to the MacCabe Affair, but focusing on 'the issue of teaching, and the issue of theory and its relation to practice' (1983: vii).

31 Williams was very likely thinking of two chapters in Eagleton's *Criticism and Ideology*: Chapter 2, 'Categories for a Materialist Criticism', and Chapter 3, 'Towards a Science of the Text', in which Eagleton follows the Althusserian emphasis of Pierre Macherey's *A Theory of Literary Production* (Macherey 1966).

32 For further elements of that 'wider reorganisation', see the essays gathered together in Williams (1981c). In the 'Introduction', Williams explains how 'the study of communications, in its modern forms, is a convergence, or attempted convergence, of people who were trained, initially, in very different fields: in history and philosophy, in literary and cultural studies, in sociology, technology, and psychology' (1981c: 11). Contributors include – amongst others – Jack Goody on 'Alphabets and Writing', and Ferrucio Rossi-Landi on 'Language'.

33 Nicholas Tredell, in his rather neglected study, *Uncancelled Challenge*, rightly observes that 'To some extent, Culture both challenges and incorporates an idealizing (and by this time failing) Althusserisme' (Tredell 1990: 73).

34 There are many points of contact between Williams and Giddens. Compare, for example, Giddens (1979a) and (1981a), as well as his review essays (1979b) and (1981b).

35 Williams's arguments in this regard are given more fully in one of his best single essays, 'The Bloomsbury Fraction' (1978/80).

36 This was the opening sentence of his address to the Slant Symposium *From Culture to Revolution* in 1968. See Williams (1989b: 32). It summed up just the phenomenological certitude which – aside from Williams's strictly political agenda – most perturbed Eagleton. See especially his comments on 'his consistent over-subjectivising of the social formation' in Eagleton (1976b: 32–5). Eagleton speaks more warmly of the same traits in his memorial essay, noting how 'he could be aware of the massive importance of his own work without the least personal vanity...because he had a curious ability to look on himself from the outside, to see his own life as in a Lukácsian sense "typical" rather than just individual' (Eagleton 1989b: 8).

37 The *New Left Review* team have it almost right when noting, 'Your rejection of literary criticism appears to be founded on a very narrow identification of it with one American school in the 20th century – it ignores the whole history of German, French or Italian aesthetics for example. You seem to be arguing that since New Criticism is objectionable we must reject criticism *tout court*' (Williams 1979: 337). Of course, Williams was never interested in the New Criticism as such, seeing it as only a selective repetition of some of the elements of Cambridge English.

38 See Williams (1983g), especially p. 177, and (1983h).

7 Against the new conformism

1 See, respectively, Williams (1989a, 1989d, 1984a, 1989b, 1989c, 1989e).

2 This includes the only substantial work (aside from *People of the Black Mountains*) not concerned with modernism that Williams produced in this final period: the monograph *Cobbett* (1983b). Even here, concern with the dynamics of Thatcherism pervades the book as a whole, as one can see from the following paragraph:

' "Nobody owes the British people a living", governments now regularly tell the British people. This astounding revelation is addressed to people for whom, in majority, the problem has always been how to make and keep a living through successive crises of economic disorgaisation and war. It is addressed to hard-working people by the representatives of a system which has at its best made the results of hard work uncertain and at worst nullified and squandered them. But there is deeper irony than that. The address is made by representatives of a system which insists that the possessors of capital and of privilege are, precisely, owed a living by everybody else. This no doubt accounts for the sense of a novel truth, as it forms in their mouths. For it is no surprise to anybody else. It was only the great proprietors of the "National Debt" and the Funds who believed and took steps to ensure that a living was owed to them. It was a debt, as we have seen, which Cobbett wanted to repudiate, in the real interests of the nation' (1983b: 73–4). The book is also noteworthy for Williams's return to the Marxist debate regarding the understanding between the forces and relations of production: see especially pp. 59–68.

3 Personal communication (1987). With characteristic generosity, Williams was kind enough to lend me the only typescript copies of a series of essays intended for *The Politics of Modernism*. For an account of our discussion, see Higgins (1989).

4 The point was first argued in a lecture given in 1974, which sadly remains unpublished in any of the collections of Williams's essays. See Williams (1974b). Standard accounts of the origins of Cambridge English and its inaugural break from the study of language include Mulhern (1979), Baldick (1983) and Doyle (1982).

5 See Tillyard (1958) and Willey (1968).

6 See Mulhern (1979), Baldick (1983), Doyle (1982) and Eagleton (1983) for useful general accounts.

7 For a useful guide to the literary deployment of the term, see Bradbury and McFarlane (1991).

8 Compare, for instance, the contents of three popular readers in literary theory: David Lodge's *Modern Criticism and Theory: A Reader* (1988), which has essays and selections by Saussure, Shklovsky and Lacan; Robert Con Davis's *Contemporary Literary Criticism: Modernism through Post-Structuralism* (1986), which features Shklovsky and Lévi-Strauss as well as several essays on Freud and Lacan; and Dan Latimer's *Contemporary Critical Theory* (1989). Terry Eagleton's *Literary Theory: An Introduction* (1983) is the best overall introduction to the field; see also Jefferson and Robey (1982).

9 See the conclusion of this book for a discussion of Williams's renewed interest in the idea of literacy.

10 See, classically, Victor Shklovsky's extraordinary essay, 'Art as Technique' (1917), and, more generally, the summary account and defence (against Trotsky's influential critique (1923)) by Eichenbaum (1926). For a useful discussion of the term itself, see Jameson (1972: 75–9).

11 Compare Williams's similar accounts in (1979: 337) and (1981b: 206). Moriarty is, I think, rightly sceptical of the logic of Williams's genealogy here when he writes that, not content with the plausible argument 'of a congruence between New Criticism and structuralism' he 'insists to a striking extent on a suppositious actual influence of the former on the latter', but is in the end unable to offer any 'empirical or textual evidence for his account' (Moriarty 1995: 102–3).

12 See, for instance, Barthes (1968); Foucault (1969); Derrida (1965). For an account of 'death of the author' theory which also seeks to place it historically, see Jameson (1991: 14–15).

13 Something of a comparable position – though articulated in a very different conceptual idiom, and with a very different range of cultural references – is to be found in Jameson's work on postmodernism. See, for instance, his remarks concerning the Brecht–Lukács debate, and particularly his provocative assertion 'there is

some question whether the ultimate renewal of modernism, the final dialectical subversion of the now automatized conventions of an aesthetics of perceptual revolution, might not simply be…realism itself! For when modernism and its accompanying techniques of "estrangement" have become the dominant style whereby the consumer is reconciled with capitalism, the habit of fragmentation needs itself to be "estranged" and corrected by a more totalizing way of viewing phenomena' (Jameson 1977: 211).

14 The well-prepared attack on the National Union of Mineworkers, as well as the general curbing of trade union activity was initiated through the Employment Acts of 1980 and 1982, and completed by the Trade Union Act of 1984; attacks on the autonomy of local government; the 'increasing militarization of the police force' (Hayes 1994: 79) was effected by the Criminal Justice Act of 1982, the Police and Criminal Evidence Act of 1984 and the Public Order Act of 1986.

15 See especially Hall (1983, 1988).

16 Compare Riddell's judgement: 'There was therefore no upsurge of popular support for Mrs Thatcher and her administration….The 1983 election did not suggest there was yet any new consensus about British society and the management of the economy…Mrs Thatcher and her administration have aroused as much bitter antagonism as fervent support' (Riddell 1983: 4–5). Of course, Hall's point was precisely to examine the dynamics of that 'alliance of disparate forces' as that is precisely the role of the hegemonic in his Gramscian-based theory.

17 See Milner (1993: 76–84) for a useful discussion of Hall and Williams's differences. As Milner puts it, 'A structuralist understanding of discourse as necessarily "polysemic" is thus combined, in Hall's account, with an equally structuralist sense of popular passivity, so as to "construct" much of the British working class itself as positively Thatcherite. Unsurprisingly, the substantive analysis appeared to Williams even more wrongheaded than the theoretical' (1993: 82). For an account more sympathetic to Hall, see Dworkin 1997: 255–60.

18 This essay was the occasion for some dispute regarding Williams's stature as a public intellectual. 'One must ask what good is a critical intellectual if he won't criticize his own side?' stated R.W. Johnson in a 1990 review essay. Johnson found 'no mention' in the essay 'of the fact that a substantial minority of miners had broken away over the issue of the denial of democracy, and that some had suffered violence as a result' (1990: 6), and all in all 'complete failure, indeed refusal, to confront the cardinal facts of the strike' (1990: 6). As always, the selection of what counts as 'cardinal facts' is often the expression of a prior political perspective. There is no mention, in Johnson's account, of the Thatcher government's long preparation for inflicting a defeat on the National Union of Mineworkers for their part in the downfall of the Heath administration: a much more significant 'denial of democracy'. See Young (1989: 365–78) for a detailed account. Several aspects of the review are, to say the least, odd: the charge that the historical labour movement was 'a truly sacred cow to Williams' is not supported by the criticisms which Williams had levelled at it since the 1950s (see Williams 1979 for examples), nor does this accusation quite fit with the critical stance taken in many of the essays in *Resources of Hope* which Johnson is reviewing. Similarly, Johnson's claim that after the 1960s Williams managed to write only 'one good book' of literary and cultural criticism, *Orwell*, is decidedly eccentric, ignoring as it does *The Country and the City*. Robin Blackburn's response, despite its fury, is undoubtedly correct here: 'It is not Williams who is "vacuous", but your reviewer if he fails to see the effort to spell out alternatives in these essays [from *Resources of Hope*, edited by Blackburn] or in *Towards 2000*' (Blackburn 1990: 4). See Hall *et al.* (1978) for the policing argument.

19 Adorno's discussion of Samuel Becket makes an interesting point of comparison. For Adorno, the force of Becket's work is located precisely in the ways in which it embodies the new cultural and political situation without the comfort of the usual

bourgeois illusions. See for example, his remarks that 'all subject matter appears to be the sign of an inner sphere, but the inner sphere of which it would be a sign no longer exists.... *Endgame* is the epilogue to subjectivity...The only aspect of freedom still known to it is the powerless and pitiful reflex action of trivial decisions' (Adorno 1991: 251, 259).

20 See Stedman Jones (1984a) for some critical comments on this procedure.

21 See Briggs (1961: 387): 'Mr Williams's last chapter seems to suffer also from being confined to an English framework of reference.'

22 Gorak emphasises the book's 'unusual combination of progressive analysis and sympathetic human understanding' (1988: 118), while Morgan finds that 'balanced discussion...is followed by pages of appallingly loose argument' (Morgan 1983: 1223). The most thorough account and analysis of Williams's proposals is to be found in Mulhern (1984).

23 See Williams (1958a: 285–94); and again, more harshly, in (1971a). As he admits in 1979, 'I must say I cannot bear much of it [Orwell's writing] now' (William 1979: 391).

24 In addition to the essays it appeared Williams intended for publication, Pinkney adds transcripts of a lecture given in Bristol in 1987, 'When was Modernism', and of a discussion between Williams and Edward Said in 1986, 'Media, Margins and Modernity'. It excludes 'Country and City in the Modern Novel', a text which Williams told me he intended for the book in our discussion in 1987. This essay is available in *Pretexts: Studies in Writing and Culture*, vol. 3, nos. 1–2 (1989).

25 See Pinkney (1989a, 1989b, 1991).

26 For a classic staging of their opposed views, see the two essays 'Discussing Expressionism' (Bloch) and 'Realism in the Balance' (Lukács) in Bloch *et al.* 1977. The debate as a whole is best framed by Lukács's 1934 essay, 'Expressionism: Its Significance and Decline', in Lukács (1980). See Lunn (1985: 78–90) for a useful general discussion of Lukác's position.

27 Robbins grasps this dimension of the argument well in his interesting discussion of the dynamics of literary professionalism. See, for instance, his acute remark 'Rather than tracing a fall from modernism into professionalism, Williams suggests that in its essence modernism already was professionalism' (Robbins 1993: 59). In this sense, Williams's arguments may be read against Anderson's claim that Britain produced no significant modernist formation. The institution of the discipline of English studies itself corresponds to at least two of Anderson's three criteria for modernism (Anderson 1984: 105).

28 See Williams's 1972 lecture, 'Social Darwinism', for a fine anticipation of many of the ways in which conservative thinkers tried to draw on Darwin's thought. Indeed, the concluding sentences of the lecture can be read as anticipating the main lines of argument at work in *The Politics of Modernism*: Social Darwinism is a part of 'the social theory of that system which had promised order and progress and yet produced the twentieth century. Instead of facing that fact, in all its immense complexity, the rationalizers and the natural rhetoricians have now moved in to snap at and discourage us: not to ratify an imperialist and capitalist order, but to universalize its breakdown and to persuade us that it has no alternatives, since all "nature" is like that' (Williams 1974d: 102).

29 For some further development of this, see 'The Legacy of Raymond Williams' (Higgins 1998).

30 Compare Williams (1977e). As we shall see below, Williams's remarks should be read in the context of MacCabe's assault on the 'classic realist text' (MacCabe 1974). For a useful overview (though they neglect Williams's distinctive contribution) of the *Screen* debate on realism in film, see Lapsley and Westlake (1988).

31 The post-lecture discussion is not given in Williams (1989a). For this, see Britton (1991: 27).

32 Or, for that matter, his own response to Eagleton's criticisms, as I discussed in Chapter 1.

33 See, for instance, Heath (1981). Many of Williams's oblique criticisms are met in Heath (1991).

34 This useful phrase is Anthony Easthope's, who has commented, in several accounts, on the importance of MacCabe's arguments in the development of British post-structuralism (see Easthope (1988)). He describes *James Joyce and the Revolution of the Word* as contrasting 'the classic realist text with Joyce's modernism' and as 'prepared to argue that Joyce's modernism, specifically that of *Finnegans Wake*, leads to a revolutionary politics because in denying the reader's pleasure it opens the reader's desire' (Easthope 1988: 136, 138). Lodge (1981) presents the best critical account of MacCabe's arguments from an orthodox literary perspective.

35 For the fullest statement of this case, see Walsh (1981).

36 Some of the strains and tensions in the position had already become apparent by 1976 when MacCabe asserted, in adjacent sentences, both that 'the breaking of the imaginary relation between text and viewer is the first pre-requisite of political questions in art', and also 'that the breaking of the imaginary relationship can constitute a political goal in itself is the ultra-leftist fantasy of the surrealists and of much of the avant-garde work now being undertaken in the cinema' (MacCabe 1976: 73).

37 See, for instance, Belsey (1982); Dollimore (1985); Durant (1981); Easthope (1983).

38 The conference papers as a whole are brought together in Fabb *et al.* (1988).

39 For discussion of Williams's views on psychoanalysis, see Higgins (1990, 1991, 1995).

40 See especially Williams (1986c).

41 See Derrida (1965, 1966) for two fascinating accounts of Artaud which in some ways confirm, and in others contradict, Williams's general argument. His general argument is confirmed in so far as Derrida uses Artaud for a general attack on the notion of representation (1966: 343–52), but Derrida's arguments as a whole are considerably more subtle than those attacked by Williams here.

42 To this extent, Pinkney's claims for Williams's interest in expressionism are partially correct, though his serious distortions of the evidence remain a problem.

43 Williams might have sought support here from Bakhtin and Medvedev. As they rightly note in their discussion of Shklovsky's conception of poetic language in *The Formal Method in Literary Scholarship*, 'Every word, as such, is involved in inter-course and cannot be torn away from it without it ceasing to be a word of language' (Bakhtin and Medvedev 1928: 94). Many of the arguments have resurfaced and been given considerable redefinition in recent debates surrounding the LANGUAGE poets and their tradition. See, for instance, Perloff (1985) and Perelman (1996).

44 He had earlier acknowledged the need for such a correction, noting that 'it was impossible for me to write adequately about dramatic forms until I fully understood the nature of the historical movement of naturalism and realism, which I did not at the time' of writing *Drama from Ibsen to Eliot* (Williams 1979: 202).

45 In the spirit of Williams's remarks on Lacan, so central to the *Screen*-theory approach, in *Politics and Letters*. 'What is needed is not a blending of concepts of literature with concepts from Lacan, but an introduction of literary practice to the quite different practice of experimental observation. That would be the materialist recovery' (1979: 341). And see especially his endorsement of Timpanaro (Williams 1978b), particularly on the related questions of psychoanalysis and linguistics.

Conclusion

1 On race, see Gilroy's comment that the 'distinction which Powell and Worsthorne [two notable British right-wing ideologues] make between authentic and inauthentic types of national belonging, appears in an almost identical form in the work of Raymond Williams' (1987: 49); on questions of gender and feminism, see the discussion and debate between Jardine and Swindells (1989), Watts (1989), Taylor (1990) and Shiach (1995); and regarding imperialism, see Said, who asks why Williams writes (of Dickens, but also more generally) 'without reference to India, Africa, the Middle East, and Asia' (Said 1993: 14); Dworkin and Roman (1993b), Viswanathan (1993), Pyle (1993) and Radhakrishnan (1993).

2 The term seems deliberately provocative, as is the tone of the whole review. (See Chapter 7, footnote 18 for further discussion.) Johnson is referring primarily to the collections of Williams's essays which appeared after his death (Williams 1989a, 1989b, 1989c, 1989d) and their respective introductions, and to Alan O'Connor's thin study (O'Connor 1989). He in fact praises Gorak's study (Gorak 1988) as 'an excellent little book' (Johnson 1990: 5). Later collections by Dworkin and Roman (1993a) and Prendergast (1995a) present an interesting variety of critical opinion and assessment on Williams. Milner (1993) seems to me to have the most balanced assessment of Williams's overall importance.

3 Amongst many others, see Parrinder (1977), Barrell (1980), Simpson (1987), Crowley (1989a, 1989b), Shiach (1989), de Bolla (1995), and Liu (1989).

4 Nonetheless, some of the essays in the collection take a more positive attitude towards Williams: perhaps not surprisingly, those which address educational policy and practice most directly. As Michael Apple put it, 'the development of educational scholarship…owes a major debt to Williams…No figure has been as powerful in setting the path that critical education studies has taken in the past two decades' (Apple 1993: 91); Leslie G. Roman, in a fascinating account argues that Williams's 'socially transformative critical realism is preferable, in its political, ethical, and educational consequences…to the relativism of post-modernist discourse and to the allegedly antithetical reactionary discourses empowering nonadvocacy and neutrality' (Roman 1993: 183), while Kohli remarks on the ways in which Williams's thinking informs her discussion of 'the power of educational institutions and practcies in the process of class identity formation and the concomitant processes of internalized oppression' (1993: 115), and Rizvi (1993) comments on the relevence of Williams's educational arguments in the context of Thatcher's educational policies. See also Brenkman, who pays tribute elsewhere to how Williams 'turned the arrogant, traditionalist, class-bound idea of a common culture into a radical, open-ended vision of people's widening participation in changing forms of literacy and learning' (1995: 254).

5 As Gorak rightly remarks, 'other self-professed "cultural materialists" have reduced Williams's program to little more than a slogan, harnessing it to Foucaultian or Althusserian analyses of the sort that he himself would hardly practice' (Gorak 1988: 90).

6 For useful warnings in this regard, see Frank (1989) and Dews (1987).

7 Parrinder – whose insights on Williams's work are too often ignored by leftist critics – is dismayed by this 'deconstructive' aspect of Williams's later work, writing, in disappointed terms, that 'Williams's negativity, his criticism of concepts, has become part of the general deconstructive tendency' (Parrinder 1987b: 82).

8 For developments on 'critical library', in relation to Williams's work and beyond, see Higgins (1992, 1996a, 1996b, 1998).

Bibliography

Works by Raymond Williams

Williams, Raymond (1947a) 'A Dialogue on Actors', *The Critic* 1:1, pp. 17–24.

—— (1947b) 'Saints, Revolutionaries, Carpetbaggers', review of *The New Spirit*, by E.W. Martin, and *Writers of Today*, edited by Denys Val Baker, *The Critic* 1:1, pp. 52–4.

—— (1947c) 'The Soviet Literary Controversy in Retrospect', *Politics and Letters* 1:1, pp. 21–31.

—— (1947d) 'Lower Fourth at St. Harry's', *Politics and Letters* 1:2–3, pp. 105–6.

—— (1947e) 'Ibsenites and Ibsenite-Antis', review of *Ibsen: The Intellectual Background*, by Brian W. Downs, and *Ibsen the Norwegian*, by M.C. Bradbrook, *The Critic* 1:2, pp. 65–8.

—— (1947f) 'Radio Drama', *Politics and Letters* 1:2/3, pp. 106–9.

—— (1948) 'A Note on Mr Hoggart's Appendices', *Adult Education* 21, pp. 96–8.

—— (1950) *Reading and Criticism*, London: Frederick Muller.

—— (1952) *Drama from Ibsen to Eliot*, London: Chatto 2nd edn, 1954.

—— (1953a) 'The Idea of Culture', *Essays in Criticism* 4, pp. 239–66.

—— (1953b) 'The Teaching of Public Expression', *The Highway*, April, pp. 42–8.

—— (1953c) 'Film as a Tutorial Subject', in J. McIlroy and S. Westwood (eds.) *Border Country: Raymond Williams in Adult Education*, Leicester: National Institute of Continuing Education, 1993.

—— (1954) *Drama in Performance*, London: Frederick Muller.

—— (1957a) 'The New Party Line?', review of *The Outsider* by Colin Wilson, *Essays in Criticism* 7: 68–76.

—— (1957b) 'Fiction and the Writing Public', review of *The Uses of Literacy* by Richard Hoggart, *Essays in Criticism* 7: 422–8.

—— (1957c) 'The Uses of Literacy: Working Class Culture', *Universities and Left Review* 1:2, pp. 29–32.

—— (1958a) *Culture and Society 1780–1950*, London: The Hogarth Press; repr. 1990 with a new foreword by Williams.

—— (1958b) 'Culture is Ordinary', in Williams, *Resources of Hope*, London and New York: Verso, 1989.

—— (1959a) 'Critical Forum', *Essays in Criticism* 9, pp. 432–7.

—— (1959b) 'Our Debt to Dr Leavis', *Critical Quarterly* 1, pp. 245–7.

—— (1961a) *The Long Revolution*, Harmondsworth: Penguin; repr. 1975.

—— (1961b) 'The Future of Marxism', *The Twentieth Century* 170, pp. 128–42.

—— (1961c) 'Communications and Community', in Williams, *Resources of Hope*, London and New York: Verso, 1989.

—— (1962a) *Communications*, Harmondsworth, Penguin; 3rd edn with new 'Reading and Retrospect, 1975', published 1976.

—— (1962b) 'A Dialogue on Tragedy', *New Left Review* 13–14, pp. 22–35.

—— (1962c) 'Books of the Year', *The Guardian*, 21 December, p.8.

—— (1965) 'The British Left', in Williams, *Resources of Hope*, London and New York: Verso, 1989.

—— (1966) *Modern Tragedy*, London: Verso; new edition without the play *Koba* and with new afterword, 1979.

—— (1967a) 'Literature and Rural Society', *The Listener* 78, 16 November, pp. 630–2.

—— (1967b) 'Literature and the City', *The Listener* 78, 23 November, pp. 653–6.

—— (1967c) Public Inquiry, *Stand* 9: 15–53.

—— (1968a) *Drama from Ibsen to Brecht*, Harmondsworth: Penguin (a revised and extended edition of Williams 1952).

—— (1968b) 'Culture and Revolution: A Comment', in Williams, *Resources of Hope*, London and New York: Verso, 1989.

—— (1968c) 'Culture and Revolution: A Response', in *From Culture to Revolution: The Slant Symposium*, ed. Terry Eagleton and Brian Wicker, London and Sydney: Sheed & Ward, pp. 296–308.

—— (1969a) 'On Reading Marcuse', review of *Negations* by Herbert Marcuse, *The Cambridge Review* 90, pp. 366–8.

—— (1969b) 'Notes on English Prose 1780–1950', in Williams, *Writing in Society*, London and New York: Verso, 1984.

—— (1970) *The English Novel from Dickens to Lawrence*, London: The Hogarth Press; new edition, 1984.

—— (1971a) *Orwell*, Fontana Modern Masters Series, Glasgow: Collins; new edition with new afterword by Williams, 1984.

—— (1971b) 'Dutschke and Cambridge' in *The Cambridge Review*, 29 January, pp. 94–5.

—— (1971c) 'The Dutschke Case and Intellectual Freedom: Two Statements', *The Cambridge Review*, 29 January, pp. 95–6.

—— (1971d) 'Literature and Sociology: In Memory of Lucien Goldmann', in Williams (1980a).

—— (1971e) A Letter from the Country, *Stand* 12: 17–34.

—— (1972a) 'Lucien Goldmann and Marxism's Alternative Tradition', *The Listener* 87, 23 March, pp. 375–6.

—— (1972b) 'Ideas of Nature', in Williams, *Problems in Materialism and Culture: Selected Essays*, London: Verso, 1980.

—— (1973a) *The Country and the City*, St Albans: Paladin; 2nd edn, 1975.

—— (1973b) 'Base and Superstructure in Marxist Cultural Theory', in Williams, *Problems in Materialism and Culture: Selected Essays*, London: Verso, 1980.

—— (1974a) *Television: Technology and Cultural Form*, Glasgow: Fontana.

—— (1974b) 'The English Language and the English Tripos', *Times Literary Supplement*, 15 November, pp. 1293–4.

—— (1974c) 'The Frankfurt School', a review of *The Dialectical Imagination*, by Martin Jay, *Negative Dialectics*, by Theodor Adorno, and *The Jargon of Authenticity*, by Theodor Adorno, *The Guardian*, 14 February, p. 14.

—— (1974d) 'Social Darwinism', in Williams, *Problems in Materialism and Culture: Selected Essays*, London: Verso, 1980.

—— (1974e) 'Drama in a Dramatised Society' in Williams, *Writing in Society*, London and New York: Verso, 1984.

—— (1975) ' "You're a Marxist, Aren't You?" ' in Williams, *Resources of Hope*, London and New York: Verso, 1989.

—— (1976a) *Keywords: A Vocabulary of Culture and Society*, Glasgow: Fontana; 2nd edn, revised and extended, 1983.

—— (1976b) 'Notes on Marxism in Britain since 1945', in Williams, *Problems in Materialism and Culture: Selected Essays*, London: Verso, 1980.

—— (1977a) *Marxism and Literature*, Oxford: Oxford University Press.

—— (1977b) 'Two Interviews with Raymond Williams', *Red Shift* 2, pp. 12–17; 3, pp. 13–15.

—— (1977c) 'Form and Meaning: Hippolytus and Phèdre', in Williams, *Writing in Society*, London and New York: Verso, 1984.

—— (1977d) 'My Cambridge', in Williams, *What I Came to Say*, London: Hutchinson Radius, 1989.

—— (1977e) 'A Defence of Realism', in Williams, *What I Came to Say*, London: Hutchinson Radius, 1989.

—— (1977f) 'Foreword', to Fekete, *The Critical Twilight*, London: Routledge & Kegan Paul.

—— (1978a) 'Means of Communication as Means of Production', in Williams, *Problems in Materialism and Culture: Selected Essays*, London: Verso, 1980.

—— (1978b) 'Problems of Materialism', in Williams, *Problems in Materialism and Culture: Selected Essays*, London: Verso, 1980 .

—— (1978c) 'A Man Confronting a Very Particular Kind of Mystery', *Times Higher Educational Supplement*, 5 May, p. 10.

—— (1978/80) 'The Bloomsbury Fraction', in Williams, *Problems in Materialism and Culture: Selected Essays*, London: Verso, 1980.

—— (1979) *Politics and Letters: Interviews with New Left Review*, London: New Left Books.

—— (1980a) *Problems in Materialism and Culture: Selected Essays*, London: Verso.

—— (1980b) 'Problems in Materialism', in Williams, *Problems in Materialism and Culture: Selected Essays*, London: Verso, 1980.

—— (1981a) *Culture*, Fontana New Sociology Series, Glasgow: Collins; 2nd US edn, *The Sociology of Culture*, with foreword by Bruce Robbins, Chicago: University of Chicago Press, 1992.

—— (1981b) 'Crisis in English Studies', in Williams, *Writing in Society*, London and New York: Verso.

—— (ed.) (1981c) *Contact: Human Communication and its History*, London: Thames & Hudson.

—— (1982) 'Distance', in Williams, *What I Came to Say*, London: Hutchinson Radius, 1989.

—— (1983a) *Towards 2000*, London: Chatto and Windus.

—— (1983b) *Cobbett*, Past Masters Series, Oxford and New York: Oxford University Press.

—— (1983c) 'Marx on Culture', in Williams, *What I Came to Say*, London: Hutchinson Radius, 1989.

—— (1983d) 'The Estranging Language of Post-Modernism', *New Society*, 16 June, pp. 439–40.

—— (1983e) 'Problems of the Coming Period', in Williams, *Resources of Hope*, London and New York: Verso, 1989.

—— (1983f) 'Adult Education and Social Change', in Williams, *What I Came to Say*, London: Hutchinson Radius, 1989.

—— (1983g) 'Cambridge English, Past and Present', in Williams, *Writing in Society*, London and New York: Verso, 1984.

—— (1983h) 'Beyond Cambridge English', in Williams, *Writing in Society*, London and New York: Verso, 1984.

—— (1983i) 'On Dramatic Dialogue and Monologue (particularly in Shakespeare)', in Williams, *Writing in Society*, London and New York: Verso, 1984.

—— (1983j) 'Film History' in Williams, *What I Came to Say*, London: Hutchinson Radius, 1989.

—— (1984a) *Writing in Society*, London and New York: Verso.

—— (1984b) 'The Resonance of Antigone', *The Guardian*, 20 July, p. 14.

—— (1984c) 'Seeing a Man Running', in Williams, *What I Came to Say*, London: Hutchinson Radius, 1989.

—— (1984d) 'Writing, Speech and the Classical', in Williams, *What I Came to Say*, London: Hutchinson Radius, 1989.

—— (1985a) 'Cinema and Socialism', in Williams, *The Politics of Modernism: Against the New Conformists*, London and New York: Verso, 1989.

—— (1985b) 'Metropolitan Perceptions and the Emergence of Modernism', in Williams, *The Politics of Modernism: Against the New Conformists*, London and New York: Verso, 1989.

—— (1985c) 'Mining the Meaning: Key Words in the Miners' Strike', in Williams, *Resources of Hope*, London and New York: Verso, 1989.

—— (1986a) 'Language and the Avant-Garde' in Williams, *The Politics of Modernism: Against the New Conformists*, London and New York: Verso, 1989.

—— (1986b) 'The Future of Cultural Studies', in Williams, *The Politics of Modernism: Against the New Conformists*, London and New York: Verso, 1989.

—— (1986c) 'The Uses of Cultural Theory', in Williams, *The Politics of Modernism: Against the New Conformists*, London and New York: Verso, 1989.

—— (1986d) 'Media, Margins and Modernity', in Williams, *The Politics of Modernism: Against the New Conformists*, London and New York: Verso, 1989.

—— (1986e) 'An Interview with Raymond Williams', in T. Modleski, *Studies in Entertainment: Critical Approaches to Mass Culture*, Bloomington and Indianapolis: Indiana University Press; repr. in C. Prendergast (ed.), *Cultural Materialism: Essays on Raymond Williams*, Minneapolis: University of Minnesota Press, 1995.

—— (1987a) 'When was Modernism?', in Williams, *The Politics of Modernism: Against the New Conformists*, London and New York: Verso, 1989.

—— (1987b) 'Country and City in the Modern Novel', *Pretexts: Studies in Writing and Culture* 2:1, pp. 3–13, 1990.

—— (1987c) 'The Practice of Possibility', in Williams, *Resources of Hope*, London and New York: Verso, 1989.

——(1987d) 'The Future of English Literature', in *What I Came to Say*, London: Hutchinson Radius, 1989.

—— (1987e) 'The Politics of Literacy', *Pretexts: Studies in Writing and Culture* 3:1–2, pp. 136–43, 1991.

—— (1988a) 'The Politics of the Avant-Garde', in Williams, *The Politics of Modernism: Against the New Conformists*, London and New York: Verso, 1989.

—— (1988b) 'Theatre as Political Forum', in Williams, *The Politics of Modernism: Against the New Conformists*, London and New York: Verso, 1989.

—— (1989a) *The Politics of Modernism: Against the New Conformists*, ed. Tony Pinkney, London and New York: Verso.

—— (1989b) *Resources of Hope*, ed. Robin Gable, London and New York: Verso.

—— (1989c) *What I Came to Say*, ed. Francis Mulhern, London: Hutchinson Radius.

—— (1989d) *Raymond Williams on Television: Selected Writings*, ed. A. O'Connor, London: Routledge.

—— (1989e) 'Fact and Fiction', in *International Encyclopedia of Communications*, ed. E. Barnouw, Oxford: Oxford University Press.

—— (1991) *Drama in Performance*, revised and extended edition of the original (1954), with introduction by Graham Holderness, Milton Keynes: Open University Press.

—— (1992) *The Sociology of Culture*, 2nd edn, introduction by Bruce Robbins, Chicago: Chicago University Press.

Williams R., and Garnham, N. (1986) 'Pierre Bourdieu and the Sociology of Culture: An Introduction' in R. Collins, *Media, Culture and Society*, London: Sage.

Williams, R., and Hoggart, R. (1960) 'Working Class Attitudes', *New Left Review* 1: 26–30.

Williams, R., and Orrom, M. (1954) *Preface to Film*, London: Film Drama Limited.

Williams, R., Hall, S. and Thompson E. (1968) *May Day Manifesto*, Harmondsworth: Penguin, 2nd edn.

Williams, R., Mankowitz, W. and Collins, C. (1947a) 'For Continuity in Change', editorial, *Politics and Letters* 1:1, pp. 3–5.

—— (1947b) 'Culture and Crisis', editorial, *Politics and Letters* 1:2–3, pp. 5–8.

Secondary sources

Apple, M.W. (1993) 'Rebuilding Hegemony' in Dworkin and Roman (eds.) 1993.

Abercrombie, N., Hill, S. and Turner, R.S. (1983) 'Determinacy and Indeterminacy in the Theory of Ideology', *New Left Review* 142, pp. 55–66.

Ackroyd, P. (1985) *T.S. Eliot*, London: Abacus.

Adorno, T. (1991) *Notes to Literature: I*, trans. S.W. Nicholsen, New York: Columbia University Press.

Ahmad, A. (1994) *In Theory: Classes, Nations, Literatures*, London and New York: Verso.

Althusser, Louis (1965) *Pour Marx*, Paris: Francois Maspero; 2nd edn, 1977.

—— (1966) 'A Letter on Art in Reply to Andre Daspre', in L. Althusser, *Essays on Ideology*, London: Verso, 1984.

Amigoni, D. (1989) Review of Robert Sullivan, *Christopher Caudwell, Textual Practice* 3:2, pp. 287–90.

Amis, Kingsley (1962) 'Martians Bearing Bursaries', *The Spectator*, 27 April, 554–5.

Anderson, P. (1965) 'Origins of the Present Crisis', in P. Anderson and R. Blackburn (eds), *Towards Socialism*, London: Collins.

—— (1969) 'Components of the National Culture', in *Student Power: Problems, Diagnosis, Action*, A. Cockburn and R. Blackburn (eds), Harmondsworth: Penguin and New Left Review.

—— (1976) *Considerations on Western Marxism*, London: New Left Books.

—— (1976/77) 'The Antinomies of Antonio Gramsci', *New Left Review* 100, pp. 5–78.

—— (1993) *In the Tracks of Historical Materialism*, London: Verso.

—— (1984) 'Modernity and Revolution', *New Left Review* 144, pp. 96–113.

—— (1990a) 'A Culture in Contraflow', *New Left Review* 180, pp. 41–78.

—— (1990b) 'A Culture in Contraflow II', *New Left Review* 182, pp. 85–137.

Annan, N.G. (1955) 'The Intellectual Aristocracy', in J.H. Plumb (ed.), *Studies in Social History: A Tribute to G.M. Trevelyan*, London and New York: Longman.

—— (1991) *Our Age*, London: Fontana.

Arac, J. (ed.) (1986a) *Postmodernism and Politics*, Minneapolis: University of Minnesota Press.

—— (1986b) 'Introduction', in Arac, *Postmodernism and Politics*, Minneapolis: University of Minnesota Press.

Aronowitz, S. (1992) 'On Catherine Gallagher's Critique of Raymond Williams', *Social Text* 30, pp. 90–7.

—— (1995) 'Between Criticism and Ethnography: Raymond Williams and the Intervention of Cultural Studies' in C. Prendergast (ed.), *Cultural Materialism: Essays on Raymond Williams*, Minneapolis: University of Minnesota Press.

Asher, K. (1995) *T.S. Eliot and Ideology*, Cambridge: Cambridge University Press.

Attridge, D. (1987) 'Language as History/History as Language: Saussure and the Romance of Etymology', in D. Attridge, G. Bennington and R. Young (eds), *Post-structuralism and the Question of History*, Cambridge: Cambridge University Press.

Bakhtin, M. and Medvedev, P.N. (1928) *The Formal Method in Literary Scholarship*, trans. A.J. Wehrle, Cambridge, MA: Harvard University Press, 1985.

Baldick, C. (1983) *The Social Mission of English Criticism 1848–1932*, Oxford: The Clarendon Press.

—— (1989) 'An Extending Humanism', *Times Literary Supplement*, 3–9 November, p. 1205.

Barnett, Anthony (1976) 'Raymond Williams and Marxism: A Rejoinder to Terry Eagleton', *New Left Review* 99, pp. 47–64.

—— (1977) 'Towards a Theory', *New Society*, 21 July, pp. 145–6.

Barrell, J. (1972) *The Idea of Landscape and the Sense of Place: An Approach to the Poetry of Clare*, Cambridge: Cambridge University Press.

—— (1980) *The Dark Side of the Landscape: The Rural Poor in English Painting, 1730–1840*, Cambridge: Cambridge University Press.

—— (1983) *English Literature in History 1730–80: An Equal, Wide Survey*, London: Hutchinson.

Barrell, J., and Bull, J. (eds) (1973) *The Penguin Book of English Pastoral Verse*, Harmondsworth: Penguin.

Barry, P. (1995) *Beginning Theory*, Manchester: Manchester University Press.

Barthes, R. (1968) 'The Death of the Author', in D. Lodge (ed.), *Modern Criticism and Theory: A Reader*, London and New York: Longman, 1988.

—— (1978) *Leçon*, Paris: Éditions du Seuil.

Becker, J. (1996) *Hungry Ghosts: China's Secret Famine*, London: John Murray.

Bell, C. (1928) *Civilization: An Essay*, Harmondsworth: Penguin, 1947.

Bell, D. (1960) *The End of Ideology*, New York: Glencoe Free Press.

Bell, M. (1988) *F.R. Leavis*, London and New York: Routledge.

Belsey, C. (1980) *Critical Practice*, London: Methuen.

—— (1982) 'Re-reading the Great Tradition', in P. Widdowson (ed.) *Re-Reading English*, London and New York: Methuen.

—— (1985) *The Subject of Tragedy*, London: Methuen.

Benedict, R. (1934) *Patterns of Culture*, Boston: Houghton Mifflin Company, 1989.

Benjamin, W. (1969a) *Illuminations*, trans. H. Zohn, New York: Shocken Books.

—— (1969b) 'Franz Kafka: on the Tenth Anniversary of his Death', in W. Benjamin, *Illuminations*, New York: Shocken Books.

—— (1969c) 'Some Reflections on Kafka', in W. Benjamin, *Illuminations*, New York: Shocken Books.

Bennet, J. (1973) ' "How It Strikes a Contemporary": The Impact of I.A. Richards' Literary Criticism in Cambridge, England', in R. Brower, H. Vendler and J. Hollander (eds), *I.A. Richards: Essays in His Honour*, New York: Oxford University Press.

Bennet, T. (1979) *Marxism and Formalism*, London: Methuen.

Benveniste, E. (1966) *Problèmes de linguistique générales*, Paris: Gallimard.

Berman, M. (1973) Review of *The Country and the City, New York Times Book Review*, 15 July, p. 1.

Blackburn, R. (1988) 'Raymond Williams and the Politics of a New Left', *New Left Review* 168, pp. 12–22.

—— (1989) 'Introduction', in R. Williams, *Resources of Hope*, London and New York: Verso.

—— (1990) Reply to R.W. Johnson, *London Review of Books*, 8 March, p. 4.

Bloch, E., Lukács, G., Brecht, B., Benjamin, W. and Adorno, T. (1977) *Aesthetics and Politics*, translation editor R. Taylor, London: New Left Books.

Bourdieu, P. (1990) *The Logic of Practice*, trans. R. Nice, Cambridge: Polity Press.

Bradbury, M. and McFarlane, J. (eds) (1991) *Modernism, 1890–1930*, Harmondsworth: Penguin.

Bradbrook, M.C. (1946) *Ibsen the Norwegian*, London: Chatto & Windus.

—— (1973) 'I.A. Richards at Cambridge' in R. Brower, H. Vendler and J. Hollander (eds), *I.A. Richards: Essays in His Honour*, New York: Oxford University Press.

Brenkman, J. (1995) 'Raymond Williams and Marxism', in C. Prendergast (ed.), *Cultural Materialism: Essays on Raymond Williams*, Minneapolis: University of Minnesota Press.

Briggs, Asa (1961) 'Creative Definitions', *New Statesman* 61, pp. 386–7.

Britton A. (ed.) (1991) *Talking Films: The Best of The Guardian Film Lectures*, London: Fourth Estate.

Brower, R., Vendler, H. and Hollander, J. (eds) (1973) *I.A. Richards: Essays in His Honour*, New York: Oxford University Press.

Bryson, N. and Kappeler, S. (eds) (1983) *Teaching the Text*, London: Routledge & Kegan Paul.

Burchfield, R.W. (1976) 'A Case of Mistaken Identity: Keywords', *Encounter* 46, pp. 57–64.

Carey, J. (1992) *Intellectuals and Masses: Pride and Prejudice among the Literary Intelligentsia 1880–1939*, London: Faber.

Casey, J. (1966) *The Language of Criticism*, London: Methuen.

Caudwell, C. (1937) *Illusion and Reality: A Study of the Sources of Poetry*, London: Lawrence & Wishart, 1958.

—— (1938) *Studies in a Dying Culture*, in C. Caudwell, *Studies and Further Studies in a Dying Culture*, London and New York: Monthly Review Press.

—— [1949] *Further Studies in a Dying Culture*, in C. Caudwell, *Studies and Further Studies in a Dying Culture*, London and New York: Monthly Review Press.

—— (1971) *Studies and Further Studies in a Dying Culture*, London and New York: Monthly Review Press.

Clark, K. and Holquist, M. (1984) *Mikhail Bakhtin*, London and Cambridge: The Belknap Press of Harvard University Press.

Colletti, L. (1972) *From Rousseau to Lenin: Studies in Ideology and Society*, trans. J. Merrington and J. White, London: New Left Books

Connolly, Cyril (1945) *The Condemned Playground: Essays 1927–44*, London: Routledge.

—— (1953) *Ideas and Places*, London: Weidenfield.

Coombes, H. (1973) Review of *The Country and the City*, *Human World* 13, pp. 69–72.

Cooper, John Xiros (1995) *T.S. Eliot and the Ideology of Four Quartets*, Cambridge: Cambridge University Press.

Coward, R. and Ellis, J. (1977) *Language and Materialism: Developments in Semiology and the Theory of the Subject*, London: Routledge & Kegan Paul.

Cowling, M. (1961) 'Mr Raymond Williams', *The Cambridge Review*, 27 May, pp. 546–51.

Crabbe, G. (1851) *The Poetical Works of the Rev. George Crabbe*, London: John Murray.

Crowley, T. (1989a) *The Politics of Discourse: The Standard Language Question in British Cultural Debates*, Basingstoke: Macmillan Education.

—— (1989b) 'Language in History: That Full Field', *News from Nowhere* 6, pp. 23–37.

Cunningham, V. (1988) *British Writers of the Thirties*, Oxford and New York: Oxford University Press.

Dahrendorf, R. (1988) 'Changing Social Values under Mrs Thatcher', in R. Skidelsky (ed.), *Thatcherism*, London: Chatto & Windus.

Davey, K. (1989) 'Fictions of Familial Socialism', *News from Nowhere* 6, pp. 38–49.

David, R.C. (ed.) (1986) *Contemporary Literary Criticism: Modernism through Post-Structuralism*, London and New York: Longman.

Davis, R.C. (ed.) (1986) *Contemporary Literary Criticism: Modernism through Structuralism*, New York and London: Longman.

Day-Lewis, C. (ed.) (1937a) *The Mind in Chains: Socialism and the Cultural Revolution*, London: Fredrick Muller.

—— (1937b) 'Introduction', in Day-Lewis (ed.), *The Mind in Chains: Socialism and the Cultural Revolution*, London: Fredrick Muller.

de Bolla, P. (1995) 'Antipictorialism in the English Landscape Tradition: A Second Look at *The Country and the City*', in C. Prendergast (ed.), *Cultural Materialism: Essays on Raymond Williams*, Minneapolis: University of Minnesota Press.

Derrida, J. (1965) 'La Parole Soufflée', in Derrida, *L'écriture et la différence*, Paris: Éditions du Seuil.

—— (1966) 'Le Théatre de la Cruauté et la Clôture de la Representation', in Derrida, *L'écriture et la différence*, Paris: Éditions du Seuil.

—— (1967) *L'écriture et la différence*, Paris: Éditions du Seuil.

—— (1994) *Spectres of Marx*, trans. P. Kamuf, London and New York: Routledge.

Deutscher, I. (1949) *Stalin*, Oxford: Oxford University Press.

Dews, P. (1987) *Logics of Disintegration: Post-structuralist Thought and the Claims of Critical Theory*, London: Verso.

Di Michele, L. (1993) 'Autobiography and the "Structure of Feeling" in Border Country' in D.L. Dworkin and L. Roman (eds), *Views Beyond the Border Country: Raymond Williams and Cultural Politics*, London and New York: Routledge.

Docker, J. (1989) 'Williams's Challenge to *Screen* Studies', *Southern Review* 22:2, p. 420–32.

Dollimore, J. (1984) *Radical Tragedy*, Brighton: Harvester.

—— (1985) 'Shakespeare, Cultural Materialism, and the New Historicism', in J. Dollimore and A. Sinfield (eds), *Political Shakespeare: New Essays in Cultural Materialism*, Manchester: Manchester University Press.

Dollimore, J. and Sinfield, A. (eds) (1985) *Political Shakespeare: New Essays in Cultural Materialism*, Manchester: Manchester University Press.

Donoghue, D. (1984) 'Examples', *London Review of Books*, 2–15 February, pp. 20–2.

Doyle, B. (1982) 'The Hidden History of English Studies', in P. Widdowson (ed.) *Re-Reading English*, London: Methuen.

Durant, A. (1981) *Ezra Pound, Identity in Crisis: A Fundamental Reassessment*, Brighton: Harvester.

Dworkin, D.L. (1993) 'Cultural Studies and the Crisis in British Radical Thought', in Dworkin and Roman (eds), *Views Beyond the Border Country: Raymond Williams and Cultural Politics*, London and New York: Routledge.

—— (1997) *Cultural Marxism and Postwar Britain*, Durham and London: Duke University Press.

Dworkin, D.L. and Roman, L.G. (eds) (1993a) *Views Beyond the Border Country: Raymond Williams and Cultural Politics*, London and New York: Routledge.

—— (1993b) 'Introduction: The Cultural Politics of Location', in Dworkin and Roman (eds), *Views Beyond the Border Country: Raymond Williams and Cultural Politics*, London and New York: Routledge.

Eagleton, T. (1976a) 'Criticism and Politics: The Works of Raymond Williams', *New Left Review* 95, pp. 3–23.

—— (1976b) *Criticism and Ideology: A Study in Marxist Literary Theory*, London: New Left Books.

—— (1982) 'Wittgenstein's Friends', *New Left Review* 135, pp. 64–90.

—— (1983) *Literary Theory: An Introduction*, Oxford: Basil Blackwell.

—— (1984) *The Function of Criticism: From the Spectator to Post-structuralism*, London: Verso.

—— (1985) 'Capitalism, Modernism and Postmodernism', *New Left Review* 152, pp. 60–73.

—— (1988) 'Resources for a Journey of Hope: The Significance of Raymond Williams', *New Left Review* 168, pp. 3–11.

—— (1989a) 'Introduction', in T. Eagleton (ed.), *Raymond Williams: Critical Perspectives*, Oxford: Polity Press.

—— (1989b) 'Base and Superstructure in Raymond Williams', in T. Eagleton (ed.), *Raymond Williams: Critical Perspectives*, Oxford: Polity Press.

—— (ed.) (1989c) *Raymond Williams: Critical Perspectives*, Oxford: Polity Press.

—— (1991) *Ideology: An Introduction*, London: Verso.

Eagleton, T. and Milne, D. (eds) (1996) *Marxist Literary Theory: A Reader*, Oxford: Blackwell.

Eagleton, T. and Wicker, B. (eds) (1968) *From Culture to Revolution: The Slant Symposium 1967*, London and Sydney: Sheed & Ward.

Easthope, A. (1983) *Poetry as Discourse*, London: Methuen.

—— (1988) *British Post-Structuralism Since 1968*, London and New York: Routledge.

Edgar, D. (1984) 'Bitter Harvest', in J. Curran (ed.) *The Future of the Left*, Cambridge: Polity Press and New Socialist.

Eichenbaum, B. (1926) 'The Theory of the "Formal Method"', in *Russian Formalist Criticism: Four Essays*, ed. and trans. L.T. Lemon and M.J. Reis, Lincoln and London: University of Nebraska Press, 1965.

Ehrlich, V. (1955) *Russian Formalism: History–Doctrine*, The Hague: Mouton.

Eldridge, John and Eldridge, Lizzie (1994) *Raymond Williams: Making Connections*, London and New York: Routledge.

Eliot, T.S. (1919a) ' "Rhetoric" and Poetic Drama', in Eliot, *Selected Essays*, London: Faber.

—— (1919b) 'Tradition and the Individual Talent', in Eliot, *Selected Essays*, London: Faber.

—— (1921) 'The Metaphysical Poets', in Eliot, *Selected Essays*, London: Faber.

—— (1924) 'Four Elizabethan Dramatists: A Preface to an Unwritten Book', in Eliot, *Selected Essays*, London: Faber.

—— (1928) 'A Dialogue on Dramatic Poetry', in Eliot, *Selected Essays*, London: Faber.

—— (1934) *After Strange Gods*, London: Faber.

—— (1939) 'The Idea of a Christian Society', in Eliot, *The Idea of a Christian Society and Other Writings*, London: Faber.

—— (1948) *Notes Towards the Definition of Culture*, London: Faber, 1983.

—— (1966) *Selected Essays*, London: Faber.

—— (1982) *The Idea of a Christian Society and Other Writings*, London: Faber.

Elliot, Gregory (1987) *Althusser: The Detour of Theory*, London: Verso.

Ellmann, M. (1987) *The Poetics of Impersonality*, Cambridge, MA: Harvard University Press.

Empson, W. (1977) 'Compacted Doctrines', *The New York Review of Books*, 27 October, pp. 21–2.

Engels, F. (1894) *Anti-Dühring*, trans. E. Burns, Moscow: Progress Publishers, 1978.

Fabb, N., Attridge, D., Durant, A. and MacCabe, C. (eds) (1988) *The Linguistics of Writing: Arguments between Language and Literature*, Manchester: Manchester University Press.

Fekete, J. (1977) *The Critical Twilight: Explorations in the Ideology of Anglo-American Literary Theory from Eliot to McLuhan*, London: Routledge & Kegan Paul.

—— (ed.) (1989) *The Structural Allegory: Reconstructive Encounters with the New French Thought*, Manchester: Manchester University Press.

Ferrara, F. (1989) 'Raymond Williams and the Italian Left', in T. Eagleton (ed.), *Raymond Williams: Critical Perspectives*, Oxford: Polity Press.

Foucault, M. (1966) *The Order of Things*, trans. Sheridan-Smith, A., New York: Random House 1970.

—— (1969) 'What is an Author?', in D. Lodge (ed.), *Modern Criticism and Theory: A Reader*, London and New York: Longman.

Forster, E.M. (1927) *Aspects of the Novel*, Harmondsworth: Pelican 1972.

Fox, R. (1937) *The Novel and the People*, London: Lawrence & Wishart, 1979.

Frank, M. (1989) *What is Neo-Structuralism?*, trans. S. Wilke and R. Gray, Minneapolis: University of Minnesota Press.

Gallagher, C. (1980) 'The New Materialism in Marxist Aesthetics', *Theory and Society* 9:4, pp. 633–46.

—— (1992) 'Raymond Williams and Cultural Studies', *Social Text* 30, pp. 79–89; repr. in C. Prendergast (ed.), *Cultural Materialism: Essays on Raymond Williams*, Minneapolis: University of Minnesota Press.

Giddens, Anthony (1979a) *Central Problems in Social Theory*, London: Macmillan.

—— (1979b) 'Raymond Williams's Long Revolution', in Giddens, *Profiles and Critiques in Social Theory*, London: Macmillan, pp. 133–43.

—— (1981a) *A Contemporary Critique of Historical Materialism*, London: Macmillan.

—— (1981b) 'The State of Sociology', *Times Literary Supplement*, 27 February, pp. 215–16.

—— (1982) *Profiles and Critiques in Social Theory*, London: Macmillan.

—— (1996) *In Defence of Sociology: Essays, Interpretations, and Rejoinders*, Cambridge: Polity Press.

Gilroy, P. (1987) *'There Ain't no Black in the Union Jack': The Cultural Politics of Race and Nation*, Chicago: University of Chicago Press.

Godzich, W. (1994) *The Culture of Literacy*, Cambridge, MA, and London: Harvard University Press.

Goldmann, L. (1952) *Sciences Humaines et Philosophie*, Paris: Presses Universitaires de France.

—— (1956) *The Hidden God: A Study of Tragic Vision in the Pensées of Pascal and the Tragedies of Racine*, trans. P. Thody, London: Routledge & Kegan Paul, 1964.

—— (1963) 'Introduction aux problèmes d'une sociologie du roman', in Goldmann, *Pour une sociologie du roman*, Paris: Collection Idees.

—— (1964) 'La méthode structuraliste génétique en histoire de la litterature', in Goldmann, *Pour une sociologie du roman*, Paris: Collection Idees.

—— (1969) *Pour une sociologie du roman*, Paris: Collection Idees.

—— (1970) *Cultural Creation*, trans. B. Grahl, Oxford: Basil Blackwell and Mott Ltd.

Goody, J. (1977) *The Domestication of the Savage Mind*, Cambridge: Cambridge University Press.

—— (1981) 'Alphabets and Writing', in R. Williams (ed.), *Contact: Human Communication and its History*, London: Thames & Hudson.

—— (1986) *The Logic of Writing and the Organization of Society*, Cambridge: Cambridge University Press.

Gorak, J. (1988) *The Alien Mind of Raymond Williams*, Columbia, MO: University of Missouri Press.

Gordon, L. (1988) *Eliot's New Life*, Oxford: Oxford University Press.

Gramsci, A. (1971) *Selections from the Prison Notebooks*, trans. Q. Hoare and G. Nowell-Smith, London: Lawrence & Wishart.

Green, M. (1968) 'Literary Values and Left Politics: a Liberal Criticism', in T. Eagleton and B. Wicker (eds) *From Culture to Revolution: The Slant Symposium 1967*, London and Sydney: Sheed & Ward.

Gregor, I., Pittock, M., and Williams, R. (1959) 'Critical Forum', *Essays in Criticism* 9, pp. 425–37.

Grossberg, L., Nelson, C. and Treichler, P. (eds) (1992) *Cultural Studies*, London and New York: Routledge.

Hall, S. (1980) 'Politics and Letters', in T. Eagleton (ed.), *Raymond Williams: Critical Perspectives*, Cambridge: Polity Press.

—— (1983) 'The Great Moving Right Show', in S. Hall and M. Jacques (eds), *The Politics of Thatcherism*, London: Lawrence & Wishart.

—— (1988) 'The Toad in the Garden: Thatcherism among the Theorists', in C. Nelson and L. Grossberg (eds), *Marxism and the Interpretation of Culture*, Urbana: University of Illinois Press.

—— (1989) 'The "First" New Left: Life and Times', in R. Archer *et al. Out of Apathy*, London and New York: Verso.

Hall, S. and Jacques, M. (eds) (1983) *The Politics of Thatcherism*, London: Lawrence & Wishart.

Hall, S., Thompson, E.P. and Williams, R. (1968) *May Day Manifesto*, Harmondsworth: Penguin.

Hall, S., Critcher, C., Jefferson, T., Clarke, J., and Roberts, T. (1978) *Policing the Crisis: Mugging, the State, and Law and Order*, London: Macmillan.

Hare, D. (1976) *Fanshen*, London: Faber.

Harrison, J.F.C. (1959) 'The Great Debate', in S.G. Raybould (ed.), *Trends in Higher Education*, London: Heinemann.

Hartley, A. (1958) 'The Loaf and the Leaven', *Manchester Guardian*, 7 October, p. 10.

—— (1959) 'Philistine to Philistine?', in J. Wain (ed.), *International Literary Annual 2*, London: Calder.

—— (1962) 'The Intellectuals of England', *The Spectator*, 4 May, pp. 577–81.

Hayes, M. (1994) *The New Right in Britain*, London and Boulder, CO: Pluto Press.

Heath, S. (1981) *Questions of Cinema*, London: Macmillan.

—— (1984) 'Modern English Man', *Times Higher Education Supplement*, 20 July 1984, p. 17.

—— (1991) 'The Turn of the Subject', in R. Burnett (ed.) *Explorations in Film Theory*, Bloomington and Indianapolis: Indiana University Press.

Held, D. (1997) *Models of Democracy*, Oxford: Polity Press.

Hewison, Robert (1981) *In Anger: British Culture in the Cold War 1945–60*, New York: Oxford University Press.

Hibbard, G.H. (1956) 'The Country House Poem of the Seventeenth Century', *Journal of the Warburg and Courtauld Institute* 19, pp. 159–74.

Higgins, J. (1985) Review of *Writing in Society* and *Beyond 2000* in *the minnesota review* N.S. 24, pp. 168–71.

—— (1986) 'Raymond Williams and the Problem of Ideology', in J. Arac (ed.), *Postmodernism and Politics*, Minneapolis: University of Minnesota Press.

—— (1989) 'Raymond Williams 1921–1988', *Pretexts: Studies in Writing and Culture* 1:1, pp. 79–91.

—— (1990) 'A Missed Encounter: Raymond Williams and Psychoanalysis', *Journal of Literary Studies* 6:1–2, pp. 62–76.

—— (1991) ' "In Short, Poststructuralist Freudianism": Misreading as Reading Through', *Journal of Literary Studies* 7:1, pp. 76–81.

—— (1992) 'Critical Literacies: English Studies Beyond the Canon', *Journal of Literary Studies* 8:3/4, pp. 86–100.

—— (1995) 'Forgetting Williams', in C. Prendergast (ed.), *Cultural Materialism: Essays on Raymond Williams*, Minneapolis: University of Minnesota Press.

—— (1996a) 'Critical Literacy in Action', *Southern African Review of Books*, January–February, pp. 26–7.

—— (1996b) '*Keywords* and Critical Literacy', paper given at *Crossroads in Cultural Studies Conference*, Tampere, Finland, July.

—— (1998) 'The Legacy of Raymond Williams', *English Academy Review* 14, pp. 30–48.

Hill, C. (1976) Review of *Keywords*, *New Society*, 5 February.

Hinton, W. (1966) *Fanshen: A Documentary of Revolution in a Chinese Village*, New York: Vintage.

Hirschkop, K. (1989) 'A Complex Populism: The Political Thought of Raymond Williams', *News from Nowhere* 6, pp. 12–22.

Hirst, P. (1979) *On Law and Ideology*, London: Macmillan.

Hitchcock, P. (1995) 'Information in Formation: Williams/Media/China', in C. Prendergast (ed.) *Cultural Materialism*, Minneapolis: University of Minnesota Press.

Hoggart, R. (1948) 'Some Notes on Aim and Method in University Tutorial Classes', in McIlroy and Westwood (eds), *Border Country: Raymond Williams in Adult Education*, Leicester: National Institute of Continuing Education 1993.

—— (1959) 'An Important Book', *Essays in Criticism* 9, pp. 171–9.

Holderness, G. (1991) 'Introduction to This Edition' in Williams, *Drama and Performance*, Milton Keynes: Open University Press, 1–14.

Holquist, M. (1990) *Dialogism: Bakhtin and his World*, London and New York: Routledge.

Hutchinson, E.M. (ed.) (1971) *Aims and Action in Adult Education*, London: National Institute of Adult Education.

Ibsen, H. (1974) *Ghosts and Other Plays*, trans. P. Watts, Harmondsworth: Penguin.

Inglis, F. (1989) 'Border Country', *Times Higher Education Supplement*, 22 December, p. 19.

—— (1995) *Raymond Williams*, London and New York: Routledge.

Innes, C. (1992) *Modern British Drama 1890–1990*, Cambridge: Cambridge University Press.

James, C.L.R. (1961) 'Marxism and the Intellectuals' in *Spheres of Existence*, London: Allison & Busby, 1980.

Jameson, F. (1972) *The Prison House of Language*, Princeton, NJ: Princeton University Press.

—— (1977) 'Reflections in Conclusion', in Bloch *et al.*, *Aesthetics and Politics*, London: New Left Books.

—— (1991) *Postmodernism, or, The Cultural Logic of Late Capitalism*, London and New York: Verso.

Jardine, L. and Swindells, J. (1989) 'Homage to Orwell: The Death of a Common Culture, and Other Minefields', in T. Eagleton (ed.), *Raymond Williams: Cultural Perspectives*, Oxford: Polity Press.

Jay, M. (1984) *Marxism and Totality*, Berkeley and Los Angeles: University of California Press.

Jefferson, A. and Robey, D. (eds) (1982) *Modern Literary Theory: A Comparative Introduction*, London: Batsford.

Jessop, B., Bonnet, K., Bromley, S. and Ling, T. (1984) 'Authoritarian Populism, Two Nations and Thatcherism', in *New Left Review* 147, pp. 32–60.

—— (1985) 'Thatcherism and the Politics of Hegemony: A Reply to Stuart Hall', in *New Left Review* 153, pp. 87–101.

Johnson, L. (1979) *The Cultural Critics: From Matthew Arnold to Raymond Williams*, London: Routledge & Kegan Paul.

Johnson, R.W. (1990) 'Moooovement', *London Review of Books*, 8 February, pp. 5–6.

Joseph, K. (1976) *Stranded on the Middle Ground?*, London: Centre for Policy Studies.

Julius, A. (1995) *T.S. Eliot, Anti-Semitism and Literary Form*, Cambridge: Cambridge University Press.

Kappeler, S. (1986) *The Pornography of Representation*, Cambridge: Polity Press.

Kermode, F. (1959) Review of *Culture and Society*, *Encounter* 12, pp. 86–8.

—— (1966) 'Tragedy and Revolution', *Encounter* 27, pp. 83–5.

—— (1971) *The Romantic Image*, London: Fontana.

Kettle, A. (1961) 'Culture and Revolution: A Consideration of the Ideas of Raymond Williams and Others', *Marxism Today*, 5: 301–7.

—— (1977) Review of *Marxism and Literature*, *Red Letters* 6, pp. 71–3.

—— (1979) Review of *Politics and Letters*, *Marxism Today* 23, pp. 28 –9.

Kiernan, Victor (1959) 'Culture and Society', *The New Reasoner* 9, pp. 74–83.

Knights, L.C. (1937) *Drama and Society in the Age of Jonson*, New York: Barnes & Noble.

Kohli, W. (1993) 'Raymond Williams: Affective Ideology and Counter Hegemonic Practices', in D.L. Dworkin and L.G. Roman, *Views Beyond Border Country*, London and New York: Routledge.

Kolakowski, (1981) *Main Currents of Marxism: Its Origins, Growth and Dissolution II: The Golden Age*, trans. P.S. Falla, Oxford: Oxford University Press.

Kruger, Loren (1991) 'Modernism in Exile: Raymond Williams's *The Politics of Modernism*', *Pretexts: Studies in Writing and Culture* 3:1–2, pp. 144–51.

—— (1993) 'Placing the Occasion: Raymond Williams and Performing Culture', in D.L. Dworkin and L.G. Roman (eds), *Views beyond the Border Country*, London and New York, Routledge.

Lapsley, R. and Westlake, M. (1988) *Film Theory: An Introduction*, Manchester: Manchester University Press.

Larrain, Jorge (1979) *The Concept of Ideology*, London: Hutchinson.

Lasch, C. (1973) 'The Cultural Cold War: A Short History of the Congress for Cultural Freedom', in C. Lasch *The Agony of the American Left*, Harmondsworth: Penguin.

Latimer, D. (ed.) *Contemporary Critical Theory*, New York and London: Harcourt Brace Jovanonich.

Leavis, F.R. (1932) *New Bearings in English Poetry*, Harmondsworth: Penguin.

—— (1933) *For Continuity*, Cambridge: Minority Press.

—— (1936) *Revaluation: Tradition and Development in English Poetry*, Harmondsworth: Penguin.

—— (1943) *Education and the University*, London: Chatto & Windus.

—— (1948) *The Great Tradition: George Eliot, Henry James, Joseph Conrad*, Harmondsworth: Penguin, 1983.

—— (1952) *The Common Pursuit*, Harmondsworth: Penguin.

—— (1953) 'The Responsibility of the Critic, or, the Function of Criticism at Any Time', in Leavis, F.R. (ed.) *A Selection from Scrutiny*, 11.

—— (ed.) (1968) *A Selection from Scrutiny II*, Cambridge: Cambridge University Press.

Leavis, F. and Thompson, D. (1933) *Culture and Environment: The Training of Critical Awareness*, London: Chatto & Windus.

Lefebvre, H. (1969) *The Sociology of Marx*, Harmondsworth: Allen Lane, The Penguin Press.

Lerner, L. (1973) 'Beyond Literature: Social Criticism versus Aesthetics', *Encounter* 41, 4 July, pp. 62–5.

Lewis, J. (1946–7a) 'Editorial', *The Modern Quarterly* 2:1, pp. 3–15.

—— (1946–7b) 'The Soviet Literary Controversy', *The Modern Quarterly* 2:1, pp. 74–84.

Letwin, S.R. (1992) *The Anatomy of Thatcherism*, London: Fontana.

Lichtheim, G. (1967) *The Concept of Ideology and Other Essays*, New York: Vintage.

—— (1970) *Lukács*, London: Fontana.

Liu, A. (1989) Wordsworth: *The Sense of History*, Stanford: Stanford University Press.

Lloyd, D. and Thomas, P. (1995) 'Culture and Society or Culture and the State', in C. Prendergast (ed.), *Cultural Materialism: Essays on Raymond Williams*, Minneapolis: University of Minnesota Press.

KING ALFRED'S COLLEGE
LIBRARY

Lodge, D. (1981) 'Middlemarch and the Idea of the Classic Realist Text', in Arnold Kettle (ed.) *The Nineteenth Century Novel: Critical Essays and Documents*, London: Heinemann

—— (ed.) (1988) *Modern Criticism and Theory: A Reader*, London and New York; Longman.

Lovell, T. (1989) 'Knowledgeable Pasts, Imaginable Futures', *History Workshop Journal* 27, pp. 136–40.

Lukács, G. (1954) *Die Zerstorung der Vernunft*, East Berlin: Aufbau Verlag.

—— (1980) *Essays on Realism*, trans. D. Fernbach, London: Lawrence & Wishart.

Lunacharsky, A. (1933) 'On Socialist Realism', in *Socialist Realism in Literature and Art*, Moscow: Progress Publishers, 1971.

Lunn, E. (1985) *Marxism and Modernism*, London: Verso.

Lusted, D. (ed.) (1989) *Raymond Williams: Film TV Culture*, London: NFT/BFI Education.

MacCabe, C. (1974) 'Realism and the Cinema: Notes on Some Brechtian Theses', in MacCabe, *Theoretical Essays: Film, Linguistics, Literature*, Manchester: Manchester University Press, 1985.

—— (1976) 'Theory and Film: Principles of Realism and Pleasure', in MacCabe, *Theoretical Essays: Film, Linguistics, Literature*, Manchester: Manchester University Press, 1985.

—— (1979) *James Joyce and the Revolution of the Word*, London: Macmillan.

—— (1985) *Theoretical Essays: Film, Linguistics, Literature*, Manchester: Manchester University Press.

McCabe, C., Mulvey, L., and Eaton, M. (ed.) (1981) *Godard: Images, Sounds, Politics*, London: BFI/ Macmillan.

MacDonald, D. (1961) 'Looking Backward', *Encounter* 16, pp. 79–84.

Macherey, P. (1966) *A Theory of Literary Production*, trans. G. Wall, London: Routledge & Kegan Paul, 1978.

McIlroy, J. (1993a) 'The Unknown Raymond Williams', in McIlroy and Westwood (eds), *Border Country: Raymond Williams in Adult Education*, Leicester: National Institute of Continuing Education, 1993.

—— (1993b) 'Border Country: Raymond Williams in Adult Education', in McIlroy and Westwood (eds), *Border Country: Raymond Williams in Adult Education*, Leicester: National Institute of Continuing Education, 1993.

McIlroy, J. and Westwood, S. (eds) (1993) *Border Country: Raymond Williams in Adult Education*, Leicester: National Institute of Continuing Education.

McLellan, D. (1969) *The Young Hegelians and Karl Marx*, London: Macmillan.

Marx, K. (1844) *Economic and Philosophical Manuscripts* in *Early Writings*, ed. Q. Hoare, Harmondsworth: Penguin 1974.

—— (1851) *The Eighteenth Brumaire of Louis Bonaparte*, in *Karl Marx Surveys from Exile: Political Writings II*, ed. D. Fernbach, Harmondsworth: Penguin 1973.

Marx, K. and Engels, F. (1888) *Manifesto of the Communist Party*, in *Karl Marx The Revolutions of 1848: Political Writings I*, ed. D. Fernbach, Harmondsworth: Penguin 1973.

—— (1975) *Selected Correspondence*, ed. S.W. Ryazanskaya, trans. I. Lasker, Moscow: Progress Publishers.

Mason, H.A. (1938) 'The Illusion of Cogency', *Scrutiny* 6:4, pp. 429–33.

Merrill, M. (1978/9) 'Raymond Williams and the Theory of English Marxism', *Radical History Review* 19, pp. 9–31.

Middleton, Peter (1989) 'Why Structure Feeling?', *News from Nowhere* 6, pp. 50–7.

Milner, Andrew (1993) *Cultural Materialism*, Carlton: Melbourne University Press.

Minogue, K. (1988) 'The Emergence of the New Right', in R. Skidelsky (ed.), *Thatcherism*, London: Chatto & Windus.

Montrose, L. (1989) 'The Poetics and Politics of Culture', in H.A. Veeser (ed.) *The New Historicism*, London: Routledge.

Moretti, F. (1983) *Signs Taken for Wonders: Essays in the Sociology of Literary Forms*, trans. S. Fischer, D. Forgacs and D. Miller, London: Verso.

—— (1995) *Modern Epic*, trans. Q. Hoare, London and New York: Verso.

Morgan, J. (1983) 'Unquestioned Questions', *Times Literary Supplement*, 4 November, p. 1223.

Moriarty, M. (1995) ' "The Longest Cultural Journey": Raymond Williams and French Theory' in C. Prendergast (ed.), *Cultural Materialism: Essays on Raymond Williams*, Minneapolis: University of Minnesota Press.

Morrison, Blake (1980) *The Movement: English Poetry and Fiction of the 1950s*, Oxford: Oxford University Press.

Mulhern, Francis (1974) 'The Marxist Aesthetics of Christopher Caudwell', *New Left Review* 85, pp. 37–58.

—— (1979) *The Moment of 'Scrutiny'*, London: New Left Books.

—— (1984) 'Towards 2000, or News from You-Know-Where', in T. Eagleton (ed.), *Raymond Williams: Critical Perspectives*, Oxford: Polity Press.

Nairn, T. (1983) 'Britain's Living Legacy', in S. Hall and M. Jacques (eds), *The Politics of Thatcherism*, London: Lawrence & Wishart.

New Formations (1988) 'Identities', no. 5, Summer 1988, pp. 3–4.

Nussbaum, F. and Brown, L. (1987) 'Revising Critical Practices: An Introductory Essay', in Nussbaum and Brown (eds) *The New Eighteenth Century: Theory/Politics/English Literature*, London and New York: Methuen.

O'Connor, A. (1989) *Raymond Williams: Writing, Culture, Politics*, Oxford: Basil Blackwell.

Orwell, G. (1945) Review of *The Unquiet Grave* by 'Palinurus', in G. Orwell *The Collected Essays, Journalism and Letters of George Orwell: Volume III*, ed S. Orwell and I. Angus, Harmondsworth: Penguin.

Oxford University Socialist Group, (1989) *Out of Apathy: Voices of the New Left Thirty Years On*, London and New York: Verso.

Parrinder, P. (1977) *Authors and Authority*, London: Routledge & Kegan Paul.

—— (1981) 'Politics and Letters', in *Literature and History* 7, pp. 124–6.

—— (1987a) *The Failure of Theory: Essays on Criticism and Contemporary Fiction*, Brighton: Harvester Press.

—— (1987b) 'Culture and Society in the 1980s', in Parrinder, *The Failure of Theory: Essays on Criticism and Contemporary Fiction*, Brighton: Harvester Press.

—— (1987c) 'Utopia and Negativity in Raymond Williams', in Parrinder, *The Failure of Theory: Essays on Criticism and Contemporary Fiction*, Brighton: Harvester Press.

—— (1988) 'Diary', in *London Review of Books*, February 18, p. 25.

Pechey, G. (1985) '*Scrutiny*, English Marxism and the Work of Raymond Williams', *Literature and History* 11:1, pp. 65–76.

Perelman, B. (1996) *The Marginalisation of Poetry: Language Writing and Literary History*, Princeton: Princeton University Press.

Perloff, M. (1985) *The Dance of the Intellect: Studies in the Poetry of the Pound Tradition*, Cambridge: Cambridge University Press.

Pinkney, T. (1989a) 'Editor's Introduction: Modernism and Cultural Theory', in Williams, *The Politics of Modernism: Against the New Conformists*, London and New York: Verso.

—— (1989b) 'Raymond Williams and the "Two Faces" of Modernism', in T. Eagleton (ed.), *Raymond Williams: Critical Perspectives*, Oxford: Polity Press.

—— (ed.) (1989c) *Raymond Williams: Third Generation*, a special issue of *News from Nowhere*.

—— (1991) *Raymond Williams*, Cardiff: Poetry Wales Press.

Pittock, M. (1962) 'The Optimistic Revolution', *Essays in Criticism* 12, pp. 82–91.

Plekhanov, G. (1953) *Art and Social Life*, London: Lawrence & Wishart.

Prendergast, C. (1988) *The Order of Mimesis*, Cambridge: Cambridge University Press.

—— (ed.) (1992) *Social Text 30: Special Issue on Raymond Williams*.

—— (ed.) (1995a) *Cultural Materialism: Essays on Raymond Williams*, Minneapolis: University of Minnesota Press.

—— (1995b) 'Introduction: Groundings and Emergings', in C. Prendergast (ed.), *Cultural Materialism: Essays on Raymond Williams*, Minneapolis: University of Minnesota Press.

—— (1995c) 'Raymond Williams and the Culture of Nations', *Pretexts: Studies in Writing and Culture*, 5:1/2, pp. 191–204.

Pyle, F. (1993) 'Raymond Williams and the Inhuman Limits of Culture', in D.L. Dworkin and L.G. Roman (eds), *Views Beyond the Border Country: Raymond Williams and Cultural Politics*, London and New York: Routledge.

Radhakrishnan, R. (1993) 'Cultural Theory and the Politics of Location', in D.L. Dworkin and L.G. Roman (eds), *Views Beyond the Border Country: Raymond Williams and Cultural Politics*, London and New York: Routledge.

Raybould, S.G. (1948) *University Standards in WEA Work*, London: WEA.

—— (1949) *The WEA: The Next Phase*, London: WEA.

—— (1951) *The English Universities and Adult Education*, London: WEA.

—— (ed.) (1959) *Trends in Higher Education*, London: Heinemann.

Richards, I.A. (1929) *Practical Criticism: A Study of Literary Judgement* London: Routledge & Kegan Paul, 1970.

Riddell, P. (1985) *The Thatcher Government*, Oxford: Basil Blackwell.

Rizvi, F. (1993) 'Williams on Democracy and the Governance of Education', in D.L. Dworkin and R.L. Roman, *Views Beyond the Border Country*, London and New York: Routledge.

Robbins, B. (1990) 'Espionage as Vocation: Raymond Williams's Loyalties', in B. Robbins (ed.) *Intellectuals: Aesthetics, Politics, Academics*, Minneapolis: University of Minnesota Press.

—— (1992) 'Foreword', to R. Williams *The Sociology of Culture*, Chicago: University of Chicago Press (second American edition of *Culture*).

—— (1993) *Secular Vocations: Intellectuals, Professionalism, Culture*, London and New York: Verso.

Robin, R. (1992) *Socialist Realism: An Impossible Aesthetic*, trans. C. Porter, Stanford, CA: Stanford University Press.

Roman, L.C. (1993) ' "On the Ground" with Antiracist Pedagogy', in Dworkin, D.L. and Roman, L.C. (eds) *Views Beyond the Border Country*, London and New York: Routledge, 1993.

Rosen, M. (1996) *On Voluntary Servitude*, Cambridge: Polity Press.

Ross, A. (1992) 'Giving Culture Hell: A Response to Catherine Gallagher', *Social Text* 30, pp. 98–101.

Rossi-Landi, F. (1981) 'Language' in R. Williams (ed.), *Contact: Human Communication and its History*, London: Thames & Hudson.

Said, E. (1975) *Beginnings: Intention and Method*, Baltimore and London: John Hopkins University Press.

—— (1983) *The World, the Text and the Critic*, London: Faber.

—— (1989) 'Jane Austen and Empire', in T. Eagleton (ed.), *Raymond Williams: Critical Perspectives*, Oxford: Polity Press.

—— (1990) 'Narrative, Geography and Interpretation', *New Left Review* 180, p. 81–97.

—— (1991) 'Identity, Authority and Freedom: The Potentate and the Traveller', *Pretexts: Studies in Writing and Culture* 3:1–2, pp. 67–81.

—— (1993) *Culture and Imperialism*, London: Chatto & Windus.

—— (1994) *Representations of the Intellectual*, New York: Viking.

Samuel, R. (1986a) 'The Lost World of British Communism I', *New Left Review* 155, pp. 119–24.

—— (1986b) 'The Lost World of British Communism II', *New Left Review* 156, pp. 63–113.

—— (1989) 'Philosophy Teaching by Example: Positions Present in Raymond Williams', *History Workshop* 27, Spring, pp. 141–53.

—— (1996) 'Making it Up', *London Review of Books*, 4 July, 18:13, pp. 8–10.

Schalkwyk, D. (1992) 'The Shock of the Old: Theory and the Renaissance', *Pretexts: Studies in Writing and Culture* 4:1, pp 85–97.

Scrivener, M. (1978–80) Review of *Marxism and Literature*, *Telos* 38, pp. 190–8.

Scruton, R. (1984) *The Meaning of Conservatism*, London: Macmillan.

—— (1985) *Thinkers of the New Left*, London: Longman.

Sharrat, B. (1982) 'Poisson: A Modest Review', in B. Sharrat, *Reading Relations*, Brighton: Harvester Press.

—— (1989) 'In Whose Voice? The Drama of Raymond Williams', in T. Eagleton (ed.), *Raymond Williams: Critical Perspectives*, Oxford: Polity Press.

Shaw, R. (1959) 'Controversies', in S.G. Raybould (ed.), *Trends in Higher Education*, London: Heinemann.

Shelden, M. (1989) *Friends of Promise: Cyril Connolly and the World of Horizon*, London: Hamish Hamilton.

Shiach, M. (1989) *Discourse on Popular Culture: Class, Gender and History in Cultural Analysis, 1730 to the Present*, Oxford: Polity Press.

—— (1995) 'A Gendered History of Cultural Categories', in C. Prendergast (ed.), *Cultural Materialism: Essays on Raymond Williams*, Minneapolis: University of Minnesota Press.

Shklovsky, V. (1917) 'Art as Technique', in D. Lodge (ed.), *Modern Criticism and Theory: A Reader*, London and New York: Longmans.

Simpson, D. (1987) *Wordsworth's Historical Imagination: The Poetry of Displacement*, New York and London: Methuen.

—— (1990) 'New Brooms at Fawlty Towers: Colin MacCabe and Cambridge English', in B. Robbins (ed.), *Intellectuals: Aesthetics, Politics, Academics*, Minneapolis: University of Minnesota Press.

—— (1995a) *The Academic Postmodern and the Rule of Literature: A Report on Half-Knowledge*, Chicago and London: University of Chicago Press.

—— (1995b) 'Raymond Williams: Feeling for Structures, Voicing "History" ', in C. Prendergast (ed.), *Cultural Materialism: Essays on Raymond Williams*, Minneapolis: University of Minnesota Press.

Sinfield, Alan (1989) *Literature, Politics, and Culture in Postwar Britain*, Oxford: Blackwell.

Skidelsky, R. (ed.) (1988) *Thatcherism*, London: Chatto & Windus.

Skinner, Q. (1988) 'Language and Social Change', in J. Tully (ed.), *Meaning and Context: Quentin Skinner and His Critics*, Cambridge: Polity Press.

Stedman Jones, G. (1977a) 'Engels and the Genesis of Marxism', *New Left Review* 106, pp. 79–104.

—— (1977b) 'The Early Lukács', in *Western Marxism: A Reader*, London: New Left Books.

—— (1984a) Review of *Towards 2000* and *Wigan Pier Revisited, Marxism Today*, July, pp. 38–40.

—— (1984b) 'Marching into History?', in J. Curran (ed.), *The Future of the Left*, Cambridge: Polity Press and New Socialist.

Stein, W. (1969) *Criticism as Dialogue*, Cambridge: Cambridge University Press.

Steiner, G. (1961) *The Death of Tragedy*, London: Faber.

—— (1977) 'Introduction', in W. Benjamin, *The Origin of German Tragic Drama*, trans. J. Osborne, London: New Left Books.

—— (1986) *Antigones*, London: Faber.

—— (1989) *Real Presences*, London: Faber.

Sullivan, R. (1988) *Christopher Caudwell*, London and New York: Routledge.

Surin, K. (1995) 'Raymond Williams on Tragedy and Revolution', in C. Prendergast (ed.), *Cultural Materialism: Essays on Raymond Williams*, Minneapolis: University of Minnesota Press.

Tawney, R.H. (1934) 'Opening Address to the WEA', *The Highway* 27, pp. 67–71.

Taylor, C. (1985) *Philosophical Papers I: Human Agency and Language*, Cambridge: Cambridge University Press.

—— (1989a) *Sources of the Self: The Making of Modern Identity*, Cambridge: Cambridge University Press.

—— (1989b) 'Marxism and Socialist Humanism', in Archer *et al.* (eds), *Out of Apathy: Voices of the New Left Thirty Years On*, London and New York: Verso.

Taylor, J.B. (1990) 'Raymond Williams: Gender and Generation', in *British Feminist Thought: A Reader*, ed. T. Lovell, London: Basil Blackwell.

Thatcher, M. (1977) *Let Our Children Grow Tall*, London: Centre for Policy Studies.

Therborn, G. (1980) *The Ideology of Power and the Power of Ideology*, London: Verso.

Thompson, E.P. (1961) 'The Long Revolution' in *New Left Review* 9 and 10, pp. 24–33, 34–9.

—— (1975) 'A Nice Place to Visit' *New York Review of Books,* 6 February, pp. 34–7.

—— (1977) 'Caudwell', in R. Milliband and J. Saville (eds), *The Socialist Register* 14, London: Merlin Press.

Thompson, J. (1993) 'Realisms and Modernisms: Raymond Williams and Popular Fiction', in D.L. Dworkin and L.G. Roman (eds), *Views Beyond the Border Country: Raymond Williams and Cultural Politics*, London and New York: Routledge.

Thomson, J.O. (1980) 'Tragic Flow: Raymond Williams on Drama', *Screen Education* 35, pp. 45–58.

Tillyard, E.M.W. (1952) *The Elizabethan World Picture*, London: Chatto & Windus.

—— (1958) *The Muse Unchained: An Intimate Account of the Revolution in English Studies at Cambridge*, Cambridge: Bowes & Bowes.

Times Literary Supplement (1961) 'Notes Towards the Definition What?', 10 March, p. 147.

Times Literary Supplement (1966) 'A Time for Tragedy', 11 August, pp. 717–18.

Timms, E. and Collier, P. (1988) *Visions and Blueprints: Avant-Garde Culture and Radical Politics in Early Twentieth Century Europe*, Manchester: Manchester University Press.

Tredell, N. (1990) *Uncancelled Challenge: The Work of Raymond Williams*, Nottingham: Pauper's Press.

Trotsky, L. (1923) *Literature and Revolution*, Ann Arbor: University of Michigan Press, 1960.

Tynan, Kenneth (1964) *Tynan on Theatre*, Harmondsworth, Penguin.

Upward, E. (1937) 'Sketch for a Marxist Interpretation of Culture', in C. Day-Lewis (ed.), *The Mind in Chains: Socialism and the Cultural Revolution*, London: Frederick Muller.

Vickery, Walter N. (1963) 'Zhdanovism (1946–53)' in M. Hayward and L. Labedz (eds), *Literature and Revolution in Soviet Russia 1917–1962*, London: Oxford University Press.

Viswanathan, G. (1993) 'Raymond Williams and British Colonialism: The Limits of Metropolitan Cultural Theory', in D.L. Dworkin and L. Roman (eds) *Views Beyond the Border Country*, London and New York: Routledge.

Vološinov, V.N. (1929) *Marxism and the Philosophy of Language*, trans. L. Matejka and I.R. Titunik, London and Cambridge, MA: Harvard University Press, 1986

Walsh, M. (1981) *The Brechtian Aspect of Radical Cinema*, London: British Film Institute.

Ward, J.P. (1981) *Raymond Williams*, University of Wales Press for the Wales Arts Council.

Watkins, E. (1978) *The Critical Act: Criticism and Community*, New Haven, CN, and London: Yale University Press.

Watson, G. (1977a) *The Leavises, the 'Social', and the Left*, Swansea: Bryn Mill Publishing Co.

—— (1977b) 'Criticism and the English Idiom', *New Universities Quarterly* 31:3, pp. 316–40.

Watts, C. (1989) 'Reclaiming the Border Country: Feminism and the Work of Raymond Williams', *News from Nowhere* 6, pp. 89–108.

Wellek, R. (1937) 'Literary Criticism and Philosophy', *Scrutiny* 5:4, pp. 375–83.

West, C. (1989) 'In Memoriam: The Legacy of Raymond Williams', in C. Prendergast (ed.), *Cultural Materialism: Essays on Raymond Williams*, Minneapolis: University of Minnesota Press, 1995.

Widdowson, P. (ed.) (1982) *Re-Reading English*, London: Methuen.

—— (1989) *Hardy in History: A Study in Literary Sociology*, London and New York: Routledge.

Willey, B. (1968) *Cambridge and Other Memories*, London: Chatto & Windus.

Williams, J.R. (1953) Review of *Drama from Ibsen to Eliot*, in J. McIlroy and S. Westwood (eds), *Border Country: Raymond Williams in Adult Education*, Leicester: National Institute of Continuing Eduction, 1993.

Wilson, S. (1995) *Cultural Materialism*, Oxford: Blackwell.

Wilson Knight, G. (1930) *The Wheel of Fire: Essays in the Interpretation of Shakespeare's Sombre Tragedies*, London: Oxford University Press.

Woodcock, G. (1978) 'The Two Faces of Modern Marxism', *The Sewanee Review* 86, pp. 588–94.

Woolf, V. (1968) *The Common Reader: First Series*, London: The Hogarth Press.

Wright, E.O. (1983) 'Giddens's Critique of Marxism', *New Left Review* 138, p. 11–35.

Young, H. (1989) *One of Us: A Biography of Margaret Thatcher*, London: Macmillan.

Zhdanov. Z. (1947) 'The Responsibility of the Russian Writer', *The Modern Quarterly* 2:2, pp. 104–12.

Index

KING ALFRED'S COLLEGE
LIBRARY